'PICTURES BRING US MESSAGES' / SINAAKSSIIKSI AOHTSIMAAHPIHKOOKIYAAWA: PHOTOGRAPHS AND HISTORIES FROM THE KAINAI NATION

In 1925, Beatrice Blackwood of the University of Oxford's Pitt Rivers Museum took thirty-three photographs of Kainai people on the Blood Indian Reserve in Alberta as part of an anthropological project. In 2001, staff from the museum took copies of these photographs back to the Kainai and worked with community members to try to gain a better understanding of their perspectives on the images. *'Pictures Bring Us Messages'* is about that process, about why museum professionals and archivists must work with such communities, and about some of the considerations that need to be addressed when doing so.

Exploring the meanings that historic photographs have for source communities, Alison K. Brown, Laura Peers, and members of the Kainai Nation develop and demonstrate culturally appropriate ways of researching, curating, archiving, accessing, and otherwise using museum and archival collections. The very process of building ties between museum and community has been crucial to the research and to the current and future benefits of this new relationship. Although the *'Pictures Bring Us Messages'* project was based in Canada, its dynamics are relevant to indigenous peoples and heritage institutions around the world.

ALISON K. BROWN is a research fellow with the Department of Anthropology at the University of Aberdeen.

LAURA PEERS is a lecturer and curator with the Pitt Rivers Museum and the School of Anthropology at the University of Oxford.

'Pictures Bring Us Messages'/ Sinaakssiiksi Aohtsimaahpihkookiyaawa

Photographs and Histories from the Kainai Nation

ALISON K. BROWN AND LAURA PEERS
WITH MEMBERS OF THE KAINAI NATION

UNIVERSITY OF TORONTO PRESS
Toronto Buffalo London

Toronto Buffalo London
Printed in Canada

ISBN 0-8020-9006-0 (cloth)
ISBN 0-8020-4891-9 (paper)

Printed on acid-free paper

Library and Archives Canada Cataloguing in Publication

Brown, Alison K. (Alison Kay), 1971–
Pictures bring us messages = Sinaakssiiksi aohtsimaahpihkookiyaawa : photographs and histories from the Kainai nation / Alison K. Brown and Laura Peers with members of the Kainai nation.

Includes bibliographical references and index.
ISBN 0-8020-9006-0 (bound) ISBN 0-8020-4891-9 (pbk.)

1. Kainai Indians – Portraits. 2. Kainai Indians – Pictorial works. 3. Kainai Indians – History. 4. Blood Indian Reserve No. 148 (Alta.) – History. 5. Pitt Rivers Museum – Catalogs. I. Peers, Laura Lynn, 1963– II. Title. III. Title: Sinaakssiiksi aohtsimaahpihkookiyaawa.

E99.K15B76 2006 971.23'400497352 C2005-902578-6

University of Toronto Press acknowledges the financial assistance to its publishing program of the Canada Council for the Arts and the Ontario Arts Council.

This book has been published with the help of a grant from the Canadian Federation for the Humanities and Social Sciences, through the Aid to Scholarly Publications Programme, using funds provided by the Social Sciences and Humanities Research Council of Canada.

University of Toronto Press acknowledges the financial support for its publishing activities of the Government of Canada through the Book Publishing Industry Development Program (BPIDP).

Contents

Illustrations

(Plates 1–32 of Beatrice Blackwood's photographs follow page 126)

Map

Figures

Table

Foreword

Eighty years ago, an Oxford scholar named Beatrice Blackwood came to the Blood Reserve, in southern Alberta, on a mission to challenge some of the predominant notions of her time. With funding support from a Laura Spelman Rockefeller Scholarship, she travelled through a number of First Nations communities, in both the United States and Canada, during an era when European women were not considered to be able explorers or scholars. Along this route, Blackwood collected samples of material culture for the Pitt Rivers Museum, and at the Blood Reserve it would be her camera that took something away. In thirty-three photographs, Blackwood captured a population in the midst of transition, and the emotion that accompanied that change.

After Blackwood's photographs reached the Pitt Rivers Museum, they were catalogued and archived, and would not attract anyone's interest again for nearly a century. That was when two researchers, Alison Brown and Laura Peers, came upon them. Wanting to know what these images represented, Brown and Peers could have easily turned to the dense scholarly literature on the Blackfoot Confederacy, one of the most heavily written cultures of Native North America. But they didn't. Following in their predecessor's footsteps, Brown and Peers decided to challenge the methodology of their own time, to try something new: they contacted the Blood Tribe, outlined a protocol agreement, and brought the photographs to Alberta for the community to examine.

Very quickly, all the individuals in Blackwood's images were identified, and their descendants traced. Had Brown and Peers relied upon available literature, the story produced by the photographs would have been one of anonymous people, trapped in a history of colonial institutions. But when the elders of the Blood Tribe saw these faces, they found their parents looking back at them. They knew those expressions intimately, and could read their emotions, recollect their stories, and describe how the pictures represented these realities. They noticed that their relatives who maintained their traditional appearance, their braids and blankets, all had a look of confidence in their eyes and postures. Conversely, the young people, students of the early residential schools, with cropped hair and foreign uniforms, appeared saddened, afraid—their shoulders slumped in exasperation, their eyes betraying loss and grief. The influence of the missionaries was all too apparent in the faces of these youths.

The account Brown and Peers heard from the elders of the Blood Tribe was unlike anything they could have learned from even the best ethnohistories in their archives and libraries. When they did the obvious, approaching the descendants of the people in these photographs and asking who they were, and what was happening in their lives, a wonderful synchronicity was created: a woman beyond her times, using her camera to challenge racial notions connecting physical appearance with intelligence, influenced – almost a century later – two women who stood against the biases of their own era, and were willing to put their careers at some risk to demonstrate how two worlds can see a singular image quite differently.

Because of their respectful and caring approach, Brown and Peers have, with this book, shown all of us how both Blood and Western societies can reap great benefit by making a simple change in standard research methods, doing the obvious, and going to the source. This work should stand as a message to wider academia, a testament to the equal importance of oral histories against those documented. The photographs themselves represent the issue at hand, for in the faces of these grandmothers and grandfathers we can see with blatant apparentness what results from a unilinear conversation between cultures, and likewise what beauty there is when two voices speak equally. For the members of Blood families, the message in Brown and Peers's book is important, and we hope that it is an indication of better relationships to come. For their contributions, Brown and Peers will forever be a part of the Blood Tribe as my sisters.

Kinaksaapo'p Narcisse Blood
Chair, Mookaakin Foundation

Acknowledgments

This project has been about cross-cultural encounters in its nature as well as in its subject matter. It has involved bridging several communities – in the United Kingdom and Canada – who have not had much previous experience of working together, and its success has therefore stemmed from a number of people who have been willing to take risks, to support people they barely knew, and to believe in the potential benefits of a new kind of research. Most of all, we would like to thank our Kainai research partners, elders, mentors, and friends for being willing to allow us to work with them, for being so kind and hospitable, and for teaching us so much. We would especially like to thank those who agreed to be interviewed as part of the project, and who are named in the list of Project Participants, but in addition would like to acknowledge the many Kainai people who also contributed to the project more informally; their comments on Blackwood's photographs, often made during social visits or fleeting conversations, have been equally important in helping us to understand the different narratives photographs can evoke. The Mookaakin Cultural and Heritage Foundation has supported this project from its outset and continues to do so, and we would especially like to thank board members Pete Standing Alone, Frank Weasel Head, Francis First Charger, Martin Heavy Head, Narcisse Blood, and Dorothy First Rider for their thoughtful suggestions and advice as the project has developed, and also for their editorial skills while we have been writing this volume. The Red Crow Community College Elders Advisory Committee provided much-needed guidance and we thank them for so generously sharing their thoughts about the project with us. Georgette Fox kindly arranged our meetings with the Elders Advisory Committee, and also organized the supper we enjoyed at Red

Crow Community College on the occasion of the handover of the copies of Blackwood's photographs and the project materials. We thank Marie Smallface Marule, President of Red Crow Community College, for allowing us the use of the College facilities on this occasion, and Myrna Chief Moon for preparing the meal. The catering staff at the Blood Tribe Continuing Care Centre must be gratefully acknowledged for preparing the food we enjoyed during meetings with the Red Crow Elders Advisory Committee. We would like to thank Shirley Bruised Head, Education Officer at Head Smashed In Buffalo Jump Interpretative Centre, for sharing so generously her own encounters with images from the past. Alvine Mountain Horse kindly provided transcriptions of the Blackfoot names and phrases used in the text and Duane Mistaken Chief provided explanatory background for a number of these terms, as well as thoughtful commentary on the draft manuscript. Most especially, we would like to acknowledge the contribution of Andy Blackwater, whose interest in the project and belief in its importance for the Kainai community has been central to its success.

Staff at the Glenbow Museum, Calgary, have been incredibly supportive and hospitable, both professionally and personally, and created an important and stimulating museum base for us in Canada. Gerry Conaty, Senior Ethnologist at the Glenbow Museum and also a board member of the Mookaakin Cultural and Heritage Foundation, gave generously of his long experience working with Kainai people. Beth Carter, Doug Cass, Nancy Cope, Clifford Crane Bear, Irene Kerr, Ron Marsh, Lindsay Moir, Pat Molesky, and Camille Owens all contributed to the project in countless ways, and we would like to thank them for their many kindnesses.

At the Pitt Rivers Museum, Michael O'Hanlon, Director, has supported the project from the outset and was willing to allow us to negotiate and sign the protocol agreement with the Mookaakin Cultural and Heritage Foundation, thus engaging the Museum in an unprecedented long-term relationship with the Kainai people. Elizabeth Edwards, Curator of Manuscripts and Photographs, was exceptionally generous with her knowledge and provided thoughtful and stimulating theoretical insights at every step of the way. Her approach to curating historical anthropological photographs as artefacts, her critical analysis of the problematic colonial framework of so many anthropological photographs, and her understanding of the importance of historic images to indigenous source communities has in many ways made the project possible. Claire Freeman, Marina de Alarçon, Lynn Parker, and

Jocelyne Dudding helped us access Blackwood's photographs, teaching slides, and manuscripts. Julia Cousins and Sue Brooks assisted greatly by administering the project, and Museum photographer Malcolm Osman scanned and printed Beatrice Blackwood's images and provided them on disk for our and the Kainai's use. Chris Gosden and Chantal Knowles generously shared with us their research on Beatrice Blackwood's career. Norman Weller, at the PRM Research Centre, facilitated the project in many ways, and we thank him for his daily assistance. Other colleagues and our students at Oxford have been encouraging and supportive, and have helped us to keep going with the work.

The Arts and Humanities Research Board of the United Kingdom provided generous funding for this project, and kindly understood when we had to change plans. At the grant application stage we had to go against their policy of not having any contact with potential reviewers, for without the knowledge and support of the Kainai community and our contact Gerry Conaty of the Glenbow Museum (whom we listed as a potential reviewer), it would not have been ethically possible to proceed with the project. The AHRB accepted this, and we hope that in many other small ways this project serves to educate funding bodies about the need to work with cultural protocols in indigenous communities.

Paul Hackett drew the map for us; Irene Kerr prepared the index. To both we offer our thanks.

We would like to thank Jill McConkey and Frances Mundy of the University of Toronto Press for their advice and support throughout the publication process and Judy Williams, copy editor, for her careful work. We would also like to acknowledge the thoughtful suggestions of the two anonymous reviewers.

Alison would especially like to thank Narcisse Blood and Alvine Mountain Horse, Jenny Bruised Head, Charlie and Betty Crow Chief, Beth Carter and Irene Kerr and their families for their friendship and continued support during her visits to Alberta, and Tom and Joy Brown for their constant encouragement. Drew Davey, Laura's husband, provided further photographic support both in Oxford and on the Blood Reserve; copied tapes to send back to community members; and supported us all the way.

Alison K. Brown
Laura Peers

March 2005

Project Participants

Immi'tsimaakii, Annie Bare Shin Bone
Interviewed on 27 August 2001; 30 August 2002

Naatoisipisttohkomi, Mary Stella Bare Shin Bone,
Interviewed on 13 August 2002; 14 August 2002

Sikapinaakii, Betty Bastien
Interviewed on 27 November 2001

Aatso'to'aawa, Andy Blackwater
Interviewed on 26 November 2001; 15 August 2002

Kinaksaapo'p, Narcisse Blood
Interviewed on 6 December 2001; 20 August 2002

Shirley Bruised Head
Interviewed on 28 November 2001

Omahkokomi, Charlie Crow Chief
Interviewed on 20 November 2001; 30 November 2001;
1 September 2002

Mamio'kakiikin, Adam Delaney
Interviewed on 4 December 2001; 28 August 2002

Tanataakii, Angeline Eagle Bear
Interviewed on 3 December 2001

Ninaisipisto, Francis First Charger
Interviewed on 2 December 2001

Iitomomaahkaa, Dorothy First Rider
Interviewed on 4 December 2001; 6 September 2002

Niipomaakii, Georgette Fox
Interviewed on 5 December 2001; 27 August 2002

Maanina, Stephen Fox
Interviewed on 9 September 2002

Sowa'tsaakii, Celina Goodstriker
Interviewed on 19 November 2001

Piinakoyim, Rufus Goodstriker
Interviewed on 19 November 2001; 20 August 2002

Ponokaiksiksinam, Martin Heavy Head
Interviewed on 16 November 2001; 8 September 2002

Issokoiyo'maahkaawa, Bill Heavy Runner
Interviewed on 3 December 2001

Otakkoyiisaapo'p, Allan Prairie Chicken
Interviewed on 5 December 2001; 27 August 2002

Tsiinaaki, Rosie Red Crow
Interviewed on 21 November 2001; 17 August 2002

Piitaikiihtsipiimi, Louis Soop
Interviewed on 30 November 2001

Ni'takaiksamaikowan, Pete Standing Alone
Interviewed on 27 November 2001

Sipistapi, Bernard Tall Man
Interviewed on 10 December 2001; 6 September 2002

Matsistaotoikamo'saakii, Rita Tall Man
Interviewed on 10 December 2001; 6 September 2002

Miyanisstsaamiaaki, Margaret Weasel Fat
Interviewed on 5 December 2001; 10 September 2002

Mi'ksskimm, Frank Weasel Head
Interviewed on 28 November 2001

Napia'koisi, Francis Whiteman Left
Interviewed on 7 December 2001; 9 September 2002

Makoiyiipoka, Bruce Wolf Child
Interviewed on 20 November 2001; 4 September 2002

‘PICTURES BRING US MESSAGES’ / SINAAKSSIIKSI AOHTSIMAAHPIHKOOKIYAAWA

Introduction

What you have brought us; I would say you have brought us a lot of our history. Just by bringing these photographs.

Margaret Weasel Fat, 5 December 2001

In August 1925, Beatrice Blackwood, a staff member from the Pitt Rivers Museum of the University of Oxford in England, spent two days at the Blood Indian Reserve in southern Alberta, Canada, where she took thirty-three photographs of Blood people. She intended them to illustrate anthropological ideas about racial difference and cultural change. In the autumn of 2001, Alison Brown and Laura Peers, a researcher and a curator from the Pitt Rivers Museum, took copies of these photographs back to the Blood Reserve and worked with members of the community, who call themselves Kainai,[1] to try to understand their perspectives on the images and their importance to Kainai people today. This book is about that process, about why museum professionals and archivists should work with such communities, and about some of the considerations that need to be addressed when doing so. We use the Kainai-Oxford Photographic Histories Project as a case study to explore some of the meanings historic photographs have for source communities, and also to explore new ways of working with such materials: developing collaborative methodologies for research, and culturally appropriate ways of curating, archiving, accessing, and otherwise using museum and archival collections. As we are based in the UK, we are aware that such developments are proving especially challenging for museums here and in Europe, and hope that this book will be used by heritage professionals working on this side of the

Atlantic who generally have little experience of working collaboratively with source communities based overseas.[2] However, we also hope that its messages will reach all museum and archival staff, regardless of their location, who wish to make the collections they care for more accessible and relevant to these audiences. While this particular project has linked the Pitt Rivers Museum with a First Nations[3] community in Canada, the dynamics of the project are applicable to other indigenous peoples and other heritage institutions elsewhere. At its deepest level, this project has turned out to be not about photographs at all, but about relationships – both the historic cross-cultural relationships documented in the photographs and the potential relationships which can be developed around such materials in the present. It is also about the current and future benefits of these new relationships both to First Nations communities and to museums and archives.

Beatrice Blackwood's photographs of Kainai people are part of the Photograph and Manuscript Collections of Oxford University's Pitt Rivers Museum, a museum dedicated to the study of human cultures founded by General Augustus Henry Lane Fox Pitt Rivers in 1884 (Chapman 1985). Blackwood took these images during a three-year research trip to Canada and the United States between 1924 and 1927. She had trained as an anthropologist, with special interests in physical anthropology, and the core of her research on this trip involved gathering genealogies and collecting measurements to try to understand which behaviours and physical appearances were responses to social and economic circumstances and which were inherited. Blackwood also took photographs to illustrate physical features of the peoples with whom she worked and to show changing Native cultures, and from some communities she collected hair samples and children's drawings as well. Her photographs of First Nations people focus on reserve communities located throughout the western part of the continent including Norway House and Oxford House in Manitoba; the Kainai (Blood) and Tsuu T'ina (Sarcee) Nations in Alberta; Kispiox and Alert Bay on the Northwest Coast; Red Lake and Nett Lake in Minnesota; and several villages in the American southwest. In addition, she worked with African-American and white communities in parts of the United States, and took photographs in several communities in Kentucky and North Carolina.

Out of all the material Blackwood collected on this trip, we focus on her thirty-three photographs of the Blood Reserve and her related fieldnotes and diary, and explore the very different meanings and uses such collections have had for Kainai people and for anthropologists. At the theoretical level, we explore the differences and productive tensions between the interpretations assigned to photographs of First Nations people by non-Native scholars, and how these same images can be understood quite differently by First Nations peoples themselves.

Within Kainai contexts, an understanding of the Blackfoot term for photograph – *Sinaakssin* – has been helpful in understanding how images can encompass different sets of meanings at any one time. Blackfoot is a descriptive language and *Sinaakssin* is a term that is also used to describe writing and drawings. As *Ai'ai'stahkommi* (Duane Mistaken Chief) has explained, when translated literally, *Sinaakssin* refers to an image that has been produced. The term for camera – *Isstaisinnakyo'p* (or *Iihtaisinaakio'p*) – describes 'what we use to [create] an image' (Duane Mistaken Chief to Brown, pers. comm. 20 July 2004). As with the Blackfoot language, where words are used to create and build up images within the mind of the listener, photographs – and the words woven around them – can also be used by Kainai people to explore and understand their past. Just as those images evoked by words will be understood differently by different listeners, photographs are historically and culturally contingent records which can be read according to one's position, background, and purpose: the anthropological context and meanings of the images taken by Beatrice Blackwood on the Blood Reserve in 1925 have been viewed quite differently by the Kainai, both then and now, and indeed by Museum staff over the years. The moment in time recorded in these images is the same, but is tied to historical narratives that vary depending on who is viewing the image. The photographs thus serve as a focus for understanding the different stories about Kainai culture and history told by anthropologists, historians, and the Kainai, and how these narratives have changed over time (see Zuyderhoudt 2004 for an overview of approaches to Blackfoot history).

Perhaps most interestingly, the photographs have allowed us to explore how such materials, produced to have meaning within and contribute to particular scholarly interests and discourses, might be reframed and reused within very different sets of interests and discourses within academia and the Kainai community. That images intended to refer to issues of race and acculturation, with all the implications of colonial control these interests implied, could be used today to address not only the nature of revisionist history but also the need of Kainai people to articulate to themselves their experiences of the past and, ultimately, to speak to their children about the strength of their community suggests again the importance of such collections to indigenous peoples. Such dynamics also have important theoretical implications for scholars working with materials of this nature, urging us to pay attention to what historic photographs suggest about the relationships between photographer and subject, to the intellectual and political contexts in which images were composed, and – while bearing these contexts in mind – to the possibilities of reading against the grain and original intellectual intentions of photographs in ways that can benefit both academic scholars and Native communities (see Stoler and Strassler 2000).

In the process of undertaking this project, we were asked by Kainai people to work in a way that is more accountable to them than many social science researchers have been to First Nations in the past. Over the last century and a half, there has been a problematic tradition of scholars from the dominant society extracting cultural knowledge from Native communities for their own purposes. Too frequently, academics have failed to ensure that the communities with whom they work benefit from their research, and, as a result, First Nations people have begun to object to traditional social science methods, saying that they have been 'studied to death':

> These feelings are very common – most researchers have had the experience of being questioned about the relevance of their work, or have been taken to task by Aboriginal people for building their career on ideas taken from Aboriginal people. To say that communities feel 'researched to death' is to state, powerfully and metaphorically, that words and ideas ... can kill, disempower, or destroy. As anthropologists are all too aware, research is easily associated with the colonial project. But ... this research lament is more about the way research has been conducted (the lack of native direction and control over the research process) and about the lack of applied research, than it is about research per se. (Warry 1998: 245–6)

By adopting a collaborative, community-based methodology in which Kainai worked with us to shape the research questions and process, advised us on cultural protocol, and reviewed research findings at every step of the way, we have been able to work in a manner which serves both scholarly and community needs. We document this process as part of this book, to serve as a guide for other researchers contemplating similar projects, and we heartily endorse such participatory approaches. This has been a tremendously exciting project that not only has enriched our knowledge of these images, but has brought us as individuals, and the Pitt Rivers Museum, together on a long-term basis to work with a dynamic source community. We have been gratified to see people on the Blood Reserve discussing the photographs at length, displaying them in their homes, remembering their ancestors, and thinking about how to use the images in the present. Their responses to the photographs have much to teach us.

Similar visual repatriation projects have shown that materials of this sort have important meanings for and uses to indigenous people. When indigenous communities reconnect with ancestral images – most especially through the act of bringing copies of archival photographs home and allowing them to be viewed within their cultural and geographical context rather than in an archival space – these meanings are even more acutely expressed. As indigenous peoples seek to heal from the difficult past of the previous few centuries and to strengthen their cultural vitality for future generations, photographs – often obtained during times of intense cultural pressures – can inspire the telling of community and cultural histories which are otherwise little documented and difficult to retrieve, submerged as they often are by mainstream historical analyses and by the processes of colonialism. Looking at historic images and photographs of objects in museum collections can therefore provide opportunities for the transfer of cultural knowledge across generations (Binney and Chaplin 1991; Edwards 1994 and 2003; Poignant 1996; Fienup-Riordan 1998; Brown 2000; Thompson et al 2001; Bell 2003; Kingston 2003). Despite such potential, it can be very difficult for indigenous community members to locate and work with historic collections, which are scattered in museums and archives in cities around the world, and are frequently incompletely catalogued and unpublished. Many people often have no idea that material pertaining to their community resides in certain archives, and seldom have the resources to hunt it down for community use. We argue that the meanings, and the community discourses that encounters with such images spark, are so important to indigenous communities that it is imperative that archivists and museum professionals find ways of creating access to these forms of cultural heritage for source communities – and it is well worth their doing so, because of the tremendous gains in knowledge that research partnerships can bring.

Visual repatriation projects have also shown the potential for important theoretical contributions and revisions to non-Native scholarship, by challenging mainstream interpretations which too often have been developed without direct indigenous input, and with documents and photographs generated entirely by non-Natives. Community-based projects exploring photographs add considerably to perspectives and techniques developed in recent decades by ethnohistorians, social historians, and other social scientists which seek to interpret documentary evidence from the point of view of the indigenous people concerned. These techniques acknowledge that materials such as photographs and documents can be read at many levels: they are records of societies in transition and provide commentary on social conditions and relationships between indigenous and non-indigenous peoples. The stories they elicit contribute immeasurably to a more balanced interpretation of the past, as well as critical commentary on the biases brought to the interpretation of photographs and of historical information by non-Native scholars. Most importantly, they can provide parallel, culturally oriented historical narratives, with fascinating resonances and dissonances between them. In this volume, we show how the anthropological context and meanings of Blackwood's Kainai photographs are very different from the meanings and contexts seen by the Kainai themselves. The differences between the narratives tell us much about the Native-white relations which produced the historical moment in which the photographs were taken.

Outline and Goals

As an important model for both this research project and this book, we have found Roslyn Poignant's *Encounter at Nagalarramba* (1996) – her account of returning photographs to an Australian Aboriginal community where they had been taken several decades earlier by her husband, Axel Poignant – to be most stimulating. It seems, therefore, both appropriate and useful to quote a key statement from her work explaining the approach that she took and on which we have drawn:

> The starting point for this book has been ... to re-engage with the whole archive of published and unpublished photographs, and to attempt to recover the ethnohistorical past of their production. The use of these photographs as sources of documentation, however, requires that particular consideration be given to the relationship between the content and construction of these images. Consequently, there are several intersecting histories with which this book is concerned: the piece of ethnohistory apparently contained within the frame, the nature of the photographic

> practices of the period, and the socio-economic and cultural constraints within which the photographer worked ... An essential part of the reconstructive process underlying the project has been the reintroduction of the photographs to the Arnhem Land community in 1992, and the beginning of the community's re-engagement with them. (Poignant 1996: 6)

Poignant's statement raises the complex realities of projects which seek to engage, or re-engage, with historic photographs, projects which necessarily work across historical contexts, across cultures, and which raise the very different sets of meanings attached to such images by anthropologists (then and now) and members of the communities (then and now) in which anthropologists photographed. In order to understand what historic images were intended to mean, what they have meant, and how they can be used today by community members and by outside researchers, it is absolutely necessary to consider the historical, political, and social contexts in which images were produced and subsequently used (Poignant 1996: 60ff; Schwarz 1997: 18; Edwards 2001: 88). As will become clear in subsequent chapters, what is depicted in a photograph can mean very different things depending on these contexts.

The structure of this book reflects the multiple contexts within which Blackwood's photographs can be situated. We begin in chapter 1 by examining the immediate context in which the photographs were produced, which is the history of the Kainai people, of their experiences on the Blood Reserve, and of resistance to attempts by colonial officials to assimilate them. We also discuss their experiences of being represented in photography and art by non-Native people. Not only did these histories affect what Blackwood saw and recorded when she passed through, but they continue to affect how Kainai people read the images today.

In chapter 2, we explore the other set of contexts in which Blackwood's images were created: her own career and her work within the broader contexts of anthropological interests and the genre of anthropometric photography. Blackwood's interest in race and both traditional and assimilated elements of Native cultures meant that she was interested in obtaining certain kinds of images which conveyed information relevant to these scholarly concerns. Her relationship with these discourses and with the colonial dynamics behind them was ambiguous, however, and we explore the ways in which she both relied on and rejected them across her career.

In chapter 3, we describe how we worked when we took the images back to the Kainai community, and why. We describe our methodology and its development, looking closely at how, together, we created a formal protocol agreement which has provided a framework for the Kainai-Oxford Photographic Histories Project and a means of ensuring that mutual goals are met. We have chosen to present this material in some detail, not only to contextualize the discussion which follows, but also to indicate how Kainai people and the Pitt Rivers Museum have together found solutions to some of the challenges of undertaking collaborative projects; challenges which often are embedded within research culture itself.

In chapter 4, Alison Brown, who conducted the interviews with Kainai community members, discusses their responses to the photographs. Five strong themes emerged in these interviews, and are discussed in detail. One was the importance of restoring Blackfoot names of individuals depicted, and the links between these names to elements of Kainai history and kinship, and the importance of such knowledge in the present. A second theme was what people called the 'transitional period,' the experiences and histories of Kainai in the 1920s. Several other themes stemmed from these: the experience of disruption and loss, symbolized by Blackwood's images of girls at residential school; the pride and hard work associated with the survival of the people during this time; and the core cultural values which many Kainai read in the images, and the importance of these in the present for educating today's youth.

Chapter 5 explores the implications of these Kainai meanings of the photographs. Some of these have to do with the Kainai today, such as the uses they are making of the images to transmit historical and cultural knowledge across generations, and the ways in which the photographs permit the articulation of Kainai perspectives, narratives, and world view. These deeper meanings of the photographs, the way in which they facilitate Kainai ideas about the past and how history should be narrated and understood, have relevance for the methods and theories of academic researchers, and we discuss in this chapter several ways in which Kainai responses to these photographs challenge outside scholars' attempts to understand First Nations histories.

This section has important implications for museums and archives, which we go on to discuss in chapter 6, for it underscores the need to take indigenous critiques on board and make collections more accessible in order to trigger the very positive benefits historic materials have for source communities today. In chapter 6 we discuss issues of access and stewardship, and the ways in which ordinary operational procedures can be barriers for indigenous source communities – and how these might be altered to facilitate access. Finally, in the Conclusion, we discuss some of the lessons we ourselves have learned through this project, some of the difficulties – entirely typical of cross-cultural research – we encountered, and our solutions to these.

Working with Kainai people on the Kainai-Oxford Photographic Histories Project has been a transformative experience for us both, and we are committed to strengthening the connections we have made with community members, both formally and informally, as the next phase of the project is developed. Although the project has built upon research methods that we have both tried to enact at varying levels throughout our careers, the focus on discussing appropriate methodology with our Kainai research partners prior to undertaking the formal interviewing process has consolidated much of our thinking on these issues, and has allowed us to develop a deeper understanding of the practicalities of undertaking collaborative research. Our subsequent conversations with community members concerning their views on how the project has progressed and how they would like to see it develop further have added to our understanding of the nature of the shifting relationships between museums and First Nations communities.

A Note on Language and Terminology

Blackfoot is an Algonquian language which is spoken by many hundreds of people in Alberta and Montana. All the Blackfoot communities in Alberta and Montana have developed immersion programs to help younger generations learn how to communicate in Blackfoot. At Kainai, the development of teaching materials for school and college students and several projects to record words and phrases that are infrequently used are contributing to language retention within the community. Few people write Blackfoot, however, and there is some debate among Blackfoot speakers over the standardization of spellings which do not take into account regional dialects.

When we discussed the issue of how to proceed with spelling the Kainai names used in this book with the Mookaakin Foundation, we were advised to use the spellings that are taught in Kainai schools. Alvine Mountain Horse, a teacher with the Kainai Board of Education, worked with us as a language consultant, and we would like thank her for advice as we prepared the manuscript. We are also grateful to Duane Mistaken Chief for his comments on the Blackfoot expressions used within this volume. Mistaken Chief has extensive experience of researching Blackfoot language and culture and incorporating both older and more modern forms of Blackfoot into curricula across a range of disciplines and at all levels of the education system (see also Bastien 2004).

There is one term we use in this book which requires further explanation: 'elder.' Within Blackfoot culture, *Aawaaahsskataiksi* are those individuals who have acquired specific forms of spiritual knowledge through having been initiated into sacred societies or through caring for sacred pipes or bundles. This word is not used as a general term, and each individual has certain specialities, based on the sacred knowledge he or she has acquired and the ceremonies they have been through (First Charger to Brown, pers. comm. 25 March 2005). They are the people who *A'kaomatapaaahsskata*, a term which translates as 'people have begun to use them as advisors [for sacred knowledge],' and they have the rights to teach about this knowledge and to transfer it to others. In the Blackfoot language, they are referred to as *Aawaaahsskataiksi* or *Kaaahsinnooniksi*, and in English the terms 'elders,' 'spiritual elders', 'ceremonialists,' 'ceremonial teachers,' and 'spiritual grandparents' are often used. Duane Mistaken Chief has provided the following explanation of the terms *Kaaahsinnooniksi* and *Aawaaahsskataiksi*:

> *Kaaahsinnooniksi* means 'our grandparents.' It is used for both ceremonial grandparents and biological or relational grandparents. *Aawaaahsskataiksi* (plural) *Aawaaahsskatawa* (singular) are more specific terms as they are used only in the context of ceremonial grandparents (those that are past members of a society or are former bundle owners). However, they are also referred to as *Kaaahssinnooniksi* too. (Duane Mistaken Chief to Brown, pers. comm. 22 March 2005)

It is important to note that the term 'elder,' in the context of the sacred and ceremony, does not imply an elderly person, but is directly connected to the specific spiritual teachings which a person has acquired. Additionally, some individuals may prefer to use terms other than 'elder' when speaking English. Following consultation with the Mookaakin Foundation, we have been advised to use the term 'elder' in this book to refer to these ceremonial grandparents on the understanding that it has wider meanings that are not easily translatable into English. For a fuller explanation of the role of *Kaaahsinnooniksi* within Blackfoot culture, we direct readers to chapter 15 of Betty Bastien's recent book *Blackfoot Ways of Knowing* (Bastien 2004: 147–50).

CHAPTER ONE

The Photographs and Their Contexts: Kainai History

Introduction

Just as the Blackfoot language builds up images in the minds of listeners – slightly different images, according to associations made by each individual listener – so Blackwood's photographs of Kainai people take on different meanings according to the contexts in which they have been placed. While our conclusions from the Kainai-Oxford Photographic Histories Project are that photographs have the potential to slip between different contexts and meanings, gathering new resonances along the way, it is crucial to understand the circumstances in which Blackwood's photographs were created, for these shape the images as much as does their content. Only when we understand these social, cultural, historical, and intellectual contexts does the rest of the project make sense: our way of working with Kainai people in the present, the resonance the photographs have for Kainai people, and the implications of all this for scholarship and for heritage institutions.

In this and the following chapter we explore these contexts: Beatrice Blackwood's background, and her research goals, which influenced what she saw and recorded, and the ways in which she used the images and associated information across her career; the place of Blackwood's Kainai photographs within the history of photography of Native peoples and of anthropological photography; and the forces that shaped the Blood Reserve and the lives of Kainai people to produce what Blackwood saw as she travelled through that community. Here we begin with the photographs themselves, and their relationship to the lives of Kainai people in the 1920s.

Beatrice Blackwood's Photographs

Beatrice Blackwood's photographs reflect some of the changes that were taking place within the First Nations communities she encountered at a time when they were undergoing cultural, social, and economic stress caused by pressures from the dominant society to assimilate. The brevity of her visits to each community made Blackwood by necessity an opportunistic photographer, recording people during the course of their ordinary daily activities. She took her photographs of Kainai people on the 3rd and 4th of August 1925, when she was part-way through a three-year research trip to Canada and the United States between 1924 and 1927. Blackwood had trained as an anthropologist, with special interests in physical anthropology, and on this trip she gathered genealogies and body measurements to try to understand which behaviours and physical appearances were responses to social and economic circumstances and which were inherited. Her photographs, as we discuss in greater detail in chapter 2, were intended to illustrate physical features of the peoples with whom she worked and to show changing Native cultures.

Blackwood's thirty-three Kainai photographs were taken at the Indian Agency (the administrative centre of the Reserve), at the office of the Indian Agent, the government official responsible for overseeing Department of Indian Affairs (DIA) policies, and during a tour of the Reserve with the agent himself, Joseph Faunt.[1] Some are informal portraits of couples or groups of women with their children and grandchildren. Most, however, are loosely of the anthropometric style used by anthropologists in the late nineteenth and early twentieth centuries to classify peoples from around the world – paired frontal and side views of individuals and, sometimes, couples. In addition to the portraits, Blackwood also took a single landscape image on the Reserve.

The photographs show men in the fields, women collecting rations, a family group beside a tipi, children with their mothers. In most cases the subjects were presumably requested to interrupt what they were doing, asked to pose, and then photographed. One group put on their dress clothing to stand by a painted tipi. Blackwood also took four class photographs of schoolgirls at the Roman Catholic Residential School, located at this time near the community of Standoff. Most of these girls, having reached adolescence, were forbidden by staff to go home for the summer holidays lest they get into 'trouble.' Younger girls who had lost one or both parents were also frequently compelled to stay at school over the summer months. Most of the girls in these images appear tense

1.1 Beatrice Blackwood on fieldwork in Yoho Valley, British Columbia, 1925. Photographer unknown. (Pitt Rivers Museum, University of Oxford, PRM. BB.A3.102)

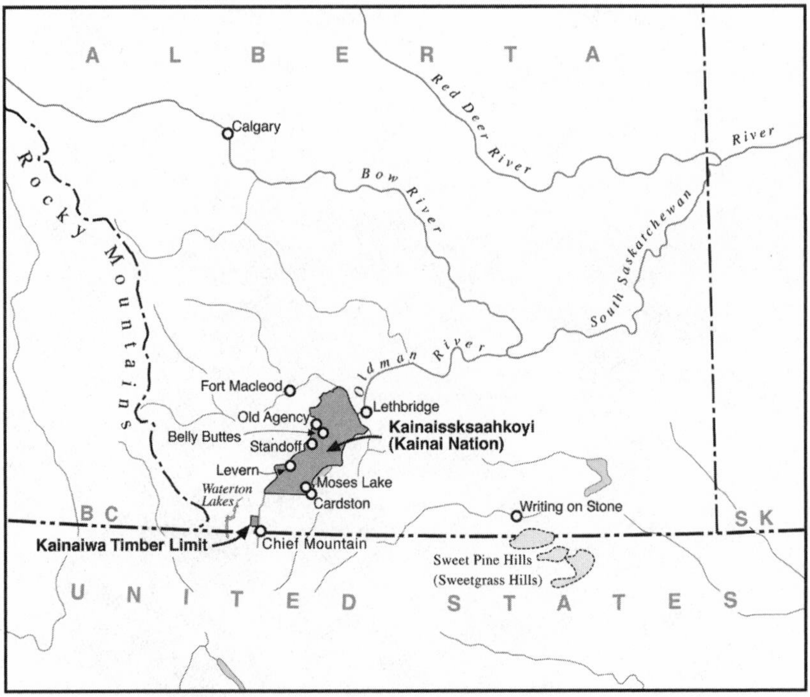

Map 1 The Blood Reserve (drawn by Paul Hackett)

and uneasy, uncertain of the implications of posing for this stranger. Taken together, and especially with the narratives Kainai people bring to them today, Blackwood's photographs do not just demonstrate cultural loss or 'vanishing peoples,' as she would have seen it, but make a remarkable portrait of a strong community in transition and encapsulate Kainai history and lives. To understand how this is so, it is necessary to explore something of Kainai history, and the historical trajectories of the Kainai people.

The Blood Reserve: Experiencing Change

The people Blackwood photographed were survivors of a difficult history,[2] reflected both in the content of her photographs and the very fact that she drove around the Blood Reserve with the Indian Agent in order to take them. The last quarter of the nineteenth century was a time of tremendous change and upheaval for the Blackfoot nations, and they had every reason to be deeply protective of their traditional territory, which stretches from *Ponokasisahta* (Elk River, the North Saskatchewan River) south to *Otahkoitahtayi* (the Yellowstone River) (Blackfoot Gallery Committee 2001: 4). Much of their distrust stemmed from tension between Blackfoot bands and whisky and fur traders and, increasingly, other settlers, which often created unstable relationships and an atmosphere of suspicion. Oral accounts relate how during the 1860s and 1870s, Kainai people were frequently subjected to brutal and traumatic attacks in which entire families were slaughtered, women were raped, and camps were burned (Rufus Goodstriker to Brown, pers. comm. 15 November 2001). Although the Kainai maintained a range of relationships with outsiders, most of which were entered into for the benefit of their own people (see for example Wischmann 2004), it was not until *Mi'kai'sto* (Chief Red Crow) befriended Colonel James Macleod, of the North West Mounted Police, who arrived with his troops in the area in 1874 with the intention of stemming the whisky trade, that their interactions with outsiders generally assumed less violent dimensions (Dempsey 2002).

Recurring waves of sickness, especially smallpox, which almost obliterated their populations, the destruction of the bison herds, which had sustained them for generations,[3] and the gradual reduction of other game, combined with the unceasing encroachment of non-Native society, compelled band leaders to negotiate Treaties with the British Crown. Along with other provisions, such as educational facilities, rations, and agricultural assistance, each Treaty provided for the establishment of a reserve, where the Native signatories believed the rights they had been promised would be safeguarded and their people would be able to retain some level of autonomy while adapting to the changes taking place around them. Native people continue to regard the Treaties signed during this era as sacred agreements which, from their perspective, constituted an act of friendship and established peaceful relationships between nations; for the Kainai, Treaty 7 is part of the tradition of *Innaisstssiisinni*[4] whereby a good and lasting relationship is created between peoples who have previously been at war (Treaty 7 Elders et al. 1996: 67–9).[5] Kainai expectations of their relationship with Canada are shaped by this concept and the notion that the Treaty is 'a solemn and binding undertaking, existing in perpetuity' (Shade 2002).

The Crown representatives, however, and later those of the Canadian government, viewed the Treaties differently, and believed that they amounted to land surrenders. This argument has been repeatedly, consistently, and forcefully denied by the Blackfoot, who argue that the Euro-Canadian legal terms used by the Crown had no meaning for a people that had no concept of land ownership but instead regarded themselves as being placed within their territory by *Ihtsitapitapiiyo'pa*,[6] and regarded the land as a source of knowledge and survival (Blackfoot Gallery Committee 2001: 66; see also Treaty 7 Elders et al. 1996; Bastien 2004; Duane Mistaken Chief to Brown, pers. comm. 8 September 2004). From the government perspective, freeing up vast amounts of land would allow for the opening up of the west for immigrants who were arriving in increasing numbers, and who would settle and cultivate the land, thereby improving the country's economic prosperity. The erroneous and widely held assumption that the Native population was dying out, even though the declining census figures had reversed by the 1920s,[7] meant that designating land as reserves was intended as a temporary measure, and in good time this land would become available for the use of settlers.

Once reserves had been established and Native people moved onto the land allocated to them, their daily lives were then controlled by the provisions of the 1876 Indian Act and its subsequent amendments, which consolidated and revised all previous legislation in the existing provinces and territories, and which had been passed without any consultation with the Native population. Their new status as 'wards' of the government subjected them to a mass of legislation that attempted to mould them into good Christian, Canadian citizens. Yet they were not represented in Parliament and had no say in the schemes or laws that affected them and their children. The paternalistic attitudes of officials led to the imposition of Euro-Canadian notions of education, health care, and economic individualism upon people who traditionally had perfectly satisfactory means of dealing with these concerns (Grant 1983: 21). Policies which from the start were invasive, restrictive and unsympathetic to their needs became even more so as time passed and it became apparent that Native people were not conforming to governmental and ecclesiastical expectations.

External repression peaked in the years following the First World War when many bands were at their lowest point owing to losses from the 1918 influenza epidemic and other health crises, hunger resulting from the failure of their agricultural efforts, the prohibitions on ceremonial expression and economic development, and the subsequent collapse of traditional social and cultural organizations through missionary influence and generational differences (Samek 1987; K. Pettipas 1994; Titley 1995 [1986]; Regular 1999). Though the Department of Indian Affairs, the government agency responsible for implementing the provisions of the Indian Act, endured some criticism over its harsh methods, it persisted with its key policy of self-sufficiency, so succinctly voiced in 1931 by Duncan Campbell Scott (1862–1947), Deputy Superintendent General of Indian Affairs from 1913 to 1931:

> ... the Government will in time reach the end of its responsibility as the Indians progress into civilization and finally disappear as a separate and distinct people, not by race extinction, but by gradual assimilation with their fellow citizens. (Scott 1931: 27)

It was not till the overhaul of the Indian Act in 1951 that many of the government's schemes of assimilation, though blatantly unenforceable and ineffectual, were struck from the statute books.

Oral histories and documentary sources which address the response of the Blood Tribe to the pressures they faced at this time present a strong and proud community that was able to make the adjustment from a nomadic to a settled lifestyle because of the tenacity and adaptability of the population and the strength of its leadership. Samek, in her comparative study of US and Canadian governmental policy towards the Blackfoot-speaking peoples, cites a comment made by the Indian Agent in 1909 that his wards maintained 'a proud and imperious spirit which after 28 years of reservation life is still the dominant characteristic of the Bloods' (Samek 1987: 134). Community members today frequently refer to their strong sense of cultural identity and their pride in being Kainai (Blackwater 15 August 2002).

Following the signing of Treaty 7 in 1877, land along the north side of the Bow and Saskatchewan Rivers was set aside for the three Blackfoot tribes residing on the Canadian side of the border. However, this land was unsuitable for agriculture and different reserves were established closer to the foothills of the Rocky Mountains (F. Taylor 1989: 29).[8] The new Blood Reserve was established in 1883 and, at 547.5 square miles, is the largest in the country. Rivers flow along the west, east, and northern boundaries (the St Mary, Oldman, and Belly), and a straight surveyed line along the Canada-US border marks the southern edge. The land is undulating and the natural cover is grassland, though a variety of trees and bushes, including poplar, spruce, willow, and chokecherry, grow in the river valleys. There is an abundance of wildflowers and many plants and shrubs are gathered for their medicinal qualities or for ceremonial purposes (Johnston 1987). The Reserve and surrounding area are rich in wildlife, including deer, moose, and numerous species of birds and reptiles. The proximity of the mountains creates an extreme climate, characterized by short, but hot and dry summers and biting cold and severe snowfalls throughout the winter months, sometimes causing flooding in the spring.

In 1925, when Beatrice Blackwood visited the Reserve, Kainai people were only two generations away from the buffalo-hunting days and were still learning to adapt to a very different sedentary lifestyle, based primarily around crop cultivation and the emergence of a ranching industry. The administrative hub of the Reserve was known as *Iikaatonnio'pi* (Old Agency), and though many people still preferred to camp in clan, or band, clusters comprising extended family, particularly in the summer time, this system was beginning to break down as people began to move into wooden houses.[9] Today the Reserve supports several distinct communities, for example, Moses Lake, Levern, and Standoff, where the Blood Tribe administration (*Iitonnio'pi*) is located, and though people generally no longer live in the areas associated with their clans, clan affiliation remains important as a mark of identification for Kainai people.[10] In contrast to 1925, the Reserve today supports a range of economic activities. Kainai agricultural organizations compete effectively in international markets and ranching continues to be lucrative for some individuals; others have developed successful careers in the rodeo industry (Baillargeon and Tepper 1998). The Kainai Board of Education, health care services, policing, and Blood Tribe administration provide employment opportunities for a large number of the working population; nonetheless, despite an increasingly diverse economy, unemployment remains high and opportunities on the Reserve are few. Many individuals, for example, are prevented from entering the agricultural industry because the costs involved are frequently prohibitive (Wolf Child 20 November 2001); in other cases, a lack of appropriate skills and experience prevents people from securing good jobs.

The Land

In the decades after the signing of Treaty 7, Canadian government officials made repeated attempts to persuade the Kainai to permit land sales and leases to nearby non-Native settlers, which would have reduced considerably the size of the Reserve. Following pressure from J.A. Markle, Inspector of Indian Agencies and Reserves for the Alberta Inspectorate, land sales had occurred at the Siksika and Peigan Reserves in the early decades of the twentieth century, and the government was confident that the Kainai would follow suit and agree to exchange part of their Reserve for the money that would grant them access to the new material wealth which they could see among their relatives (Narcisse Blood to Brown, pers. comm. 20 August 2002; see also Samek 1987). In the event, though a number of leases were granted, attempts to force the Tribe to sell part of its landbase were continually resisted, though not before a referendum on the issue had been held on the Reserve in 1917, with the Kainai being forced to vote on the proposed surrender of ninety thousand acres. On this occasion the Kainai opposed the surrender, but undaunted government officials began a program of intimidation and bribery and attempted to force the surrender by a second vote. Though this vote went in favour of the surrender, *Aatso'to'aawa* (Head Chief Shot Both Sides) immediately lodged a complaint in Ottawa, and demanded that it should not go ahead until a full investigation had taken place (Wilson 1921; Fisher 1974; Dempsey 1986: 50–1). Oral history continues to recognize the strength of his leadership during this period and the respect people had for him, as these two examples recalled by *Nii'ta'kaiksa'maikoan* (Pete Standing Alone) and *Maanina* (Stephen Fox), both of whom were Band Councillors and knew the Head Chief well, demonstrate:

> There was a time in the late teens when the government tried to get us to sell the north part of the Reserve. And they had a vote on it and the vote went to sell the land ... They hired a lawyer and they went through the ballots and [having realized that the election officials had included people who had not reached the voting age of twenty-one] they started taking [out] people that were not twenty-one. And after they'd done that, the guys that didn't want to sell came on top. If he [Head Chief Shot Both Sides] had just gave up, I wouldn't be living where I'm living. That part ... was going to be sold. So he did a lot for the people. He was an honest man. (Standing Alone 27 November 2001).

> I served under this gentleman. He was, I would say, a really smart person. He doesn't say much in Council. He would sit there, probably close his eyes. At one time, there was a new Council got in, and they said, 'The

> Chief is just sleeping all through the meeting.' But he wasn't sleeping. He closed his eyes but he was listening. He knows everything that was going on. This one guy tried to tell him that he was sleeping in Council. He says, 'Son, I don't sleep. I know everything that goes on.' He was a real smart person. (S. Fox 9 September 2002)

Despite the strength of resistance to land sales among the Kainai, the government persisted in its efforts to acquire land from the Tribe through whatever means possible. In 1918 the Reserve was threatened once again by the implementation of the 'Greater Production Plan,' a scheme devised by Indian Commissioner William Graham[11] with the intention of increasing crop cultivation, ostensibly to support the war effort (Dawson 2002). 'Unused' land was to be leased to white farmers and government farms would be established on five reserves in Canada, providing employment for Native labourers. A farm of 4,880 acres was created on the Blood Reserve, and the Tribe was asked to lease a further 6,000 acres to the government as a patriotic gesture, a superfluous request as a 1918 amendment to the Indian Act gave the Kainai no say in such matters (Dempsey 1986: 51). That same year, the Soldier Settlement Act was passed, intended to provide soldiers returning from the First World War with land to begin their own farming efforts. Since the Board established to deal with the Act was granted the power to buy up uncultivated land on reserves without Native consent, this proved to be another attack on the Kainai landbase.

At the same time as efforts were being made to reduce Kainai lands, a program of agricultural development was implemented and was regarded by the government as being the means through which the Kainai, along with other Nations in western Canada, would become self-sufficient. Even though the climate could be harsh, the soil was rich, and some sections of the Blood Reserve were ideal for agricultural development. Following the lead of Chief Red Crow, one of the first on the Reserve to start farming, the Kainai began to cultivate crops shortly after signing Treaty 7, and by 1881, the first seeding, downstream from the Old Agency, was almost complete (First Charger 1998: 4). Initially, farming activity was successful, with the Kainai working hard to produce crops of good quality. However, despite their willingness to adapt to the new conditions, the climate proved to be detrimental, and a series of droughts throughout the late 1880s and early 1890s, combined with the lack of access to the necessary agricultural implements, severely impeded Kainai attempts to cultivate the land (Dempsey 1980: 200–1).

By the turn of the twentieth century, the Kainai began to move their small patches of cultivated land along the river bottom to the open prairie to provide opportunities for larger-scale farming initiatives (First Charger 1998: 4). During the subsequent decade they worked extremely hard to turn large portions of the northern part of the Reserve over to grain production, and cultivated wheat, oats, vegetables, and hay of the highest quality. Using the proceeds from grazing leases, they purchased farming machinery, such as a steam-operated plough, and were able to provide financial assistance to individuals who wished to begin farming. Though there were periods of relative prosperity for some individuals during the late 1910s and early 1920s, in general the Kainai suffered the consequences of the shift from small-scale farming to mechanization: 'With this conversion ... the average Indian had neither the education nor the cultural conditioning to compete, and he slipped farther and farther behind his white neighbours' (First Charger 1998: 6).

The Kainai did not restrict themselves to crop cultivation during this period, and entered the stock-raising business in 1894 (Wilson 1921: 17). Over the next two decades, they expanded their herd through a loan system controlled by the government and by 1907 had increased their herd to seven thousand (F. Taylor 1989: 32) and continued to improve their stocks in the following years. Despite the praise that was directed towards them for their efforts in ranching and agriculture, disaster was to befall the Kainai by the early 1920s. The harsh winters of 1919 and 1920 combined with the post-war depression and the effects of the 1918 influenza epidemic were catastrophic for the Kainai economy. Overgrazing was especially problematic, with many white farmers ignoring the boundaries between the land they had leased and that used by the Tribe. Keith Regular, in his study of the intertwined economies of the Kainai and settler communities from 1884 to 1939, has observed that illegal trespass was constant and considerable and, as a result, 'it is almost certain that, except for short periods around round-up and sale, the Reserve was continually over-stocked' (Regular 1999: 116). Although wheat prices remained high for a further two years, the cattle industry was effectively wiped out in this period, with the government's mismanagement of the Tribe's resources being widely regarded as the main cause by Kainai leaders and other critics at the time, and subsequently by historians (e.g., Samek 1987: 85–6).[12]

The most vocal contemporary critic was former Indian Agent Robert N. Wilson, whose pamphlet, *Our Betrayed Wards*, detailed the rise and fall of the Kainai livestock industry. He exposed the government's ineffectual and callous response to the crisis of 1919–20, when cattle and horses died in their hundreds, with profound economic and social implications for the Kainai.[13] Wilson regarded the government's action as a deliberate attempt to cripple the Kainai economy, thereby forcing the Tribe to agree to land sales (Wilson 1921; see also Fisher 1974), and he also criticized the Greater Production Plan and the enforced leasing of Kainai lands. His list of alleged fraudulent intentions and behaviour on the part of government representatives makes bitter reading and is an important contextualizing document for Blackwood's Kainai photographs. During this period, the continued poor weather caused many Kainai, as well as white farmers, to simply give up their attempts to cultivate the land. Having been essentially self-sufficient since the 1890s, by 1920 many Kainai were facing extreme poverty, and were issued rations paid for from the Tribe's trust fund. Historian Hugh Dempsey has stated that $21,000 from the same source was used to restock the cattle herd, despite the losses being primarily due to government incompetence (Dempsey 1986: 61). During this difficult era Kainai families supported themselves by selling the produce from small family farms, working in the sugar-beet fields in the nearby settlement of Raymond, coal-mining, freighting, hay-making, and digging bison bones for fertilizer (Regular 1999).

Although their economic situation fluctuated somewhat according to market conditions and inclement weather, by the mid-1920s the Kainai were experiencing a period of economic recovery.[14] Material wealth was, however, concentrated in the hands of a small group of farmers, known as the 'Upper Ten' (Dempsey 1997: 8), and many in the community, though their economic situation had undoubtedly improved, were by no means affluent. Cultural values, such as the importance of sharing, remained uppermost and ensured that those with less access to the emerging cash economy were still cared for. Those growing up during this era were probably largely unaware of the economic imbalances between themselves and the non-Native community, and it is notable that they tended to comment on issues such as hunger only in relation to their time in boarding school. Pete Standing Alone, for example, recalled his own family's experience during this period:

> My Dad ... started to farm in 1921 in the aftermath of ... when they tried to sell the Reserve. There was a big lease around Cardston and, in 1921, they gave it out to individuals and my Dad got some of that land and he prospered and within ten years he was pretty well off. Like, during the

> depression, Hungry Thirties, Dirty Thirties, lot of names, I would be around eight and I never knew hardship the way people describe it because my Mother and Father provided for us. (Standing Alone 27 November 2001)

The Tribe's increasing economic prosperity was frequently remarked upon by outsiders, and the Kainai were often identified in the press and in other sources as being one of the most independent and resourceful Native communities in Canada, with many band members achieving economic success through their own efforts, without the level of government assistance given to many other First Nations (e.g., Long Lance 1921: 20). Department of Indian Affairs (DIA) Annual Reports from this era point to the success of Kainai farmers, though they gloss over the fact that it was largely due to the persistence and hard work of Reserve residents who overcame the official obstructions: 'On the Blood Reserve the advancement in the way of farming has been marked. These Indians had a splendid crop in 1924, and it is believed, when the returns are in, the crop for 1925 will reach the two hundred and fifty thousand bushel mark' (Report of the Deputy Superintendent General 1925: 7). Among those who remarked on the material wealth acquired by some individuals was Beatrice Blackwood, who, with her interest in 'traditional' and 'modern' aspects of life within Native communities, observed that 'Some Indian tribes, such as the Bloods in southern Alberta, whose reservation includes some of the best wheat-bearing land in Canada, have taken more kindly to developing their agricultural procedure along the white man's lines, and are using modern machinery, modern barns and silos, and modern methods of marketing their produce' (Blackwood 1927: 18).

Missions, Churches, and Schools

Blackwood's photographs show aspects of this agrarian revolution, and the struggle for land and rights that came with it, in Kainai lives. The photographs also show other elements of struggle in the Kainai community at this time, specifically the pressures applied by government and church to assimilate the Kainai and strip them of their traditional culture. In addition to the governmental policies that invaded most aspects of people's daily lives, Native people throughout Canada also had to contend with other means through which the Department of Indian Affairs implemented its policy of 'aggressive civilization' (D.G.

Smith 2001). The government believed that the most effective way to assimilate the Native population would be to educate children according to Christian beliefs, and, with this goal in mind, teaching responsibilities were contracted out to the churches. Anglican and Roman Catholic missions were first established on the Blackfoot Reserves in the 1870s, and shortly afterwards the first mission schools were founded. On the Blood Reserve the original St Paul's Anglican Mission School was established in the 1890s and transferred in 1924 to a new building northwest of Cardston.[15] The first Roman Catholic School, the Immaculate Conception School, was founded in 1893 by Father Lacombe, and was administered by the Grey Nuns and Oblate Fathers. The original building, which Beatrice Blackwood visited, stood on the banks of the Belly River near Lower Standoff, opposite the government hospital, and a new building, renamed as St Mary's Roman Catholic Indian Residential School, was opened in 1926, close to the Farm Four area (Middleton 1953: 60). Both the schools and all other administrative buildings were relocated to the southern part of the Reserve in the mid-1920s in a move motivated by politics (Fox 2001: xii). Government officials were so convinced that the proposed sale of the northeast part of the Reserve would succeed that they believed that a new administrative centre would need to be established (Narcisse Blood to Brown, pers. comm. 20 August 2002). In the event, the land sales did not go ahead, but by then the relocation program was complete. Former staff and students from both schools recalled the drastic improvement of facilities within the new buildings; however, improvements in heating and shelter could not make up for the increased restriction on activities. Sister Odelia Lamontagne, a Grey Nun who came to the Blood Reserve in 1923, has recalled the impact of the change in location for the schoolgirls in particular:

> On Easter Monday in 1926, we moved to St Mary's. That was a big change for all of us. We had 36 girls. After a few days 19 came in the same day. We kept the girls until they were 18 years old. They never went home, not even for summer holidays. They left school after their wedding ceremony. In 1939, they were discharged at 16, it was the first time they all went home for the summer holidays.
>
> At Standoff, they enjoyed the holidays. We had the river where some would swim twice a day. In the afternoon we would go in the woods where they picked berries. There was no time to be lonesome. But here, nothing of that, they just had a few feet of shadow near the church basement and no place for picnics. (Lamontagne 1969: 9)

Boarding schools separated children from their families for lengthy periods of time, leading to social and cultural disruption, the effects of which are still being felt within the community. Though many parents and grandparents were opposed to the separation from their children and grandchildren that residential school entailed, they believed it was necessary for them to receive an education that would prepare them to deal with non-Native society and help them negotiate between the two cultures (Crow Chief 20 November 2001). The education children acquired, however, usually did not live up to these expectations. The emphasis on academic work was minimal, and many children left school with only a rudimentary grasp of writing, arithmetic, and spoken English. Girls were usually taught home-making skills such as baking and sewing while boys worked outdoors, tending animals, cultivating crops, or learning a trade. At St Mary's, learning English proved to be even more complicated than at the Anglican school, since many of the nuns, being French-Canadian, had difficulties themselves communicating in English. In addition, other non-Native people who worked at the schools, such as farming instructors, were often European immigrants and spoke accented English which was hard for Kainai children to follow.

Contemporary documents and oral accounts frequently refer to the unsanitary environment that the children were exposed to in the schools, which had much to do with the ill-health so commonly experienced. Blackwood remarked upon the extent of illness among the schoolgirls she encountered at St Mary's, observing that they 'were not a very healthy bunch, several had open wounds, and others had swollen ones which they had not reported' (Blackwood Papers, Diary 1924–7, 4 August 1925; hereafter cited as Blackwood Diary 1924–7). Many children developed strategies to cope with the difficulties of school: for example, speaking Blackfoot when in the dormitories, sneaking into the kitchens to find extra food, and in many cases, running away. Four volumes of elders' biographies published in conjunction with the Kainai Board of Education (Zaharia and Fox 1995a, b, c; Zaharia, Fox, and Fox 2003) are rich in details provided by Kainai people who attended residential school on the Blood Reserve, and in some cases, Dunbow Industrial School, which was located south of Calgary. The experiences shared by these individuals express the range of responses to the residential school system and illuminate some of the tactics adopted by children to cope with loneliness, the confusion and feelings of inadequacy brought on by the brainwashing attempts of school staff, and the fear of being punished for doing something considered 'wrong.' Some people share their recollections of lighter moments from their schooldays – picnics in the mountains and the close friendships that developed between classmates – and feel that their experiences taught them how to survive. The statements below were made by some of the women Blackwood encountered when they were small girls. Their words are a glimpse into how schoolchildren experienced the Roman Catholic Residential School during the time of Blackwood's visit, and provide alternative perspectives to those of the nuns and other staff which she recorded:

> I was nine years old when I went to the Roman Catholic Mission School in Standoff. I found the nuns very strict. I was still a student there when we moved to our new St Mary's Roman Catholic Residential School. I really didn't learn as much as I should have. I also worked around the residence. When vacation time came, I remained at school with the other senior girls. (*Mini* Minnie Chief Moon, in Zaharia and Fox 1995a: 49)

> My grandmothers didn't want me to go to school. They felt that if I was being placed at school I was being abandoned. Finally at about nine years of age, I was placed at the old Roman Catholic Mission School in Standoff. I didn't mind being at school. I was taught how to work and cook there and was well taken care of. Since our residence was close to the river, we went swimming every day during the warm weather. We also went for long walks which were most enjoyable. (*Iinakay* Annette Russell, in Zaharia and Fox 1995a: 49)

Assimilation Policy and the Kainai

From the government and church perspectives, the biggest obstacle to the assimilation of Native people into Canadian society was their insistence on continuing to celebrate their traditional ceremonies. During the first three decades of the twentieth century, despite several amendments to the Indian Act designed to eliminate Native forms of spiritual expression, Native people continued to observe their ceremonies and paid little heed to the legal consequences. The files of the DIA are filled with correspondence complaining that these ceremonies took people away from their agricultural work during the height of summer, a time when they should really be busy in their fields. Crops were said to suffer, drying up as the farmers danced for days on end instead of applying their energy to harvesting. Moreover, the gatherings were considered injurious to the health and morals of the participants, causing over-excitement and exposure to the unsavoury elements of white society such as bootleggers who would prowl the boundaries of reserves tempting people with alcohol.[16]

The correspondence of missionaries with DIA officials during this time period is particularly vitriolic, their letters being peppered with exaggerated claims – for example, that dancing was 'a known cause of mortality among children' – that not surprisingly showed little consideration for differing spiritual views (Department of Indian Affairs, Father J. Hugonard to the Secretary, 31 July 1915. NAC, RG10, vol. 3826, file 60,511-4, Pt. 1). Instead, missionaries lamented that the money and time expended on educating Native children in the image of white society was wasted, because they were encouraged by their parents to go 'back to the blanket' and participate in dances and ceremonies, undoing all the 'good' habits drilled into them at school. These concerns were shared by departmental officials. In 1931, for example, Indian Agent Pugh of the Blood Reserve wrote to Inspector William Graham informing him that he believed the holding of the annual Sun Dance would be detrimental to the Tribe's agricultural efforts, which were being hampered by poor weather conditions. Graham communicated his concerns to the Deputy Superintendent, Duncan Campbell Scott, which we quote here at length:

> [Pugh] suggests that you write to the Chief and Council, advising them of the necessity of not holding this affair until such time as their Reserve is in shape. The Indians at this point, as you know, have an idea that the holding of these dances is sanctioned by the Department, and if instructions were to come from you that they were not to dance I think it might have the effect of at least retarding the affair ... the time will come, sooner or later, when we will have to stop these dances altogether or else give up farming. It seems absurd that boys and girls that have been in residence in our boarding schools for from eight to ten years should return to the Reserve and become the ringleaders of these affairs. Inspector Christianson tells me that he has seen young men, graduates of our schools, stripped naked with the exception of a breech cloth, and oiled and painted, taking part in these dances. It is hard to believe that a boy who has professed Christianity should revert to these pagan customs inside of a few months after they return home. In my opinion it does not say very much for the effort that we are making to civilize them. (Department of Indian Affairs, W.M. Graham to D.C. Scott, 22 June 1931. NAC, RG-10, Vol. 3827, file 60,511-4B)

Scott did indeed write to Head Chief Shot Both Sides suggesting that he encourage the Kainai to pay 'the closest attention to their farming operations during this very critical period' and reminding him that 'Indians should take advantage of the opportunities that they have to improve their material conditions and welfare.' He concluded by observing:

> As a leader of your people who has their confidence, I rely upon you to use your influence with them and discourage the holding of a dance, particularly at a time which would be so detrimental to their best interests. (Department of Indian Affairs, D.C. Scott to Head Chief Shot Both Sides 29 June 1931. NAC, RG-10, Vol. 3827, file 60,511-4B)

The exchange above clearly demonstrates the DIA officials' misunderstanding of the meaning of ceremonials to the Kainai, practices which are necessary to ensure the welfare of all. Observances central to Prairie cultures such as the Sun Dance of the Blackfoot nations were regarded as detrimental by the authorities not merely because they took time to arrange and enact. Most objectionable were ceremonies such as piercing rituals, in which men who wished to fulfil a personal vow, such as asking for the recovery of a sick relative, had thongs which were attached to a central pole inserted into their chests and then danced backwards. White observers regarded piercing as a barbarous practice and failed to recognize its cultural importance and that it was not an integral part of the Sun Dance, but was undertaken by individuals who had vowed to undergo this ceremony (Blackwater 15 August 2002). Other elements of ceremonials regarded as unlawful were giveaways, which involve the exchange of goods such as horses, blankets, money, and food and often accompany dances and ceremonies. Though giveaways reflect the high regard in which generosity is held among Native people, at this time they were considered by the authorities to be wasteful and to cause impoverishment. An 1895 amendment to section 114 of the Indian Act specifically prohibited Native peoples from exercising this essential part of their ceremonial life and also declared the wounding or mutilation of human or animal bodies as part of ceremonies illegal (K. Pettipas 1994: 95; see also 113–14). Both offences were punishable with a prison sentence of at least two months and a maximum of six, though there is ample documentary and oral evidence for the strategies taken by community members to avoid the legislation.

The Kainai response to the assault on their spirituality during this era was sincere determination to continue appreciating and learning from those gifts which had been given to them by the Creator and other Spirit Beings, and which had sustained their people for generations. Though certainly some individuals converted to Christianity, spiritual leaders of the 1920s insisted on their people having the right to pray in their own way, just as non-Native people enjoyed this freedom. As Many Fingers and Venne (1987: 6) have noted, 'Indian law and government was and is part of the sacred order maintained through the unwritten customs embodied in many religious ceremonies, not a political order maintained by force.'

Blackwood recorded in her diary that the Kainai 'still have their Sun Dance but much watered down and without the torturing' (Blackwood Diary 1924–7, 2 August 1925). Although the Sun Dance was never banned outright on the Reserve, government officials repeatedly behaved in an obstructive manner, and did their best to ensure that those aspects of the ceremonials that they regarded as most objectionable were not permitted to go ahead. Twice during the period 1921 to 1931 officials threatened to depose Head Chief Shot Both Sides for disobeying their wishes and supporting the Sun Dance ceremonials. Indeed, following from the correspondence quoted above, Head Chief Shot Both Sides refused to ask the Kainai to disperse, even though Agent Pugh had prevented Blackfeet from Montana attending the ceremony, and had attempted (unsuccessfully) to have the RCMP return visitors from Siksika to their reserve at Gleichen (Many Fingers and Venne 1987). Yet threats of imprisonment and withholding of rations did not prevent the Kainai from continuing to celebrate as their ancestors had done and instead strengthened their resolve to resist the legislation.

Official complaints were not restricted to Native participation in ceremonial activity. They were also directed towards attendance at the summer fairs and agricultural exhibitions which were a common feature of the prairie social calendar but were regarded as wasting time and hindering progress towards civilization. To the delight of white spectators, Native people were often invited by organizers to participate and often wore their beaded outfits for the parades and 'wild west' shows which usually accompanied these events. In 1914 an amendment was passed to Section 149 of the Indian Act to provide legislative support for the existing informal policy of regulating off-Reserve dancing and to restrict Native participation in organized events such as stampedes and fairs by targeting both participants and organizers and levying a fine and/or threatening imprisonment to any Native person who participated in a show or exhibition or any individual who encouraged their involvement, without the consent of the Superintendent General of Indian Affairs or his authorized agent (An Act to Amend the Indian Act S.C. 1914, c. 35, 4–5 George V, in Department of Indian and Northern Affairs 1981: 132).

In addition to this amendment intended to curtail Native freedom, a pass system was introduced following the Northwest Rebellion of 1885 which further restricted the rights of residents to leave reserves for either business or social purposes. The pass system was said to protect Native people from the ills of society, such as alcohol, prostitution, and theft, but also aimed to separate them from the settler population, until tensions subsided (Barron 1988: 25). A person wishing to leave the reserve had to be in possession of a pass signed by the Indian agent which stipulated the duration and purpose of the trip. Overall, the system was plainly ineffectual, though in the early days there were certainly incidents in Blackfoot country when people were arrested for moving between reserves without a pass (Cecile Many Guns, quoted in Treaty 7 Elders et al. 1996: 150). Towards the 1920s, people were less intimidated by the system and, knowing that carrying a pass was not a legal requirement for travel, simply ignored the rule. Some agents continued to insist that passes were necessary but would issue them almost on demand and for extensive periods. By the 1930s passes were still being used in some areas, but had merely become a means of monitoring Native mobility and attempting to bolster the authority of the agent (Barron 1988: 38). *Ponokaiksiksinam* (Martin Heavy Head), for example, recalled a story he had heard about his own ancestor's disregard for the pass system:

> Martin Heavy Head: My grandfather told me a story of going to visit over here by Fort Walsh ... My great-grandfather, Heavy Head, was sort of, he was well off, he was wealthy, so in 1906 he decided to take a trip to, probably, Nekaneet. So they left and they were gone about a week. They were just taking their time going, when they looked back and there was dust coming up from the prairie, where there was a black cloud. So they sent somebody back to have a look to see what was causing this dust. And what happened was the whole Reserve was following them!
> Alison Brown: What, that was all the dust off their wagons?
> Martin Heavy Head: Yeah, from the wagons and the horses. So they immediately set up camp and started hunting to feed everybody when they got there. He said after that they travelled faster, but they did more

> hunting and they eventually got there and they had a great time. They were having dancing and they transferred stuff back and forth. So it was quite the event. But that was one of the things that people did in defiance of the government because, see then people, not only Bloods, but other people, they did ceremonies all the time, just so that they wouldn't have to do what the government was asking them to do – to farm. So they went visiting! ... Just, you know, vacate the whole Reserve. It would be vacant for however long. Because they were only maybe one generation removed from the people that didn't have a Reserve and they just travelled wherever. So it was kind of like being tied down and now they had a chance to do something so everybody went off. And they wouldn't just do it for a week. They would do it for three, four weeks, you know? Just be gone. And that was something that, like it happened all over, it wasn't just here. (Heavy Head 16 November 2001)

These were the forces and pressures to which the Kainai were responding when Beatrice Blackwood visited in August of 1925. Though the community was in the early stages of recovering from the traumatic events of the recent past and people were dealing with extreme changes to their social, cultural, and economic circumstances, the photographs taken by Blackwood and the observations she recorded nonetheless suggest that they remained strong and were seeking ways of tackling the new challenges.

Photography and the Kainai

Churches, schools, and government restrictions were obvious manifestations of attempts to control and assimilate Kainai people. One other, less obvious way of imposing control by non-Natives has been the use of representational genres that have contributed to an accumulation of visual stereotypes used to affirm messages of cultural difference. Since contact, Kainai people have been sketched, painted, and photographed, largely by outsiders who viewed them within such preconceived categories as Noble Savages, Warriors, or a Vanishing Race – or sometimes as claims of success in assimilation programs. In this section we focus on the experiences Kainai people have had being represented visually, both to explore this manifestation of their historic relations with non-Natives and to underscore their considerable experience of being photographed by the time Blackwood encountered them.

Images of First Nations people made by non-Native photographers have always reflected outsiders' understandings and perspectives of Native people. Only a tiny minority of historic images of First Nations people were made for or by First Nations people, as family photographs and tokens of pride and love (and see P. Taylor 1988: xix for a similar observation regarding photographs of Aboriginal Australians).[17] The vast majority of photographs of First Nations people have depicted them as non-Natives wanted to see them, and from a position of relative ignorance of Native cultures. As Richard W. Hill, Sr has observed: 'The invention of photography ... introduced a new dimension to Native stereotyping. Indians became collaborators, captured for eternity in strange poses that were not always of their own making. Staged poses for the camera resulted in photographs that lacked cultural depth. They were unreal (Hill 1998: 141). Thus, the stereotypes of the Romantic, the Warlike, the Vanishing, and the Noble Savage recur in various combinations in the vast majority of photographs of Native people, regardless of why these images were taken. Edward Curtis's romantic fantasies of vanishing Noble Savages, the 'before and after' portraits of Native children taken at boarding schools as proof of successful assimilation, formal images of official delegations of men in tribal dress with top-hatted colonial officials, Army photographs of captured 'hostile' prisoners, Treaty photographs of Native signatories, postcard images of men in buckskin and feathers: all show cultural difference from the photographer, either positively or negatively constructed.[18] While such images differ in purpose, they share the fact that they all claim to show 'authentic' Native peoples, but were actively constructed to make the subjects correspond with the set of visual cues which signified 'authentic' to non-Native viewers (Edwards 1992: 12; and see Scherer 1992 on the different types and commonalities of photographs of Native Americans). The clothes and ornaments worn by First Nations people in historic photographs (hide or cloth; moccasins or shoes) conveyed messages readily understood within the dominant society. To a Euro-Canadian, an image of a Native man with short hair wearing a Victorian suit and shoes generally 'meant' successful assimilation, while one depicting a Native man in hide clothing, moccasins, and long braids could 'mean' a nostalgic celebration of the Noble Savage stereotype. Perhaps the most obvious example of this is the now well-known fact that Edward Curtis dressed his subjects in 'more traditional' garments than they usually wore to create images of romantic and vanishing Noble Savages (Lyman 1982; Gidley 1998). In every case, the 'facts' recorded by the camera were deliberately selected and intended to be understood in preconceived ways within non-Native society.[19] Photographs of First Nations people therefore need to be understood as being about the problematic relationship between Native and non-Native peoples as much as they were about the details recorded on the negative.

That images of Kanai people could record such relationships and their dynamics is suggested not only by their subject matter, but by the categories of people who created them. Missionaries, traders, explorers, anthropologists, artists, teachers, and government officials – each with their own goals regarding the Kainai – all produced sketches, paintings, and photographs of Kainai people over time. Beginning in the mid-nineteenth century, scientists involved with a series of exploratory expeditions recognized the documentary potential of the camera, and those with ethnological interests began to record Native peoples just as those with interests in land and resources took landscape shots (Silversides 1994: 2). One of these was George Mercer Dawson (1849–1901), a photographer for the 1872–4 British North American Boundary Commission, who subsequently mapped the region around the Bow, Belly, and St Mary's rivers – soon to become part of the Blood Reserve – for the Geological Survey of Canada. Like many of his contemporaries, Dawson believed that collecting materials from Native peoples, whether these were photographs, stories, or artefacts, was an act of ethnographic salvage, preserving for posterity a record of people whose lives were being irreversibly altered. Though his photographs are primarily of landscapes, he also took some images of Blackfoot people.[20] Taken shortly after the signing of Treaty 7, these images give a very clear indication of the severity of conditions that Blackfoot people faced at this time; for instance, his group shot of women and children wrapped in their blankets and huddled together at Fort Whoop-Up on a bitterly cold winter's day.[21] As most visitors came to Blackfoot country in the summer months, photographs such as this, which depict the seasonal harshness of the climate, are both rare and important, revealing as they do the reality of living in a challenging environment at a time when resources were being eradicated.

Anthropologists, too, wished to record what they assumed were 'vanishing' cultures, and were drawn to Blackfoot communities on both sides of the international border[22] because of their strong traditional ways. As we explore more fully in chapter 2, anthropologists took photographs as part of their strategy of documenting the people they encountered, and while many images reflect the concerns of physical anthropology – paired frontal and profile portraits, for example – others focus on those aspects of peoples' lives which were most under threat, such as ceremonial practices. Anthropological interests are seen clearly in collections of photographs made among Blackfoot peoples. Clark Wissler of the American Museum of Natural History, for example, began an extended collaboration with David Duvall (a resident of the Blackfeet reservation of French-Piikani descent), which resulted in a series of monographs on Blackfoot culture and history (Wissler and Duvall 1908; Wissler 1910; 1911; 1912; 1913; 1918) and extensive field correspondence, notes, and some photographs. Around the same time, Walter McClintock, an employee of the U.S. Forest Service working in Montana, took extensive notes and many photographs during visits to the Blackfeet Reservation. These were published as the *Old North Trail* in 1910 and in several subsequent anthropological publications (e.g., McClintock 1930 and n.d.).[23]

Most of the professional and semi-professional anthropologists working in Blackfoot territory in the late nineteenth and the first two decades of the twentieth centuries made only very brief visits to the Blood Reserve. Some, such as Wissler and McClintock, concentrated their efforts at the Blackfeet Reservation in Montana. Others worked at the Blackfoot Reserve near Gleichen, for instance Harlan I. Smith (1872–1940) of the Victoria Memorial Museum,[24] who made two short visits in 1928 and 1929 to collect artefacts and take photographs and motion picture film which was then made into an educational documentary, *The Blackfoot Indians of Alberta* (1928). This short film includes scenes such as a demonstration of the use of bow and arrows, farming practice, and children laughing and playing. The comparison of 'traditional' and 'modern' aspects of Native cultures that characterizes Blackwood's images also informed Smith's documentary, in which 'old Aboriginal culture and modern things introduced by the white man' (Anon. 1933: 6) were contrasted. The Siksika people's transition from a nomadic to an agricultural agrarian lifestyle based on non-Native ideals was depicted by comparing a canvas tipi with a government-built frame house and blanket outfits with the increasingly common citizens' dress, while ceremonial life was described as 'mystic rituals.' Unlike Blackwood, however, Smith was careful to include extensive caption information with his images of Native peoples, and ensured that his subjects saw the photographs he took of them (Canadian Museum of Civilization 2000).

Artists and popular photographers were also interested in symbols of traditional Blackfoot culture, and in the early twentieth century many individuals worked in this region. They brought, of course, a range of styles and media to their work, but many of them created portraits of individuals in a variety of more or less romantic and nostalgic poses. Among these many artists producing romanticized images of Kainai people perhaps the best-known is Edward S. Curtis. Curtis and his team had spent some time at the Blackfeet reservation in 1909 with the anthropologist Alfred C. Haddon of Cambridge University (Gidley 1982), and returned to the area in August 1925, shortly after Blackwood (Gidley 1998: 148). They made a brief visit to the Blood Reserve before travelling to northern Alberta, collecting images which were to form part of volume 18 of *The North American Indian*, Curtis's immense project to record for posterity twenty volumes of photographs featuring eighty tribes and 'their history, life, manners, ceremony, legends and mythology' (quoted in Fleming and Luskey 1991: 216). Curtis published a small number of photographs taken at the Blood Reserve, including scenes of women preparing meat, several views of tipis with ceremonial bundles outside, and a number of named portraits in the romanticized style with which he is associated.

Of particular interest for the purposes of this project are two images of *Aistainsskii* (Coming Singer), whom Curtis, like Blackwood, photographed in frontal and profile positions. Comparing Blackwood's images with those of Curtis underscores the different intellectual approaches of these photographers to their subject. In Curtis's images little is made of the background, and the portrait of *Aistainsskii* fills the frame. In some respects, the frontal image resembles Blackwood's quite closely. *Aistainsskii* is wearing everyday work clothes, and looks straight at the camera. In the profile view, however, he wears a headdress, which is partly cut off in the image, and the viewer is drawn to this and his shell earring. In contrast, in Blackwood's profile image for which he stood with his wife, *Iikaiyissi'nikki* (Killed Before You Did), *Aistainsskii* wears a wide-brimmed hat, and does not wear earrings. Though both these images were clearly posed, the sense that Blackwood was making the most of her opportunity to photograph people during the course of their daily routines, and within a framework of scientific research that contrasted 'traditional' and 'modern' elements of Kainai life as she understood them, is perhaps most keenly expressed by juxtaposing these two images taken in the summer of 1925 (see figures 1.2 and 1.3). The dominance of the headdress and earring in Curtis's image – visible

1.2 *Astanihkyi* 'Come-singing,' 1925. Photograph by Edward Curtis. (Reproduction courtesy McCormick Library of Special Collections, Northwestern University)

1.3 *Aistainsskii* Coming Singer with *Iikaiyissi'nikki* Killed Before You Did (Mrs Coming Singer). Photograph by Beatrice Blackwood. (Pitt Rivers Museum, University of Oxford, PRM. BB.A3.70)

signs of difference – emphasizes the broad ambition of his project: to record for posterity what he viewed as fading elements of Aboriginal culture.

Curtis both inspired and reflected a popular genre of romantic imagery. In western Canada, the opening of the railways and increased tourism across the 1920s and 1930s brought all kinds of artists and photographers working in this tradition:

> As soon as the railroad was built, we had tourists already around that time. Maybe not in the same sense as tourists today, but we had people that were, what do you call them, kind of explorers in their own way. Then they came in flocks and they wanted to take pictures of us as to where we were at, at the beginning of our transition, to bring the pictures back to those people that were showing more interest in us. (Blackwater 24 November 2001)

The centre of production for genres of portraits of Blackfoot people that reflected standard colonial perceptions of otherness at this time was the artists' colony at Glacier National Park established by Winold Reiss (1886–1953) in 1934. Reiss first came to Montana in 1919 to sketch Blackfeet people, and in 1927 returned to the reservation and Glacier National Park at the request of the Great Northern Railway to paint portraits of local Blackfeet for the St Mary's Chalet Hotel as part of the GNR's advertising strategy of attracting tourists through imagery of people as well as scenery (see figure 1.4, portrait of Head Chief Shot Both Sides taken by Tomar J. Hileman, official photographer for the Great Northern Railway, to promote Glacier National Park).[25] Native people were encouraged to set up their tipis near the school and work as art models, and their presence attracted numerous amateur and professional artists. North of the border, artists such as Edward Montague Morris (1871–1913), Nicholas de Grandmaison (1895–1978), and Mildred Valley Thornton (1890–1967) all painted romantic portraits of Kainai people which continue to be exhibited in galleries throughout Canada (Dempsey 1982; Thornton 2000; Morris 1985).

One artist who worked at the Glacier art colony provides an especially interesting comparison to Blackwood: the English traveller, sculptor, and writer Clare Sheridan (1885–1970). Sheridan spent the summer of 1937 travelling in the area and was invited to stay with the family of *Aisstaohkomiaakii* (Comes Calling Woman) Ethel Tailfeathers (see fig. 12).[26] During this time she photographed and created several sculptures of Kainai and Blackfeet, some of whom Blackwood had also met several years earlier (Sheridan 1938). In her book Sheridan describes a photography session at the home of *Isstsstsiimi* (Rough Hair) and his wife, *Naipisstsaakii* (Cloth Woman), in which *Isstsstsiimi* suggested that Sheridan should also dress up in his wife's clothes for the camera (Sheridan 1938: 190).[27] Her description offers a new perspective through which to view Blackwood's remarks on dressing for the camera made twelve years earlier and emphasizes the familiar relationship that Kainai people had with photography by the early twentieth century, a relationship that was characterized as much by their understanding of the content and purpose of images as by the manner in which they were made.

In order to understand Blackwood's photography as it fits within these anthropological, artistic, and colonial contexts, it is necessary to relate it to the broader genres of images of Kainai people outlined above. Not all of these conform to preconceived categories, however, and like Blackwood's photographs, many such images open the way to reinterpretation or reveal elements of reality which were often deliber-

1.4 Portrait of Head Chief Shot Both Sides taken by Tomar J. Hileman, official photographer for the Great Northern Railway, to promote Glacier National Park. (Hastings Museum and Art Gallery 983.78.177)

ately removed by other photographers and artists who wanted to make their images fit into certain categories. Several important collections of photographs were made by non-Natives who lived for some time around Kainai people, and record different kinds of relationships from those recorded by scientists or artists: more personal, more respectful, more aware of the difficulties faced by Kainai people. Kainai today recognize differences in tone and depth between images produced by such individuals and images produced by people who spent little time in the area. As *Kinaksaapo'p* (Narcisse Blood), Chair of the Mookaakin Foundation and Kainai Studies Co-ordinator at Red Crow Community College, has remarked of Blackwood's photographs:

> These pictures just give ... you a glimpse of our lifestyle back then. I mean, it tells a lot, but even so, it's still just a glimpse. So, there's a lot that is not said in these pictures. For instance, there were some other people that wrote about us, [James Willard] Schultz,[28] people like that, that actually lived among us, so they got to see our lifestyle, as opposed to somebody that just happened to be passing through. And if they happened to be passing through at our Sun Dance, I'm sure the pictures would be quite different. (Blood 6 December 2001)

There are a number of photographic collections reflecting this greater depth of relationship. One such collection is that of Robert N. Wilson.[29] After serving with the North West Mounted Police, Wilson operated a trading post on the Belly River near Standoff throughout the 1880s and was Indian Agent at the Peigan Indian Agency from 1898 to 1903 and on the Blood Reserve from 1904 to 1911. During this time he recorded ethnological information about the Blackfoot Nations which was published by the Royal Society of Canada (Wilson 1910). He also facilitated the work of anthropologists and purchased artefacts which he later sold to the Department of Indian Affairs and to museums in the United States (VanStone 1992: 3; Brown 2000: 56). Wilson appears to have had unusual respect for the Blackfoot people and their traditions in comparison with other government officials, and he worked hard to help them develop their economic potential. His photographs include standard subjects such as portraits of Kainai personalities, for instance Chief Red Crow, but also include arrangements of objects which presumably were at one time in his possession, and a series of images taken at the Sun Dance camp of 1892.[30] Many of Wilson's photographs are documentary in that there has been seemingly little attempt to portray a romanticized view of the community; they also provide a valuable record of Kainai people's persistence in maintaining their spiritual life despite government repression. Unusually, they are marked by a sense of warmth and informality that is not apparent in many other images taken during this era.

Another historic photographer well known to Kainai today whose images reflect a real relationship with their ancestors is George T.N. Anderton (1848–1913), who was stationed with the NWMP at Fort Walsh in 1876. Anderton eventually set up a business in Fort Macleod, where he took studio portraits, but he also visited the Reserve to photograph people at their homes (Silversides 1991). Professional photographers like Anderton who could make repeat visits to the Reserve often built up close relationships with some of the people they photographed.[31] That many Kainai people today have family photographs that were taken at local studios attests to the ease which some people felt towards selected photographers at this time, and suggests that in these environments they were able to make their own choices as to how they posed.[32] Portraits of Blackfoot people who chose to sit for professional photographers often exude the same air of confidence and pride that can be observed in some of the more romanticized images taken by Edward Curtis and his contemporaries, but many sitters posed in European clothing, or with friends and family, reflecting self-defined identity and image rather than stereotype.[33]

What makes these images different, of course, is the different dynamics of power between photographer and photographed, the levelling of such dynamics through the establishment of personal relationships and feelings of respect. Very few images record such relationships, because they rarely existed. The stereotyped, superficial, exoticized, or trophy nature of the vast majority of images of First Nations people says much about the nature of Native-white relations in general. One of the largest groups of photographs of First Nations people, and of Kainai people, is that taken by mission staff and other non-Native educators, illustrating church- or school-related activities and used to demonstrate the processes of assimilation and conversion (Miller 2003; see also McMaster 1992: 79). Though there are notable exceptions, for example a series of photographs taken by Canon S.H. Middleton of schoolgirls from St Paul's Residential School enjoying themselves during trips to Waterton Lakes Park,[34] the majority of photographs of Kainai schoolchildren taken during this period are formal. As a result the children appear serious and often quite lost, with the power relationship between them and the staff being starkly exposed.

Rethinking Blackwood's Photographs

Such images of schoolchildren bring us back to Blackwood's class photographs of girls incarcerated over the summer, and the other images she took on the Blood Reserve. As we have indicated, like other anthropologists of this era, Blackwood translated what she saw into the intellectual currents of her time, focusing on 'traditional' and 'modern' elements of culture while ignoring the new manifestations of heritage and the realities of life on the Reserve in the present: in her case, she saw the girls in their uniforms as exemplifying the processes of cultural change faced by First Nations peoples. Like those taken by missionaries or other officials, her photographs of the schoolgirls also serve as documents embodying the problematic relationships between the Kainai and non-Natives, although Blackwood herself would not have intended this set of meanings. As stated above, anthropologists needed official permission to visit reserves during this era, and once they were there, the success of their work would have largely depended on the Indian agent's willingness to assist.

For Beatrice Blackwood, her Oxford status, combined with the fact that the Indian Agent was her guide, meant that she or the Agent could ask people to pose while giving the Kainai little recourse but to agree. The expressions on the faces of the schoolgirls confirm this. One also wonders about the group standing with the painted tipi: while obviously proud of the tipi and its furnishings and their dress clothing, these were not items of everyday use at the time, and were usually worn only at ceremonial events and social gatherings such as parades and stampedes which took place throughout the summer months. Were they forced by the Agent to change clothes and pose, or did they choose to dress up for the camera? Blackwood's statement that 'they all put on their "glad rags" to be photographed' (Blackwood Diary 1924–7, 3 August 1925) is ambiguous, but the power dynamic between their ancestors and officials was apparent to the Kainai:

> She wrote at the beginning [of her diary] the Indian Agent took them out and probably the Indian Agent told them, 'You have to do this.' (Weasel Head 28 November 2001)

Conclusion

Mi'ksskimm's (Frank Weasel Head's) reading of this photograph by Blackwood demonstrates the knowledge of Kainai history and relationships with non-Native peoples that exists within the Kainai community today. Within this understanding, Kainai people evaluate and critique images of their ancestors which have been created by outsiders, as we will discuss in later chapters. Their understanding of images such as Blackwood's is framed by a very different set of experiences and perspectives from what outsiders have had, of being affected by and resisting colonial processes – including processes of representation. The images Blackwood obtained during her short tour of the Blood Reserve reflect these experiences and processes. They were, in fact, partially intended to portray cultural change resulting from colonialism, as well as other information about Kainai people which fitted in to scholars' categories and debates about race. In the next chapter, we examine Beatrice Blackwood's intentions in taking these photographs, and her work within the broader contexts of her career and of anthropological interests of the era.

CHAPTER TWO

Anthropological Contexts

Introduction

Beatrice Blackwood photographed the Kainai at a specific moment in their history and in her own career. She did not come to the Blood Reserve simply to record life, but to find material which would contribute to her research on 'race' and acculturation. While it is often said that the camera never lies, as we discussed in chapter 1, it does record the intentions of the photographer in the way an image is composed. Blackwood's photographs were created and had meaning within her own research interests of her 1924–7 project, but also within the broader tradition of anthropological photography. In this chapter we explore Blackwood's background and career, and the relationship of her research to broader anthropological concerns, as contexts for her Kainai photographs, just as in the previous chapter we explored Kainai culture and history as factors which shaped these images. We emphasize especially the very complex relationship that Blackwood had with intellectual categories such as 'race,' with the discipline of anthropology, and with colonialism. While she emphatically rejected simplistic cultural hierarchies, she continued to work with such concepts, and her North American trip was made possible by colonial structures of power.

Beatrice Blackwood, Anthropology, and Oxford

Beatrice Blackwood (1889–1975) was born in London in 1889 into a successful family of publishers. She rejected the expected route of a good marriage and children for a woman of her social background, and chose to study at Oxford University instead, graduating with an undergraduate degree in English Language from Somerville College in 1912. As with other women students at Oxford during this time, Blackwood was not permitted to attend a degree ceremony or acquire a diploma until the university rules were changed in 1920, when she promptly obtained hers (Knowles 1998: 6; Brittain 1960:152). She returned to Oxford in 1916 to begin studying for the Diploma in Anthropology, which she completed in 1918. In 1923, Blackwood also took a Bachelor of Science degree with a thesis in embryology (Penniman 1976; Gosden and Knowles 2001: 140; Knowles 2004).

The teaching of anthropology and human anatomy were closely linked at this time, and it was not surprising that Blackwood would develop interests in both physical and cultural aspects of anthropology. She began work first as a volunteer and then as a research assistant for Professor Arthur Thomson in the Department of Human Anatomy, which was then based in the University Museum of Natural History. In 1920 she was promoted to Departmental Demonstrator there, and then began her B.Sc. studies (Penniman 1976; Knowles 2004). In 1924 she began the three-year research trip in North America to explore the relationship between intelligence and 'race' during which she took the Kainai photographs. During this trip she learned much about fieldwork and collecting, and for the rest of her lengthy career her interests remained focused on the details and documentation of material culture and its social production. When she returned to Oxford in 1927, Blackwood became a University Demonstrator in Ethnology and in 1935 her post was transferred to the adjoining Pitt Rivers Museum, which focuses on technology and anthropology. Blackwood is best known outside the Pitt Rivers Museum for her fieldwork and collecting in the Pacific in 1929, a much more in-depth project than her North American work had been, and for publishing the system of artefact classification used at the Pitt Rivers Museum which she had helped to develop (Blackwood 1935, 1970). She undertook one further trip to North America in 1939 to attend academic meetings in San Francisco and Mexico City and to do further collecting, but was forced to return hastily when war broke out.

Within the Pitt Rivers Museum, Blackwood did much to set the exacting professional standards at the core of the Museum's operations, and added significantly to the collection through her fieldwork and by arranging exchanges with other museums. Her meticulous documentation of the collections became an example for ethnographic museums worldwide, and for decades, more than any other member of staff, she knew the nature of the collections and the locations of artefacts within the galleries and storage areas – 'our database in the days before computers,' as one colleague recalled (S. Jones 1994: 4). Small of stature, she was something of a character, and drove a motorcycle and sidecar around Oxford in the 1920s and 1930s. While generous with her knowledge and time with those who asked for her assistance, she could be 'almost fiercely sharp with anyone who mishandled Museum specimens in her presence' (S. Jones 1994: 4). She is remembered both fondly and with some terror by those whom she hired or trained, to whom she was Miss Blackwood until her death in 1975. Although she was awarded the Rivers Memorial Medal by the Royal Anthropological Institute in 1943 in recognition of her Melanesian fieldwork, Blackwood has remained a minor figure within the history of anthropology. She never became interested in the theoretical developments occurring within anthropology in the 1920s or after, and felt uncomfortable at the discipline's drift away from material culture (Knowles 2000; Gosden and Knowles 2001: 141). Even after she was promoted to Lecturer in 1946 (Knowles 2000: 261), her teaching was on what was then felt to be the more old-fashioned 'ethnology' (defined then as the comparative study of different human populations) rather than on the new theoretical ideas in social anthropology taught by Radcliffe-Brown and others in the department.

Blackwood's North American Fieldwork

The 1924–7 North American trip was an important first professional experience for Blackwood. Funded by a Laura Spelman Rockefeller Memorial Fellowship in the social sciences, it involved physical measurements and mental tests of different cultural groups across North America. Her research had several different components which she pursued at different points in the trip. Regrettably, little documentation has survived that describes Blackwood's own understanding of its goals. Her progress reports to her funding body, for example, were not preserved, since, at the time of her research, both the Laura Spelman Rockefeller Memorial and the Rockefeller Foundation considered data pertaining to their fellowships to be confidential. All correspondence with fellows was discarded and only the most essential of information concerning the awards was retained (Ken Rose, Assistant Director, Rockefeller Archives Center to Brown, pers. comm. 13 February 2002). Blackwood's work in the American South, undertaken during the first few months of 1924, was, in her words, 'part of a survey being carried out by the National Research Council, to be made available for statistical treatment from any point of view which may arise, e.g. it is to be correlated with the results of mental and sensory tests being given to the same individuals, to study the relation [between them]' (Blackwood Papers, Correspondence, Box 27, Folio 4:202, Blackwood to Professor [Thomson], 6 April 1925). Later, in requesting permission of the Department of Indian Affairs to work on Canadian Indian reserves, Blackwood stated that her purpose was 'to make a study of the physical measurements of women of different racial stocks' (Department of Indian Affairs, Blackwood to D.C. Scott, 28 June 1925, original and copy in NAC RG 10, Vol. 6816, File 486-6-1, Pt. 1). Regrettably, these few remarks are all the documentation of her intentions that has survived. Following the trip, she also published the results of mental tests she conducted on different groups as 'A Study of Mental Testing in Relation to Anthropology' (Blackwood 1927).

Blackwood's fieldwork was ambitious in scope. During this time, she travelled from New York to Alert Bay and from northern Manitoba to the American Southwest by train, canoe, mule, car, and truck. She spent much of the first autumn based at Princeton University and the spring of 1925 at several African-American colleges in the South before embarking on a two-year whistlestop tour, during which she seldom slept in the same bed for more than two nights running. She visited more than three dozen Native communities, some for only a day, others for a week or so, and met with colleagues in cities along the way. In addition to the photographs she took to support her research (and others which were given to her by officials with whom she worked), Blackwood also recorded her experiences in an extensive diary in which she described her travels, her research, and the responses to her and her work from professional colleagues, from administrative, health, and mission staff employed at the reserve communities she visited, and also from First Nations people.

Blackwood was a candid, if sometimes terse, writer, and her diary provides a glimpse into her intellectual development and her own position as a lone female researcher working in an academic (and, in Native communities, a bureaucratic) environment in which women were very much a minority. It also records her views on the conditions experienced by First Nations and African-American people and her distress at some of the disturbing scenes she witnessed; for example, appalling health conditions on some reserves, or the racial discrimination facing Black communities in the American South. The diary is a rich source of historical and cultural information and provides insights into the relationships between Native peoples and anthropologists, the history of anthropology and the social relationships within the discipline, the institutional history of the Pitt Rivers Museum, and the histories of a number of First Nations communities. Blackwood's diary is further enhanced by the fieldnotes she made on her trip, though many of these are largely extended versions of her diary entries. We include the portion of her diary and fieldnotes pertaining to the Blood Reserve as appendix 2, together with Kainai responses to this material.

At most of her stops, Blackwood took physical measurements which she recorded on standardized forms she brought with her (see figure 2.1). When possible, she also obtained samples of hair from people whom she measured. She carefully noted genealogical information about these people on the forms and the envelopes in which the hair samples were placed. Regrettably and somewhat intriguingly, Blackwood's physical anthropological data has not survived, though her diary records that she spent many hours measuring people and recording the results. It seems likely that as she became increasingly convinced that this information had limited use, she put it to one side, and seemingly chose not to deposit it in the Museum with the rest of her papers. Likewise, the sample of baby hair that she obtained at the hospital on the Blood Reserve is no longer in the collections of the Pitt Rivers Museum (Blackwood Diary 1924–7, 3 August 1925), and indeed, it is unclear if it ever was, though hair samples from several other Native communities were accessioned into the collections (Peers 2003).

Blackwood's additional papers stored in the Pitt Rivers Museum Manuscript Collection further illuminate aspects of her research. She corresponded at length with colleagues in Oxford, the United States, and Canada who facilitated her research and supplied criticism and intellectual support; several folders of these letters remain. From some communities (but not the Blood Reserve), she collected sets of children's drawings (all depicting a man, a woman, and a child for use in cross-cultural comparison), and notes on traditional stories and other ethnographic data which she deposited with the Museum some years later. Finally, Blackwood's papers from her later career include lecture notes, along with lists of slides and museum artefacts used in lectures and demonstrations, which show her use of some of the information and photographs collected on this trip in the context of her teaching at Oxford University, and we discuss this later in the chapter.

177

No. ....

Race ....

Full Name Sex

Age: yrs. mos. Date of birth: day month yr.

Birthplace Occupation

Father's birthplace Mother's

Father's race or nationality Mother's

Father's ancestors came from

Mother's ancestors came from

Other data on ancestry

	Span	1
	Stature	2
	Shoulder height	3
	Mid. Finger	4a
	Arm length	4
	Ht. to ant. sup. il. sp.	5
	Ht. to iliac crest	6
	Sit. ht.	7
	Shoulder width	8
	Width bet. iliac crests	9
	Head length	10
	Head width	11
	Min. frontal	12
	Bizygomatic	13
	Bigonial	14
	Nasal width	15
	Nasal height	16
	Upper facial ht.	17
	Total facial ht.	18
	Lip thickness	19
	Mouth width	20
	Hand length	21
	Hand width	22
	Head height	23

Skin Colour.
N | R | W | Y

Hair Colour.
black dk. brn. med. brn.
lt. brn. fair v. fair gray
lt. red bright red dk. red

Hair Form.
straight low waves dp. waves
curly frizzly woolly

Hair Texture.
coarse med. fine

Eye Colour.
dk. brn. lt. brn. neutral
hazel green
blue gray

Eye fold.
abs. trace med. mkd.

Intercanthus width.
narrow med. wide

Nose.
Bridge: low med. high
Profile: convex str. concave
Nostril axis: ant-post. obl.
transverse

Prognathism.
None slight med. mkd.

Bite.
overhung edge-to-edge
underhung

General Condition.
Good med. bad v. bad

1-2 Rel. Span	
3-2 Rel. Shld. Ht.	
4-2 Rel. Arm L.	
5-2 Rel. Leg L.	
7-2 Rel. Sit. Ht.	
8-2 Rel. Shld. W.	
9-8 Rel. Hip. W.	
11-10 Ceph. I.	
23-10 Vert. I. L.	
23-11 Vert. I. B.	
12-11 Fr. Pa. I.	
13-11 Ceph. Fa. I.	
12-13 Zyg. Fr. I.	
14-13 Zyp. Con. I.	
17-13 Up. Fac. I.	
18-13 Tot. Fac. I.	
15-16 Nasal I.	
22-21 Hand I.	

Pathological conditions.

Notes

Where measured Date

2.1 Blackwood's form for recording physical measurements. (PRM Blackwood Papers, Box 21, Folder 2)

Blackwood and 'Race'

Blackwood's research focus on this trip seems to have arisen from interests she developed learning physical anthropology (her notebooks from the Diploma in Anthropology course include a great deal of material and practical work on physical anthropology, human evolution, and 'race') and later working for Professor Arthur Thomson, head of the University Museum of Natural History. At the same time, Blackwood had strong interests in social anthropology and material culture, and in North America she began collecting and arranging exchanges of material to augment the Pitt Rivers Museum collections. Her anthropological perceptions of Native American peoples and artefacts were very much those of the time, focusing on the tensions and shifts between elements of 'traditional' and 'modern' culture. Despite the date of her training at the beginning of an exciting period of theoretical change for anthropology that occurred during the 1920s (and her exposure, at Oxford, to these new ideas), Blackwood inherited and maintained older theoretical traditions such as the salvage paradigm. Within this long-standing paradigm of anthropology, the 'traditional' – implying pre-European contact, or at least old – was very much privileged by scholars who wished to record, collect, and preserve these elements that were assumed to be dying out. Thus, in November 1925, justifying a decision to make an uncomfortable journey in order to work in one of the Ojibwe communities in Minnesota, she wrote in her diary that 'Ponemah is still comparatively untouched & almost entirely pagan' – and therefore, of course, a tempting destination for an anthropologist (Blackwood Diary 1924–7, 9 November 1925). As discussed in greater detail elsewhere in this chapter, when collecting artefacts, stories, and other data, she tried to get older-style 'traditional' material, and in her work on race was similarly interested in how older, 'purer' groups responded to racial 'mixing': her notes on people she studied frequently refer to 'pure-blood,' 'hybrid,' and 'traditional.'

During the initial months of her research, Blackwood was exposed to difficult situations which led her to develop new ideas which existed in uneasy parallel with the preconceptions she brought with her from her training. Her first months in the United States were spent at African-American colleges, where she was disturbed to discover the discrimination faced by Blacks and began to grapple with the political implications of standard measures of 'race.' From February to late March 1925, while based in Nashville, Blackwood recorded frequently and with amazement in her diary episodes of racism and segregation which she encountered, for example on public transport. Because the rooms she took were in 'Little Africa,' close to the people she wished to study, some whites would not have Blackwood in their homes (Blackwood Diary 1924–7, 16 April 1925). During the time she was measuring and collecting genealogies on one Black college campus, tensions between the Ku Klux Klan and Black activists ran so high that there were riots and the book shop was burned. Having had no previous experience of such interracial tensions in England, she noted with frustration an incident when a promising student 'asked whether there was a college for coloured students in England where she could study music. It was quite difficult to make her realise the difference between England & America in this respect' (Blackwood Diary 1924–7, 9 March 1925). Her diary is very strongly worded during this period, and at one point her frustration spilled out into it:

> Monday June 8 1925, Tuskegee: told someone 'how I had at last obtained the entry I had been wanting into the homes of the community – & how difficult it had been. She said that in the first place people couldn't believe I really would come – & in the second they were afraid – if the white people of the district knew that I was being received socially they might come & burn down the buildings. I said they needn't know everything that went on in the campus but she said they always did. The South makes me want to go out & scream. If I were here on my own responsibility I'd like to start a row just for the sake of saying 'I am from England & I don't care a damn for your conventions. You daren't touch me, & if you touch my friends I'll make such a row as there hasn't been since the Revolution.' (Blackwood Diary 1924–7, 8 June 1925)

At several points during this period, she had to explain and justify her research very carefully indeed to the Black presidents and student leaders of these colleges, who were 'very suspicious of mental tests,' and reluctant to contribute genealogical information or to sanction her work (Blackwood Diary 1924–7, 7 March 1925; see also entry for 29 April 1925) because they feared she was trying to equate race with intelligence, to their detriment. She was forced to think about the connotations of terminology associated with her project, choosing the term 'mixed' (as in 'mixed-blood' or 'mixed-race') instead of the widely used 'mulatto' or 'octaroon' (Blackwood Diary 1924–7, 29 April 1925), terms which had been used in the slave trade. As late as the 7th of June, just two months before she arrived at the Blood Reserve, Blackwood lunched with members of the local 'Interracial Commission' at the Tuskegee Institute in Alabama (a college for African-Americans)[1] and 'Discussed tests & their legitimate uses' (Blackwood Diary 1924–7, 7 June 1925). For someone trained in theory, Blackwood's education and thinking had been greatly challenged during these months, and placed into a political context that was entirely new to her.

It was after these eye-opening months in the American South that she began working with Native American people, and she quickly discovered that they faced many of the same problems as African-Americans. By the time she began working in Native communities, she was alert to some of the social, economic, and political realities Native people faced, and early in her research trip became aware that such factors and prejudice counted for far more in determining what people's lives and abilities were like than inherited factors did. Her disenchantment with terms such as 'race' and 'intelligence' is made clear in the monograph which was the primary product of this research trip (Blackwood 1927). While her frameworks were firmly of the period, Blackwood began this report by acknowledging that scores on mental tests 'vary in direct ratio with the social status of the subject' (1927: 8), and she concluded by stating that 'intelligence ... can be defined only as what is measured by the tests' and that '"race" should carry a biological definition only' (1927: 111). In other words, along with other anthropologists of the era such as Franz Boas, she was rejecting any direct link between intelligence and physical inheritance, and saw clearly the possibility that racism and prejudice might skew the frameworks and results of intelligence tests. In these conclusions she seems to have agreed with several scholars with whom she discussed issues of intelligence testing. Early in her research, she had an interview with Dr J.C. Chapman, an educational psychology expert working in Boston, who expressed scepticism 'as to the possibility of testing intelligence apart from environment, & also of the pit-falls in interpreting the results of the tests' (Blackwood Diary 1924–7, 30 September 1924). Later, after witnessing interracial politics, Dr Mourse Work of the Tuskegee Institute told her very frankly that he thought that 'all [intelligence] tests hitherto applied have been too much dependent on language & on training – too academic & ['therefore' sign] unfair' (Blackwood Diary 1924–7, 29 April 1925). She seems, in the end, to have agreed with him.

The other evidence for her doubts about the concepts of 'race' and 'intelligence' is found more subtly in her papers and other materials arising from the 1924–7 research, many of which appear never to have been used, or even touched, following her return to Oxford. The hair samples she obtained in some Native communities as part of her physical measurements are still in the little envelopes she placed them in, and have never been opened. The children's drawings she obtained for comparative purposes did not come to the Museum until after her death, and she never published on them. The slips of paper on which she recorded physical measurements do not exist in the Museum's collection, and seem not to have been deposited there. Some of her photographs were never printed, or existed in contact-print form only. On the other hand, many of her photographs were printed as pairs of frontal and side portraits, often on the same piece of paper to emphasize the comparison (see figure 2.2). In the early 1930s these paired images were glued to large cardboard sheets to create a reference collection for the Pitt Rivers Museum which emphasized physical and cultural features, and it was in this format that Blackwood's Kainai images were most accessible to Museum staff and researchers until 2001, when they were scanned separately for this project (Edwards and Hart 2004: 50–7).

While Blackwood maintained an interest in physical analysis throughout her career, she seems to have continued such work for its own sake, as if simply to keep her hand in. In addition to the monograph which is the official report of her North American fieldwork (1927), Blackwood published some of her findings on skin colour and methodology for recording it (Blackwood 1930), and later published on the practice of infant head-binding in New Britain (1955) and on the physical measurements of Oxfordshire villagers (Blackwood et al. 1939). These publications are narrow reports of findings rather than of their real implications, and, as she was not theoretically inclined, she did not use the material to develop broader understandings of human development. Her main interests after the 1920s trip turned to material culture and to museum work and teaching.

Blackwood lectured heavily at Oxford from about 1930 to 1950; most of her teaching and lecture notes are dated in the 1940s, after she was officially made a University Lecturer in Ethnology. Her teaching included a great deal on physical anthropology and concepts of race, in which she both repeated theories of the era and qualified them in important ways. She gave lectures on 'Ethnology' (then defined as the comparative study of human populations and heavily based on physical anthropology and the effects of environment on physical and cul-

2.2 Blackwood's photographs mounted on card in PRM collections. (PRM Photograph and Manuscript Collections, Box 54, Card 20)

tural 'types'), a 'Regional Ethnology' series, and 'Lands and Peoples,' which seems to have been a similar course. She lectured on North American Plains peoples in both courses. Her notes contain a series of lectures on physical anthropology and particularly on methodology, which include references to the necessity of making measurements quickly so as not to frighten subjects, and the use of photography.[2]

Blackwood used very little of her Kainai data (or, indeed, any of her data from the 1924–7 field trip) for teaching: in six boxes of lecture scripts, slide and artefact lists, and reading notes for teaching, there are only half a dozen slides and an equal number of lines of text referring to her fieldwork on the Blood Reserve. In her notes for a lecture on North American Ethnology, given in the 1940s, she begins by describing various physical types, including the Plains type, which she describes as 'characterised by a massive and large face, aquiline nose, heavy features and tall stature. Here belong the Blackfoot, Crow, Pawnee, some Shoshones, Dakota etc.' (Blackwood Papers, Ethnology Lectures, North America, Box 16, p. 95). In a similar lecture, she also commented on 'Physical types of Plains Indians': 'They are among the tallest of the Indians. ... The Plains type I took on the Blood Reserve in 1925 is, on the whole, more homogenous than are the Indians in other parts of the country' (Blackwood Papers, Lands and Peoples Lecture Series, Box 23, 'Plains Indian' lecture, p. 10). In another lecture on the Plains, she discussed topics such as the arrival and effects of horses; social organization; warfare; subsistence; and various artefacts in the Pitt Rivers Museum, such as clothing, which illustrated aspects of Plains cultures. Following a discussion of ceremonialism, she remarked that 'A modified version of the Sun Dance is kept up, but the torturing of men and animals is forbidden'[3] – probably an adaptation of a comment in her diary, published here as appendix 2. Her slide list for these lectures includes several of the Kainai images:[4] the one of four men, possibly used to illustrate her description of a Plains physical type (although a slide list for 1954 which includes this image has her handwritten note 'Hair still worn in braids' next to it); one of the images of man, women, and child in front of a tipi, on which she notes 'Elk-teeth ornament on dress, some moccasins, some boots' (on the 1954 list this image has the notation, 'Painted tipi, Blood Reserve, 1925. Note outside pole carrying wind flaps. Talk about outfit here'). Her papers for these lectures (Blackwood Papers, Box 13) included an image of animals in a corral on the Blood Reserve that was given to her by Indian Agent Faunt and that she may have used in the lectures. In addition, the box in which she kept her slides for this lecture[5] also includes an image showing a general landscape on the Blood Reserve, probably to allow her to talk about the effect of environment in (as it was then believed) determining elements of Plains cultures.

In her teaching, then, Blackwood focused extensively on race and on the links between race, environment, and culture. However, she avoided shallow generalizations about race in her teaching, and indeed worked into her lectures the very latest findings on blood groups, archaeology, and other research which helped to refine theories about human populations and their relationships. The legacy of her disquiet with ready associations between 'race' and intelligence and other factors, which she expressed in her diary for the 1924–7 field trip, may be seen in a poignant pencilled insertion, in large letters, in a lecture on ethnology which she gave during the war years of 1942 and 1944: 'THERE IS NO ARYAN RACE.'[6]

Clearly, her work during the 1924–7 field trip gave Blackwood serious doubts about the concept of race and its political misuse, and she communicated those doubts decades later in her teaching. Despite this, she maintained her research framework for the duration of the trip. As she moved across the continent taking physical measurements, recording genealogies, measuring skin colour, and cutting and labelling hair samples, she worked with the concept of race every day. She also discussed, on almost a daily basis, theories from scholars and administrators about how to deal with the 'problem' (as it was then referred to) of Native peoples – in other words, how to manage what were assumed to be inferior races during the period of their decline. The 1920s was an interesting time for these discussions, a period of emerging theoretical interests in psychological anthropology, ethnic identity, and cultural change and assimilation on the one hand, and on the other hand the growing frustration at a pragmatic level within the Department of Indian Affairs that Native people were not availing themselves of the opportunity (as white society perceived it) to assimilate, but were instead stubbornly retaining elements of their traditional culture. Blackwood's conversations with scholars and non-Native officials revealed to her that what the dominant society in North America felt very strongly was a need for the complete assimilation of Native peoples, African-Americans, and other minorities into mainstream white society through education and intermarriage. Thus, when she 'talked shop with Dr Ralph Linton' at the Field Museum in Chicago on 24 June 1925, Linton – who later went on to publish a major monograph on acculturation[7] – stated strongly that regarding African-Americans, 'the solution of the future lay in complete absorption of the negro into the white stock' (Blackwood Diary 1924–7, 24 June 1925). Similarly, Blackwood paraphrased the attitudes of Reverend Atkinson, the missionary at Oxford House in northern Manitoba, as 'The only possible future for the Indian in Canada is complete assimilation with the whites – in blood as in culture – this is going on pretty rapidly' (Blackwood Diary 1924–7, 29 June 1925).

While such views were expressed all around her, and she frequently recorded them in her diary, Blackwood's initial experiences in the American South seem to have made her sceptical of the political and racist attitudes which underlay popular ideas about assimilation. After noting Reverend Atkinson's strong belief in the need for it, she went on to say, 'though there is nothing like the prejudice there is in the South against Negroes, there are many people who will have nothing to do with the Indians – "the darker race"' (Blackwood Diary 1924–7, 29 June 1925). Nevertheless, Blackwood constantly worked with and accepted assistance from missionaries, Indian agents, school principals, and other colonial officials who held negative views about Native people: she stayed with them, was driven around reserves in their cars and paddled upriver in their canoes, used their offices for measuring, and checked her genealogical data given by Native peoples against officials' records and knowledge. She was surrounded by their ideas and assumptions about Native peoples and sought permission for her research not from the people themselves, but from Duncan Campbell Scott, the Deputy Superintendent of Indian Affairs (Department of Indian Affairs, Blackwood to D.C. Scott, 28 June 1925, NAC Indian Affairs, RG 10, Vol. 6816, File 486-6-1, Pt. 1). Intellectually, she also participated in anthropological ways of thinking which contributed to or shared the attitudes of these colonial agents. These ways of thinking can be seen in her photographs – but so, as we explore in chapter 4, can other perspectives.

Anthropology, Photography, and Beatrice Blackwood

> Any meeting of cultures, after all, challenges and confirms expectations in ways exposed with peculiar force through the camera lens. For that is photography's single prerogative among the pictorial arts: to register all that falls within the camera's range, exposing the photographer as ineluctably as his subject, revealing furtive assumptions as tellingly as open biases. That mixed array of assumptions and biases constitutes a

> remarkable and ongoing cultural dialogue. (Schwarz 1997: 25, citing Mitchell 1994: xi)

Whatever her doubts might have been in the 1920s about the concept of 'race' and its applicability in the situations she was seeing, Blackwood continued across the entire three-year trip to photograph people in poses that related to the broader scholarly project to define race and racial difference. Her paired front and side portraits are referentially anthropometric, and together with her meticulous and constant recording of measurements suggest that she was at some levels participating in an intellectual system which linked anthropology, race, and colonialism.

Photography assumed an increasingly prominent role as anthropology developed in the later nineteenth and early twentieth centuries, making available to scholars a range of images showing aspects of ritual and daily life from peoples around the world. The first major scientific expedition sent from the United Kingdom to record a non-Western culture, the 1898 Cambridge University Expedition to Torres Strait, took moving pictures as well as still images (Herle and Rouse 1998). These images were produced to document cultural elements of interest and to facilitate analysis after the expedition returned to Cambridge. Photographs went hand-in-hand with artefacts, linguistic data, stories, and information about kinship, religion, and politics collected 'in the field' and transferred to Western academic institutions. However, one particular element of anthropological thinking dominated anthropological photography in the late nineteenth century: the attempt to understand the relationship between human physical appearance and human culture, and the origins and development of both.

The emergence of photography and anthropology in the latter half of the nineteenth century meant that both became involved in the development of theories about human origins and the relationship between different 'races.' Photography was used to document the physical appearance of human populations and thus as a tool in explanatory theories (Edwards 1998: 24; Pinney 1989). Anthropometric photography used standard poses (showing the subject in full frontal, side, and three-quarters, face or full body, naked if possible and posed against a measurement grid or with a measuring stick: see, for example, plate 12 in Wright 1992: 21). As Thomas Huxley, president of the Ethnological Society and a biologist, instructed in an 1869 memo, 'the entire figure of the subject was to be photographed, unclothed, full face and profile, and then the same aspects of the head alone. The subject was to be placed at a precise distance from the camera ... A measuring rod was to be placed in a specific position alongside the body, off which measurement of that body could be read' (Edwards 2001: 137–8). Such images were a powerful comparative tool which allowed scholars to think about the differences and similarities between peoples, including those within Europe and Great Britain (Edwards 1998: 28–33). That the nature of the power involved in such comparison was not entirely scholarly is indicated by the fact that Huxley's memo was sent out by the Colonial Office in London to all colonial governors requesting that they obtain these photographs for the furthering of scientific knowledge (Edwards 2001: 131–56).

Many of the images actually produced were relatively unscientific and crude, using only pairs of frontal and side facial images to reference scientific thinking. These images were used to describe and classify what were seen as different 'racial types,' although in real terms the images were not standardized sufficiently to permit exact comparison (Edwards 2001: 138ff). They did, however, visually encapsulate physical and cultural ways in which their subjects differed from the viewer (Edwards 2001:137; see also Banta and Hinsley 1986: 57–63), and the physical traits they depicted were linked with cultural traits in classificatory schema to speak of 'primitive' and 'civilized' peoples. An example would be the description in an 1877 volume, *Descriptive Catalogue of Photographs of North American Indians*, of Eskiminzin, an Apache, cited in W. Richard West (1998: xiii):

> Height, 5 feet 8 inches; circumference of head, 22 1/2 inches; circumference of chest, 37 inches; age 38 years. Head chief of San Carlos reservation and of the Pinal Apaches. His family was among those slain at the Camp Grant massacre in 1871. Is now taking the lead in living a civilized life, having taken up a farm on the San Carlos River.

Commenting on the crudeness of such classificatory language used to describe photographs of Native peoples, West has remarked that 'whatever Eskiminzin might have thought about "civilized life" on his San Carlos River farm, I have always had great difficulty believing that if you asked him who he was and what was important to him, he would have responded by telling you the circumference of his head and chest' (West 1998: xiii).

Clearly, though, these measurements were important to non-Native scholars, who made so many of them. At one level, such classification was a genuine search for understanding, and just part of the broader Victorian concern for developing and ordering knowledge. Classification was, however, not a neutral act. Aided by photography of non-Western peoples, it was an intellectual process related closely to the processes of enacting political and military control over colonized peoples and lands: theories about the cultural and physical evolution of humans, and about hierarchical relationships between peoples, were developed in the later nineteenth century by scholars working partly from photographs, and were used to rationalize colonization and control of indigenous peoples by European settler societies (Schwarz 1997: 24–5, citing Scherer 1992: 33; Edwards 1998: 5; Edwards 1992: 6). Anthropometric and ethnographic photographs – of colonized and otherwise disempowered people, by and for colonizers – embody the asymmetries of power inherent in such relationships (Edwards 2001: 3). Anthropologists saw photography as a scientific tool, an objective device for recording facts about non-Western cultures in which they were interested (Edwards 1992: 4; Edwards 1998: 23–5, Edwards 2001: 133). Driven by their concern to record what they saw as vanishing traditional elements of Native cultures, many were unaware that they were actively composing images which fitted with theoretical interests and omitted so much of the 'modern' or 'acculturated' realities of Native life. Their photographic techniques hid or minimized the nature of the politics involved in their taking. The use of a studio or plain backdrop to isolate the subject from his or her immediate surroundings and reality, the standard use of paired frontal and side views within this laboratory-like setting, and the emphasis on details of material culture deemed to be 'traditional' or desirable to view (and the hiding or avoidance of other details) all shifted the viewer's attention to the data presented, and obscured or denied altogether the staging, manipulation, and relations of power necessary to create such images (and see, in this vein, MacDougall 1992: 105; Schwarz 1997: 25 and citing Mitchell 1994: xiii). Such strong framing is also seen in the contemporary captioning of images of First Nations people taken during this era, which rarely comments on the political context or relationships in which the photograph was created. This deterministic use of photographs is something that scholars recognize in hindsight, however. Many anthropologists and other researchers today who take photographs as part of their data collection or who write about photographs and their meanings are very well aware of the complexities surrounding the creation and use of images of indigenous peoples, as well as of the concerns of these communities regarding the present and future use of such material.

Later in her career, Blackwood lectured to anthropology students at Oxford for a number of years and communicated to them, in a lecture series on 'Methods of Physical Anthropology,' ideas about the utility of photography and how best to take photographs that would be useful for physical analysis. Typical of the period, her lecture notes are nearly devoid of the issues of ethics and power that were so central to working in the manner she and many other anthropologists still advocated, and are worth quoting from here at length to give a sense of the certainty scholars brought to this work:

> All anthropological records are greatly increased in value by the addition of photographs. For anthropological purposes the ideal is to have three views of the same individual, full face, profile, and back. If circumstances do not allow of this, take the first two. If possible they should be full length, the subject standing in the military position of attention, but with one arm extended by the side, and the other flexed across the body horizontally from the elbow. The shoulders should be level. It adds to the usefulness of the record if the points corresponding to the ends of the long bones can be marked on the limb before the photograph is taken. If a stature standard is photographed alongside, the photograph can then be utilised to give data as to proportions. It goes without saying that the value of the photograph from the point of view of physical anthropology varies inversely with the amount of clothing worn by the subject. In any case the removal of any head covering should if possible be insisted on.[8] But the same rule holds good here as in taking measurements, it is better to photograph under unfavourable conditions than not to photograph at all ... Some attention should be given to the background, which should be as plain as possible, a drab-coloured wall is the best. Photographs should also be taken of the environment, to show the nature of the country, the vegetation, geological features, and so on, which often have an important bearing on the life of the people. Different types of villages, houses, etc. should be recorded, care being taken to choose such as are really typical, and to get them from a good view point. The taking of chance snap-shots is as a rule a waste of time and material from an anthropological standpoint. Well chosen post-cards are often worth having. It would be a great boon if any one who has the opportunity would try and get good photographs to add to our collection.[9]

In another lecture (on ethnology and the Northwest Coast, given in 1946), Blackwood showed her adherence to anthropological categories in her captioning of images that she took in the 1920s and used as lecture slides: even when she initially obtained the names of the individuals she photographed, these were dropped to emphasize the anthropological point being made by the image. Thus, a pair of photographs of shaman Billy Williams at Kispiox in British Columbia, in his regalia and with his small daughter by his side, were captioned for her lecture slide 'Man wearing Chilkat blanket. Front' (Blackwood Papers, Lecture Notes, Box 13), which demonstrates the blurring of her interests in material and physical anthropology (figure 2.3).

Blackwood's Kainai Photographs

Blackwood often noted in her diary that once she arrived in a community, she 'wandered round taking photographs' of whatever caught her professional eye. Her subject matter was not random, though. Blackwood took her photographs of Kainai people as an anthropologist who was interested in issues of race and of culture change, as well as in the nature of what she saw as 'traditional' and 'authentic' Native cultures. She intended these images to have meaning within her research – to add to other forms of data and records she brought back to Oxford with her, and to function as aides-memoire – within the contexts of scholarly conversations on race and cultural transition, and in future teaching on these topics as well as on the Native cultures involved. The content of her photographs and the way she framed images were intended to provide data on human physical types, on elements of traditional Native culture, and on material culture as an index of cultural continuity and change. Of the thousands of images she took during this three-year trip, the largest group is of references to cultural activity and material culture, followed by anthropometric-style and casual portraits and general images of landscape and local buildings or landmarks.

At the most obvious level, most of Blackwood's images have Native people in them. Some of these are casual snapshot-style portraits, but many of the images show individuals and couples in two standard poses, from the front and from the side, framing these photographs as referentially anthropometric views. Her labels and notes on these images at the time highlight these intentions. Appendix 2 (page 211) 'Blackwood's notations on her Kainai Photographs,' is a chart compiled from two separate lists made by Blackwood as part of her indexing and record-keeping work.[10] One list excludes personal names, and empha-

2.3 Billy Williams with his daughter, Kispiox Village, 1 September 1925. Photograph by Beatrice Blackwood. (Pitt Rivers Museum, University of Oxford, PRM BB.A4.34)

sizes terminology associated with anthropometric photography ('Adult male, full length, full face and profile'; 'Full face only'; 'Another man, full face and profile. Close up'), while another list includes personal names but adds racial categorizations after these: 'Charlie Wolf Plume. Full Blood.' The original lists in which Blackwood must have recorded the names of those people who posed for her as individuals or small groups no longer remain in the manuscript collections of the Pitt Rivers Museum, though the list naming the schoolgirls has been preserved. Within the compilation list that Blackwood typed up at a later stage, the personal names are submerged by a tide of anthropological categorization and meaning. The contributions that some of these Kainai people made to their community, some of which are noted in chapter 4, are dissociated from these scientific frameworks. Blackwood did not collect biographical information on these people, and spent no time getting to know them as individuals. The remarks in her diary are generalizations concerning the extent to which Kainai people had become acculturated and, on the whole, do not seem to link with the people she photographed:

> Visited a new house one of the Indians is having built, also his barn – modern in every respect. This man owns a large amount of land, 3–400 head of horses, and herd of cattle, and a six-cylinder car – with which he is at present touring in Montana. (Blackwood Diary 1924–7, 3 August 1925)

Of all the sets of photographs from all the First Nations communities she worked in, Blackwood's Kainai photographs contain the highest percentage of paired anthropometric-style portraits. Twelve of the images are part of paired front and side views; another is marked 'full face only' as if she had intended to obtain a side view but couldn't; and several others depicting small groups also look as if she thought of them as frontal images but was unable to obtain the side view as well. The emphasis on race for this group of images is possibly due to comments made by Indian Agent Faunt that the Kainai were of a truer, less hybridized physical type than other tribes:

> Talked to the Indian Agent about the Bloods. He says that they are a high type of Indian – far superior to the Crees. (Blackwood Diary 1924–7, 2 August 1925)

> They are far more like the traditional Indian than the Crees are – tall, big-boned, large faces with very high cheekbones – and big hooked noses, the

> men wear their hair in two long plaits tied together in front on their chests. The women all wear shawls except some who had European dress. (Blackwood Diary 1924–7, 3 August 1925)

The word 'traditional' here, used in relation both to physical features and to hairstyle and dress, is crucial. Given her interest in 'race,' physical types, and inheritance, Blackwood's brief visit to the Blood Reserve thus provided her with a reference point for comparing Native peoples and understanding hybridity and inheritance.[11] A few months later, in Minnesota, Blackwood visited Ojibwe communities which became for her examples of less 'pure' physical and cultural types. Dr Albert E. Jenks, a professor of anthropology at the University of Minnesota – and one of the researchers in a controversial series of court cases to determine the blood quantum of Ojibwe and mixed-blood people in Minnesota a decade earlier (see Beaulieu 1984: 293; Meyer 1994: 168; Peers 2003) – suggested a particular tour of Ojibwe communities which would give Blackwood a good sense of the ongoing process of physical and cultural change among Native people:

> Talked to Dr Jenks, Professor of Anthropology, who schemed out a trip for me to Indian Reservations. The one where there is most mixture is at White Earth ... Another, the Turtle Mountain Reserve ... [where there are various mixtures] ... a good place to study the amalgamation process. (Blackwood Diary 1924–7, 13 October 1925)

Blackwood did not actually visit either White Earth or Turtle Mountain, but her notes on the Minnesota Ojibwe communities she did work in (Nett Lake, Red Lake, Ponemah) emphasize hybridity. This focus is underscored by notes in Blackwood's handwriting which were found tucked in with children's drawings collected in Minnesota, for example:[12]

> Drawings by children of Red Lake Indian Boarding School (Chippewa Tribe). These children have some mixture of white blood – some of them a considerable amount – but all have some Indian blood or they could not be at this school.
>
> Drawings by children at Nett Lake Indian Day School (Chippewa Tribe). This reservation is one of the most isolated in Minnesota. There was no road into it till about 10 years ago. There is some white blood but much less than in any other village and the people are more primitive in their habits than elsewhere in Minnesota.

The Kainai, then, came to stand in Blackwood's mind as an example of 'purer' physical type, a concept somehow entwined with that of 'traditional' culture. This is confirmed by the captions she wrote later when she was teaching back in Oxford for the glass lantern slides that she produced from these photographs. These emphasize the terms 'full-blood' and 'traditional' and were partly based on her field lists. One such caption reads:

> Photo taken by B. Blackwood, August 1925. Taken on the Blood Indian Reserve, S. Alberta. Blood Indian man. Full-face and profile. Said to be full-blood.[13]

Her lecture notes, as discussed earlier, confirm that the Kainai represented a 'purer' 'type' than other tribes for Blackwood: 'They are among the tallest of the Indians ... The Plains type I took on the Blood Reserve in 1925 is, on the whole, more homogenous than are the Indians in other parts of the country' (Blackwood Papers, Lands and Peoples Lecture Series, Box 23, 'Plains Indian' lecture, p. 10).

While she did not include a measuring rod in her images and photographed her subjects fully clothed, unlike the most scientifically rigorous images of this genre, Blackwood's use of the paired front and side poses made them referentially anthropometric and she clearly took them in that tradition; we therefore use 'anthropometric' to describe them, while being aware that they are only loosely so by some standards. In what is perhaps one of the earliest photographs showing anthropometric techniques being implemented on the Blood Reserve, for instance, two adolescent boys sit by a tipi, watching with some curiosity as a scientist measures a Kainai man (see figure 2.4). As noted above, the most severe type of this portrait involved frontal and side views of subjects posed (preferably naked) against a measured grid (Edwards 2001: 137). Blackwood's images, by contrast, like those of many anthropologists, use the front and side views as references to this genre of imagery. They could have been used in only the most general way to compare physical types and head shapes. To be useful in physical anthropology they would have needed further associated data of facial and cranial measurements, skin colour and hair type – many of which sets she obtained, but not from all those whom she photographed, and often from people whom she did not photograph. Without such supporting data, it is unclear how these portraits would or could have been useful; at one level, then, they seem rather to be 'in the style of'

2.4 Ethnologist measuring a Blackfoot man, Macleod District, Alberta, ca. 1910–20. Photographer unknown. (Glenbow-Alberta Institute NA.668-18)

anthropometric images rather than such images themselves, and include as much detail about dress, housing, and other cultural and lifestyle features as they do about physical traits. This further distinguishes them from proper anthropometric photography, in which subjects were isolated from their physical and social environments and placed against plain backdrops as if on a laboratory slide for analysis and comparison (MacDougall 1992: 107; Edwards 2001: 137).

Blackwood's portraits rarely isolate people from their backgrounds, even when she was in a community for a longer period of time. Some portraits were taken outdoors, with the reserve landscape providing the setting; in others, the room or building against which they were taken is visible, together with furniture, porches, and, sometimes, other people. The constant inclusion of such details gives Blackwood's portraits an oddly non-scientific feel, showing instead frontal and side views of real people in real local and social contexts. In part, this may have been due to Blackwood's interest in 'traditional' culture. One gets the sense from her photographs and notes that, as her research trip progressed, she began to place more importance on understanding 'traditional' and 'modern' culture, and to see physical type and inheritance as part of this intellectual framework of understanding cultural change. Furthermore, as illustrated by the discussion above concerning figure 2.3 (of Billy Williams and his daughter), the photographs themselves increasingly emphasize material culture, even when Blackwood was ostensibly taking anthropometric-style images.

This interest in material culture is demonstrated in the entire group of Blackwood's photographs from this trip, in which the second major theme is material culture and its use as an indicator of cultural continuity and change. As an anthropologist interested in Native American and First Nations cultures, with expectations of 'authentic' and 'hybrid' cultures equating to pre-modern and modern phenomena, in many of her Kainai photographs Blackwood focused on material culture, which, for her, served as an index of authenticity. Moccasins peeking out from under skirts or trousers, a painted tipi, elk-tooth earrings, blankets worn as shawls, and long braided hair all served for Blackwood in these images as icons of 'authentic' Kainai culture and survivals from the past (as they do, although differently, for Kainai people today; see chapters 4 and 5).

In both folk culture and anthropology, human physical characteristics have long (and erroneously) been equated with culture, and the 'purity' of physical traits equated with 'purity' or authenticity of culture. Traits thought to be culturally 'authentic' were described by the term 'traditional.' This has become entangled with the anthropological salvage paradigm, in which authentic was seen to equal pre-contact, undiluted, as it were, by European influence in thought or material culture. Blackwood's photographs were composed and selected within these intellectual beliefs. The captions she added to them later, in Oxford, underline this and suggest that in her teaching (the only way in which she ever used the images), she presented them within these concepts and that the images functioned, in part, to validate and pass on the concepts themselves.

Thus, the texts on her lantern slides (which were produced from these photographs) refer to terms such as authenticity/tradition; hybrid ('hybrid costume now in everyday use'); and 'still,' as in 'still used':

> Photo taken by B. Blackwood, August 1925. Taken on the Blood Indian Reserve, S. Alberta.
>
> Blood Indians in the hybrid costume now in everyday use. From left to right their names are: Mrs Yellow Shine, Mrs Shot-on-both Sides, Mrs Rough Hair and Rough Hair with their daughter.[14] (Rough Hair is also seen on Slide No. 26, second from left.)
>
> Buffalo hair blankets are too scarce and expensive, and there are very few worn, but many people still wear (trade) blankets. Many also still prefer moccasins to trade footgear. The trimming on the blouses worn by Mrs Rough Hair and the child consists of elk teeth, these are a sign of wealth.[15]

Blackwood's Interactions with First Nations People

Clearly, Blackwood's engagement with anthropological ideas was complicated and at times ambiguous, although on the whole she worked within the dominant, intertwined sets of ideas about physical and cultural traditionalism and change. How did these ideas, her project overall, the political contexts in which she worked, and her own personality affect her interaction with the people she studied? How did they respond to her, and why, and how did their responses shape the photographs she took?

Blackwood's approaches to people and her explanations of her project varied from community to community, and were dependent on the support and permission of officials, beginning with the principals of colleges in which she worked in the southern United States and going on to Indian agents, missionaries, teachers, and medical staff. As her letter to the Deputy Superintendent of Indian Affairs shows, however, she assumed, at least partly on the basis of the prestige her Oxford affiliation gave her, that this permission would be granted, and in essence she asked for advice rather than for consent to undertake her research:

> I am an anthropologist from the University of Oxford travelling in this country with a Laura Spelman Rockefeller Fellowship. My object is to make a study of the physical measurements of women of different racial stocks. My Fellowship allows me a certain amount of travel in the summer and I wish to take the opportunity to see something of the Canadian Indians. I have a 'round-trip ticket' which takes me from Winnipeg to Vancouver on the C.P.R. Would you kindly advise me as to the best places to stop at along this route to get into touch with the Indian Reservations? I should also be grateful for the names of any persons who would assist me in this. (Department of Indian Affairs, B. Blackwood to D.C. Scott, 28 June 1925, NAC RG 10, Vol. 6816, File 486-6-1 Pt. 1)

As she had expected, permission was indeed granted for her work, and Scott's response was to direct her to J.R. Bunn, Inspector of Indian Agencies for Manitoba, who was asked to assist her if at all possible (Department of Indian Affairs, D.C. Scott to J.R. Bunn, 2 July 1925, NAC RG 10, Vol. 6816, File 486-6-1, Pt. 1). Once in Native communities, Blackwood worked with white officials to obtain and verify genealogical data in which to contextualize her physical measurements, as she wished to know the parentage and ancestry of those she measured and photographed to understand who was 'full blood' and who was 'mixed' (e.g., Blackwood Diary 1924–7, 22 July 1925, Norway House, where she describes working with Mr Blackford at Hope Island 'to have an opportunity of going over my slips [pieces of paper with names of people she had measured and the information she had obtained from them] with him & finding out all I could about the people I measured. Then wandered round taking photographs').

To these people she seems to have offered adequate explanations of her work. At Atlanta University, she noted that the students she measured were 'an intelligent crowd & were interested in what I was doing, they did not object to anything,' suggesting that she discussed her research with them in some detail, as indeed she was often obliged to do in the politically charged atmosphere of the South (Blackwood Diary 1924–7, 12 June 1925). She seems to have made less of an attempt to explain her work to Native people, and her explanations must have been even less clear because of language barriers. In some communities

Blackwood hired community members, usually young women, as interpreters or facilitators, but there is no record of how she briefed these assistants about what to say to other Native people. In some cases people seem not to have understood the purpose of the research; for example, when she visited Nett Lake, Minnesota:

> Went round measuring with the aid of Pearlie Day, a half breed girl who proved very successful in approaching the women – so that we got most of them except those who were sick & the very old. A few wouldn't, one said if I measured her I should be able to arrest her. Another said if there was a war she would be sent to fight. Another said she was too big to be measured! One thought I was measuring her for a suit of clothes – I hope she doesn't expect it to appear! (Blackwood Diary 1924–7, 2 November 1925)

In other communities, missionaries made brief and rather vague announcements of Blackwood's purpose and asked for cooperation. In the northern Cree community of Norway House in Manitoba, she attended the Sunday afternoon Cree sermon to have a chance of addressing as many members of the community as possible, but the explanation given of her work was misleading, and she made it more so in conversation with the Cree afterwards:

> Mr Atkinson [the missionary] gave out [at the Cree sermon] that there was a lady who had come from very far away 'naspich wana' [northern Cree, *naspic wahnaw*, literally 'very far away,' phrase also used to mean 'England'][16] & was travelling 'in the interests of the Indian women' & would like to see them all after the service. So about a dozen turned up on the school verandah & were measured – much to their amusement. They took it quite well – I explained that I wanted to remember exactly what they were like so as to be able to tell the people at home, who couldn't come because it was too far away – one of the school girls interpreted for me. (Blackwood Diary 1924–7, 5 July 1925)

The following week, in the neighbouring community of Oxford House, Blackwood again used the missionary to announce her work:

> in the afternoon a number of women collected in front of the church in response to Mr Atkinson's invitation on Sunday. Some turned shy and ran away, but I managed to measure about 50 of them – head & face were all I

> could manage to get – & even those were taken under difficulties – it was hard to make them hold up their heads. They were very good about it, though, & Mrs Atkinson says they will talk about it for a long time. I wondered whether I should be held responsible for making 'bad medicine' if anyone fell sick, but Mr Atkinson said he didn't think they would credit a white woman with such doings. (Blackwood Diary 1924–7, 13 July 1925)

Elsewhere, she appears to have not attempted detailed explanations of what and why she was researching, but used every opportunity to collect data. In the Ojibwe community of Red Lake in Minnesota, she counted herself fortunate to arrive when annual Treaty monies were being paid out, which meant that most of the community filed through one building to receive payments: 'Payment of annuity money. Set up my instruments in a room in the office & caught a number of the women as they came for their payment' (Blackwood Diary 1924–7, 16 November 1925).

On another occasion, Blackwood was even more forceful in obtaining information, in this case a photograph. On the Sarcee (Tsuu T'ina) Reserve near Calgary, she found that

> The women were shy & refused to be photographed – even the younger ones. One old woman objected very strongly to my trying to photograph the medicine man's tent while he was out, so I had to try a snap while Dr. Murray [the Indian Agent] was talking to her – his medicine bags were hung over the end of the bed ... (Blackwood Diary 1924–7, 30 July 1925)

And on at least one occasion, Blackwood's purpose was completely misunderstood by the people with whom she worked, and she persevered rather assertively, despite the resulting problems. Shortly after leaving the Blood Reserve, Blackwood began work in the village of Kispiox in British Columbia, where the men seem to have been sufficiently upset and uncertain to spread serious rumours about the purpose of her study:

> Measured some more women. The menfolk are taking exception to my work, especially Chief [word unclear: Sumadegs?]. They are already rather annoyed at the white man's interference with their totem poles though nothing is ever done without the consent of the owner of the pole. One woman said her husband said he would throw her out because she

> allowed me to measure her ... Rumour went round that the Government had sent me to measure the women & they were all going to be killed off. Traced it to the fact that my measuring rod when folded up in its case looks not unlike a gun! Carried it without its case after that. (Blackwood Diary 1924–7, 23 August 1925)

Rather amazingly, though – despite such unease and vague (and at times entirely absent) explanations of her work, as well as the coercive system of power within which Native peoples may have felt unable to refuse to be measured or photographed – many people responded quite positively to Blackwood. Intriguingly, a small but consistent group of her photographs taken across this trip includes images that have nothing to do with race, anthropometry, or cultural tradition and change, but are of children playing, people showing off pets, couples or families laughing, and weddings that occurred while she was visiting. Blackwood was clearly able to interact positively with a wide range of people, and was able to be the engaging person she was with the people around her, even when measuring or photographing. The officials with whom she checked information expressed surprise at the people who had allowed her to measure or photograph them:

> Went over slips with Mr Isham, getting particulars of the people measured from the annuity pay roll. He was surprised at the people who had allowed me to measure them. (Blackwood Diary 1924–7, 3 November 1925, Nett Lake, Minnesota)

> AM. Measured the school girls over 15, with the assistance of Miss Deedie the matron. PM. went round the village measuring, with Ella Anderson one of the school girls as interpreter ... Most people willing to be measured. (Blackwood Diary 1924–7, 14 November 1925, Red Lake, Minnesota)

Despite such generally positive interactions, despite the fact that Blackwood saw her work as entirely scholarly in nature, and despite her attempts to reject definitions of race which were used against Blacks and Native peoples, Blackwood's research, and her photographs, existed within and were made possible by a system which managed and controlled Native people. The photographs could not have been made without assistance from people in that network of non-Native officials, bureaucrats such as Indian Agent Faunt, and scholars who were all interested in similar topics as part of their work of managing minority groups. While Blackwood would have resisted having her work categorized within this broader political context, even intellectually her interests in physical types and cultural change were part of a system of thought which categorized Native people within imagined racial and cultural hierarchies and imposed on them a controlling grid of dominant-society knowledge. Her photographs, with their anthropometric poses and emphasis on material culture as an index of traditional versus modern, emerged out of this 'nostalgic, but obliterating, gaze' which was directly linked to and sustained colonialism (Poignant 1996: 47). These readings of Blackwood's photographs, specifically their role as documents related to the political history of the Kainai and of their relationships with the dominant society in the late nineteenth and twentieth centuries, become clear when one examines Kainai history from the time they signed Treaty in 1877 up to the time of Blackwood's visit. What she saw, and photographed, was the result of this history. It is the complex interaction of her interests and understandings, her anthropological background, and the nature of her photography with Kainai history that enables us to try to understand Kainai responses to the images in the present, and a fuller range of meanings connected with them.

In making such harsh criticisms of Blackwood's photographs, and of Blackwood herself as a participant in colonial systems of power which were wielded against the Kainai, one needs to bear in mind that the images constantly carry with them this broader range of meanings: as documents of anthropological thought; as records of the articulation of such thought in one research project; as documents of Blackwood's own career; as records of oppressive relations between the Kainai and outsiders; and as glimpses of Kainai histories and lives. There are, however, 'points of fracture' (Edwards 2001: 12) in even the most troubling and oppressive colonial power bound up in these photographs, ways in which the images do not, in fact, serve as vehicles or articulations of such power. In some respects, Blackwood's photographs are not standard anthropometric images. While they were composed to have meaning within that frame of reference, they were also taken very hastily, so that her intentions were subverted either by her personal interactions with people (some of whom are talking and laughing, in one of them [fig. 26] quite possibly at her) or else because she was moving too quickly to pause for formal anthropometric poses. In this respect, Blackwood was part of a larger anthropological imaging tradition which failed to take properly anthropometric compositions because of resistance by those photographed (Edwards 2001: 138–41). Blackwood also combined her interest in culture with her interest in physical types, so she included real backgrounds, houses and other buildings, and details of life in the community. Such details make the photographs snapshots of people's lives rather than just anthropological constructs. They are portraits, not only of real people still remembered in the community, but of the realities of First Nations life that anthropologists rarely recorded: the reality of girls being kept in school over summer; of labouring in hot dusty fields; of work clothes and everyday routine; of women collecting rations. These images cut across a day in the lives of Kainai people, just as Blackwood herself did, in 1925. They appear on the surface to be anthropological photographs taken during an oppressive period of colonization (and they are); they are also documents of that regime; and they are documents of Kainai lives and histories. As Elizabeth Edwards has noted (2001: 6), photographs are intended to convey specific meanings within specific contexts, but tend to escape those pigeonholes and to be reassigned new meanings in new contexts. These are also Kainai photographs, with Kainai meanings, and those were activated when the images were visually repatriated to the Kainai.

CHAPTER THREE

Working Together

Introduction

The photographs that Beatrice Blackwood took on the Blood Reserve in August 1925 are very much products of their time, and especially of engagements between the Kainai and various forms of colonial control, ranging from Indian agents to anthropometric photography. The Kainai-Oxford Photographic Histories Project is also a product of its own time, and of the desire on the part of scholars and First Nations people today to renegotiate relationships so that the dynamics of power reflect greater equality than they have previously. While we were both aware of other projects that had attempted to do this, and had worked with First Nations people before, we have had to learn a great deal from Kainai advisors in order to carry out this work. In the end, one of the most crucial results of this research has been this learning process and the construction of a partnership of respect and trust with Kainai people which has allowed it to happen. Mindful of James Clifford's admonition (2004: 22) that collaborative works 'need to be appreciated as fruitful, contingent coalitions rather than as performances of postcolonial virtue,' we document this learning process, and the way in which the research partnership has developed, for others who might consider similar work. In addition to discussing the guidance we have received from Kainai research partners, we also highlight other projects that have shifted the ways scholars think about working with photographs, and the intertwined histories represented in them.

Finding Our Way

The roots of this project lie in a conversation between Alison Brown and *Miyanisstsaamiaaki* (Margaret Weasel Fat) in July 1999. Brown was in southern Alberta undertaking fieldwork in connection with her doctoral dissertation and had been introduced to Mrs Weasel Fat, while visiting the encampment at the Kainai Sun Dance grounds. Mrs Weasel Fat described some of her experiences with museums and archives and mentioned that one of her colleagues at Red Crow Community College, a higher education institution located on the Reserve, was putting together a collection of archival photographs for the students' use. Brown was familiar with Blackwood's papers and photographs taken at the Blood Reserve in the Pitt Rivers Museum, and arranged to have catalogue information regarding them sent to the college for inclusion in the archival project. After receiving the catalogue details, Mrs Weasel Fat's colleague wrote to the Museum to seek further information. It later transpired that her letter was never received by Museum staff, and presumably had gone astray in the post. The query was never followed up, and so Blackwood's Kainai images remained as they had been for decades: a small collection of prints and negatives, little used and rarely seen.

In the meantime, we were both becoming more intrigued by Blackwood's fieldwork in North America and the records she made of her encounters with Native peoples. We were interested in how her use of photography intersected with her other research methods and her interpretation of her data. We were even more interested in what her photographs might mean to First Nations people today and how their perspectives could inform our own use of photographs in writing cross-cultural histories and in developing ethnohistorical methodologies (see also Malmsheimer 1987). During her doctoral research Brown had discussed with several Prairie First Nations a selection of archival footage and photographs taken by anthropologists in the late 1920s, which included images taken by Blackwood of Plains Cree people and Tsuu T'ina people just before she visited the Blood Reserve (Brown 2000). At the same time, Laura Peers had been working with two Ojibwe communities in Minnesota to identify ways of caring for materials (including photographic images) that Blackwood collected while visiting their reservations during her research (Peers 2003; see also Paiz 2004). These experiences were teaching us that the descendants of those people photographed by Blackwood so long ago had much to bring to the interpretation of the images and a great deal to say about how photographs have been used within intellectual and social contexts to define their communities. In 2001 we received a grant from the Arts and Humanities Research Board of the United Kingdom (hereafter AHRB) to pursue our questions in relation to Blackwood's Kainai photographs, and we began the project in the summer of that year.

The grant text concentrated on the scholarly elements of the research: our desire to explore the photographs as having different sets of culturally constructed meanings, and the ways such material might be used in creating cross-cultural understandings of the past. We hoped to interview Kainai people about what the photographs meant to them today and about their thoughts on the potential uses of these and similar images within their community. We also noted the importance of such images for strengthening the knowledge of history within First Nations communities as part of their broader project of increasing the vitality of First Nations cultures and identities. We noted that much of the existing work on visual repatriation and its use in these contexts came out of research in the Pacific, and that little similar work had been done in North America, offering potential for opening new lines of scholarly inquiry. We included our intention to deposit copies of interview tapes and transcripts from the research, along with a set of prints of Blackwood's images, with a repository identified by community members for community use, and stated that we expected two main outcomes from the research: a scholarly book aimed at educating non-Native heritage professionals about the importance of such materials to source communities, and a second outcome to be for the benefit of community members, the form of which was to be determined by the Kainai themselves. We explained that such an orientation was an essential part of working with indigenous communities, and that part of the book would be devoted to a discussion of the philosophy and pragmatics of such community-based research.

The fact that the Kainai have for some time been using historical images to transmit historical knowledge across generations has been an important dynamic of this project. Another important element has been the fact that many people within the community are accustomed to working with museums in an effort to regain control of their heritage and were willing to work towards building a relationship of trust with another heritage institution.[1] Like other indigenous nations, the Kainai have long been concerned about their right to shape external research that takes place within their community and have taken a series of measures over the years to protect their intellectual and cultural property and to ensure the continuance of their traditional knowledge. In the 1970s Kainai spiritual leaders initiated negotiations with museums in Alberta for the return of ceremonial bundles essential to Kainai spiritual beliefs and practices, many of which had been separated from the community during periods of extreme cultural stress earlier in the century. Their efforts were instrumental in reinvigorating some of the sacred societies and the Sun Dance, following a period of decline in the 1950s and 1960s, and in developing new forms of relationship between these museums and the community. Two decades later, in 1994, the Blood Tribe Chief and Council established a Cultural and Intellectual Properties Policy which called for any research by outside parties to be authorized by Chief and Council and for the Tribe to be given full rights of access (Crop Eared Wolf 1997: 39). This policy was motivated by concerns that cultural protocol be adhered to and that the Tribe's culture and history not be exploited. Further, with the formation of the Mookaakin Cultural and Heritage Foundation in 1998, the pioneering work of those leaders who first began seeking repatriation on behalf of the community has continued. The Kainai Nation has since secured further repatriations of pipes and bundles from museums in North America and has begun the process of repatriating sacred items currently housed in European museums (Crop Eared Wolf 1997; Bharadia 1999; Conaty 2004).[2]

The Mookaakin Cultural and Heritage Foundation is a voluntary organization whose board consists of Kainai men and women who are deeply involved in the ceremonial life of the community. Board members are committed to the preservation of Kainai culture, spirituality, and traditions and advise museums and heritage institutions about the care of Kainai collections and the need to incorporate Kainai perspectives into the interpretation of historical and archaeological resources.[3] Recently, members of the Foundation played an important role in creating new repatriation legislation in the province of Alberta (Legislative Assembly of Alberta 2000), and two Mookaakin Foundation members, Pete Standing Alone and Frank Weasel Head, participated in the Blackfoot community team that worked on an exhibition of Blackfoot culture, *Nitsitapiisinni: Our Way of Life* (Blackfoot Gallery Committee 2001; Conaty 2003; Conaty and Carter 2005), which opened at the Glenbow Museum in Calgary in 2001. As it can often be difficult for researchers and museum staff to know whom they should contact in the first instance when trying to initiate projects, the formation of an organization such as the Mookaakin Foundation provides an identifiable group of people within the community who can offer guidance in this area and can advise researchers of community protocols and appropriate ways of behaving. Annabel Crop Eared Wolf, Director of Tribal Government and External Affairs and board member of the Mookaakin Foundation, has observed the shifting relationships between museums and First Nations and has commented on how the Blood Tribe views these changes:

> The Blood Tribe believes that it is embarking on a new era that will respect and give credence to its religious rights and freedoms. This era, it is hoped, will be marked by a re-evaluation of how Indian culture and religion are viewed and treated by government and its institutions. There needs to be a maturation process and a commitment to examine existing relationships between Indian people and Euro-Canadian institutions and governments who have assumed responsibility for First Nations heritage. These institutions must realize and recognize that scientific rights of inquiry do not take precedence over cultural and religious rights. (Crop Eared Wolf 1997: 40)

Early in the planning of this project, colleagues at the Glenbow Museum[4] recommended that we contact the Mookaakin Foundation in order to discuss with them possible ways in which we might proceed, and a meeting with the Foundation was arranged to take place shortly after we arrived in Canada in the autumn of 2001. During this meeting people commented on the potential for using Blackwood's photographs in community educational contexts, and questioned us about Blackwood's motives and her intellectual background. They were also interested in our own intentions and our goals in pursuing this project, and directly and indirectly, it emerged that there was concern about some previous research and publication on Kainai culture in which they saw errors of fact, betrayal of trust, and motivations of greed. When we explained that we saw two outcomes for the project, one of which was to be this book, it was suggested that we develop a protocol agreement that would codify the aims of the Kainai-Oxford Photographic Histories Project and the responsibilities of each party.[5] While Mookaakin Foundation members were extremely positive about the potential of the project, they made it clear from the beginning that it should proceed on Kainai terms, meeting Kainai needs and not just academic ones.

Protocol agreements are part of a range of procedures which have become an increasingly standard part of research with indigenous communities, especially within the social and environmental sciences, as a means of creating trust, preventing misunderstandings, and formalizing goals. While some scholars and institutions are uncomfortable about the potential restrictions such agreements might place on them, being willing to negotiate such agreements is a crucial step in overcoming the distrust caused by unsatisfactory scholarship and its results in the past and reflects an acknowledgment that indigenous peoples have legitimate rights of control in the representation of their heritages and cultures (e.g., L.T. Smith 1999; see also chapter 5).

Although the development of our protocol agreement was a first for a British museum, and a learning experience for Pitt Rivers Museum staff, none of whom had before been involved in writing documents of this nature, it follows well-established processes within North America, which emphasize the need for collaborative research frameworks (we discuss the development of this methodology below). As we drafted the protocol, we had to ask ourselves, as researchers and as Museum staff, some of the questions which the Mookaakin Foundation was also interested in: Who would benefit from the knowledge that the pictures evoked? How could that knowledge be made available? To what extent should this knowledge be incorporated into the Museum's own records? What would the Museum receive from this project, and what might it be asked to commit to in order to meet Kainai goals? During the negotiation process, we kept in touch with the Director of the Pitt Rivers Museum, Dr Michael O'Hanlon, by e-mail and fax, and ensured that he (on behalf of the Museum), as well as the Mookaakin Foundation, was satisfied with the document. In the end, both parties have derived great satisfaction from this formalized relationship, and hope to continue working together in the future.

The process of negotiating the protocol agreement underscored for us the fact that this way of working involves a sharing and a shift of power within the traditional research relationship – in which the outside academic usually controls the research, from framing research questions to determining the form of publication – to one in which we were operating more as a team, with Kainai needs and concerns addressed at least as much as scholarly ones. Such a shift became evident, in fact, even before the interviews began, with the issue over the Museum's copyright of Blackwood's photographs. From the outset we had intended that a duplicate set of the images be presented to the community for their own use, though, as fitting with English law, the copyright remains with the Pitt Rivers Museum and is stated on a sticker which Museum protocol dictated should be attached to the reverse of each image, including those presented to individuals as gifts. Standard Museum policy requests that researchers refrain from reproducing archival photos without permission, and that those who receive copies of images in the Museum's photographic collections sign a statement agreeing to this and ensuring that full acknowledgment be made to the source of an image should they wish to publish it. Such requests, however, may not always be appropriate, especially in cases such as this, where the photographs have personal meanings for the source community and are so central to the transmission of community-focused historical knowledge: as Kainai people themselves asked us virtually the first moment they saw these images and their copyright stickers, how can university archives copyright an image of someone's grandparents? Like Roslyn Poignant, who found herself 'doing all manner of unexpected things,' including cutting up photographs to focus on certain individuals in images she worked with in a visual repatriation project with the Kunibídji people of Arnhem Land, Australia (Poignant 1996: 12), we have had to consider what is really at stake when trying to learn how resources of this sort can be utilized by source communities. We have begun to learn to balance the importance of archival integrity with the community need to make these images as widely available as possible, and to modify them, if required, for instance by reprinting to isolate one individual within a group in order to provide a portrait for a descendant.

We have also accepted that some information elicited from the images and shared during interviews will not be added to the Museum's records, or even be translated from Blackfoot. Some of this information proved to be intimate family and life stories, and in conjunction with Kainai advisors we deemed it too private for public dissemination: it is for the use of families and the Kainai community and not for a museum far away or for the researchers who may later access those records. As we discuss further in chapters 5 and 6 along with other lessons and implications of this project, we found that learning to let go of the traditional scholarly need to seek and record as much detail as possible has been central to the success of the project, and has helped to create an environment in which community members felt safe to voice (and to teach us) their understanding of the images, their historical experiences, and the kinds of meanings historical photographs can have within contemporary indigenous communities. By agreeing to respect the wishes of community members about what should be made publicly available from this research, we have gained a level of understanding about the essence of the topics in which we were most interested that would not have been possible had we taken the traditional research path. As *Ninaisipisto* (Francis First Charger), a member of the Mookaakin Foundation, has gently reminded us:

> Remember you can never be an expert on the Kainai people but you can better understand how and why they are a certain way. (First Charger to Brown, pers. comm. 13 July 2003)

All of these topics were discussed while we were negotiating the protocol agreement, and along with the agreement itself, these discussions provided an important starting point to establish a relationship of mutual trust and a means of ensuring that we respect the needs and rights of the Kainai Nation to utilize these historical resources in their own way. The feeling that we were involved in a trust-building exercise continued as we developed the protocol agreement and is ongoing; our advisors have made assurances along the way that we are 'doing okay' and that 'the elders are satisfied' with how we have approached them and the project.[6] Just as it was important for community members to feel that we could be trusted to take their wishes into account, we have also needed to know that community members were supportive of what we were trying to achieve and that we could turn to them for advice.

The protocol agreement was signed on 3 November 2001 by Pete Standing Alone for the Mookaakin Foundation and Alison Brown on behalf of the Pitt Rivers Museum (Peers having returned to Oxford to resume teaching and curatorial responsibilities and to continue with the archival research). The agreement (published as appendix 3) spells out, in a basic manner, who will contribute what to the project and what the Pitt Rivers Museum, the Mookaakin Foundation, and the Blood Tribe will receive from it. The agreement is also subject to review and revision from time to time, as the nature of our relationship changes. It states that copies of all research materials, including tapes, transcripts, and sets of the photographs, are to deposited with the Blood Tribe in a repository to be decided by them.[7] All interview transcripts are to be approved by the interviewees before being quoted or deposited, and all interviewees will receive tapes and transcripts of their interviews. The Pitt Rivers Museum has agreed not to publish materials relating to this project without first seeking feedback and approval from the Mookaakin Foundation, a process that has worked well in relation to conference papers and other publications we have worked on in addition to this book. In return, Mookaakin Foundation members have acted as cultural advisors and have facilitated introductions to other community members for the purpose of conducting interviews. It is important to note that the protocol agreement exists to provide guidance and ensure that research is conducted in a manner which is culturally appropriate and benefits both parties: it is there for guidance, not as a means of controlling the research or its outcomes. Its existence and stipulations have facilitated our work; we do not feel that we have been intellectually constrained by it in any way. Rather, it has laid a foundation for good working practice, and our willingness to enter into it opened many doors for us in the community.

Though the aims of the Mookaakin Foundation are supported by Chief and Council, the Foundation does not speak for the Kainai Nation, and the views expressed in this book are those of individuals. We have been asked by Kainai people to ensure that this point is made very clear to the reader, so that it is understood that the knowledge shared during interviews is based on the teachings that those individuals who participated in the project have received throughout their lives, and does not imply a generic 'Kainai perspective.' Furthermore, in addition to the Mookaakin Foundation, other community members work with museums and research institutions on repatriation and cross-cultural education projects, and we have tried, throughout the duration of this project, to ensure that they also had an opportunity to express their views in order to provide a fuller community response to the images. Those with whom we worked on this project encouraged us to seek out different community perspectives, and regard the diversity of views that emerged as a reflection of the reality of life in the community.[8]

In November 2001, the Mookaakin Foundation facilitated a meeting with the Elders Advisory Committee of Red Crow Community College. At this meeting the project and the role of the Mookaakin Foundation in guiding it was explained and the elders were asked for their comments on how it might benefit the community. Permission was also sought to interview them individually in the weeks ahead. Two further group meetings were held later on in the process, first to present the findings, ask for guidance about the deposition of tapes and transcripts, and present a draft outline of the plans for this book, and second to discuss the book manuscript in more detail by explaining the context in which an individual's quotations had been used, and seek approval for this. On both occasions, and in the individual interviews, members of the Elders Advisory Committee generously provided feedback and stimulating comments, and helped to ensure that the work was carried out in a respectful and culturally appropriate manner. In addition to working with these groups, we met with educators on the Reserve to discuss uses of the photographs and associated information within the school and college curricula. While the Mookaakin Foundation formally became our advisors, then, relationships were actively developed across this diverse community with many people outside the Foundation.

Our meetings with the Mookaakin Foundation and the Red Crow Community College Elders Advisory Committee provided an expression of the hopes and concerns of Kainai people regarding the involvement of outsiders in research about their culture and history. We describe these events briefly here because they emphasize the importance of such research projects to First Nations peoples, and the fact that research needs to be done in a culturally sensitive way. These meetings also taught us much about cultural protocol, and others contemplating similar projects need to be aware of the cultural expectations which operate within the communities with which they work. We held meetings in places Kainai people suggested (a hotel in the nearby city of Lethbridge that they often use for meetings; meeting rooms in the Continuing Care Centre in Standoff) and in which we were able to provide snacks or a meal in accordance with Kainai concepts of hospitality. While we rented the spaces and provided food, together with honoraria and small gifts for those who attended the meetings (in recognition of their considerable knowledge and expertise)[9] and reimbursement for mileage, we were made keenly aware that, once in these meetings, we were very much in Kainai cultural spaces. While our meetings with the Mookaakin Foundation were in English, with internal discussion in Blackfoot translated once consensus had been reached among Mookaakin members, the meetings with the Red Crow Elders Advisory Committee were held primarily in Blackfoot, with translations provided by *Aatso'to'aawa* (Andy Blackwater), a spiritual advisor, former Band Councillor, and a member of the board and Elders Advisory Committee of Red Crow Community College. Mr Blackwater's tremendous contribution to the project will be discussed in further detail below; however, it is important to note here that his skill in translating Blackfoot and academic concepts as well as the Blackfoot and English languages proved essential to our understanding of each other's perspectives, and has been crucial to the success of the project overall.

After initial chat, all our meetings were opened formally with prayer in Blackfoot, and everyone present had an opportunity to contribute to the discussion, with the formal tone of business matters being frequently interspersed with gentle humour and teasing. The seriousness, formality, and prayer were natural expressions of Kainai culture, but also served to make important points to us. To our Kainai advisors, this project involved not just scholarly research for the benefit of academia, but issues involving the health of their community, the rights of Kainai people, and the very real need within their community to think about and discuss their history and their often problematic relations with (and representations by) non-Native researchers, officials, and photographers. The hopes of elders and of leaders working in various ways to preserve Kainai culture and identity were communicated to us very forcefully in these meetings. They also permeated informal conversations during the many social and ceremonial events Brown attended during the extended fieldwork periods, and were apparent during other occasions such as the time we were taken for a tour of local industry sites on the Reserve by Francis First Charger – a tour into which he wove his own history of the Reserve, as well as a history of Kainai economic activity. This tour was Mr First Charger's way of giving us another frame of reference with which to view Blackwood's images; one which contrasted posed historical photographs and the experiences they evoked with the realities of the Reserve today and the economic industries developed by the Tribe, implemented as a means of recovering from a history of colonization. It was important to our Kainai mentors that we understood the total context – cultural, historical, social, economic, and deeply spiritual – in which the project was situated, and that we worked in ways which supported Kainai people.

Given the importance to members of the Mookaakin Foundation of the way in which we worked, we waited to begin the formal interviewing component of the research until the protocol agreement was signed, and it was agreed upon that the first interviews should be with Mookaakin Foundation members. Once Brown moved on to interviewing other Kainai people, she was greatly assisted by Andy Blackwater, who not only acted as guide and driver when the severity of the weather made the road conditions unsafe for the rental vehicle, but also suggested community members who might be able to participate, and explained cultural concepts that would help to clarify the experiences and knowledge being shared in the interviews. The first series of interviews were conducted during November and December 2001 and were followed with secondary interviews during the summer of 2002. During the interviews, which took place in the home or workplace of the interviewee, or in Brown's rented accommodation in the nearby town of Fort Macleod, photographs were presented in clear plastic wallets in a folder which also contained contact details for the Pitt Rivers Museum staff responsible for the North American collections, Photograph and

3.1 Mrs Rosie Red Crow examining Blackwood's photographs, 21 November 2001. (Photograph by Alison Brown)

Manuscript collections, and marketing (the Museum department responsible for authorizing reproductions of images in the Museum's collections), a short biography of Blackwood and her research, and copies of the diary entries and fieldnotes pertaining to her visit to Kainai. Self-adhesive notes were used to attach the identifications Blackwood had provided for some individuals, and these were added to as the interviews progressed and people's names were remembered. Interviews took the form of going through the images with the interviewees and taping their comments (see figures 3.1 and 3.2). The interviews were quite open, as we hoped people would talk freely about what the images meant to them, rather than be directed to particular topics. Some very general questions were asked of each interviewee, however, concerning the ways in which they thought the images might be used to talk about history and how they could be used within the community. Most interviews were with elderly people, who often knew those in the photographs well, and were able to speak of them through personal knowledge. In addition, they had experienced similar lifestyles to those depicted in the photographs, and were able to reflect

3.2 (l–r) Andy Blackwater and Stephen Fox discussing Blackwood's photographs, 9 September 2002. (Photograph by Alison Brown)

on these as they discussed the images. Younger people were also interviewed, however, including several educators who were keen to comment on the potential of the images for curriculum development. Although they did not necessarily know the people photographed personally, it was important that they had an opportunity to express their views on the potential of the images to promote understanding about the past and to explore generational responses to the photographs. On one occasion, a class of students at Kainai High School also viewed the photographs and were invited to think about their relevance to their own history, adding another dimension to the readings of the images, that of Kainai teenagers.[10]

In addition to the formal interviewing process, many other people across the community commented on the use of the images as a resource, and their perspectives have also contributed to the project. Although their words were not recorded on tape, their perspectives have nonetheless had an impact on our understanding of what the images meant to different generations within the community. Often, while on her way to do an interview, Brown would be approached by or would be introduced to someone with a direct family connection to a person in the photographs, and it was often during these chance meetings that the emotional impact of the photographs was most clear. This was observed early in the project by Narcisse Blood, Chair of the Mookaakin Foundation, who constantly encouraged others to come and look at the pictures and made sure that there were ample opportunities for this to happen, for instance through inviting us to attend community events:

> You've seen the reaction and the enthusiasm of some of our people, especially when they recognize people. Just before we came in [to Red Crow Community College] one of the secretaries wanted to look at that picture one more time of their relations. (Blood 6 December 2001)

As word spread that someone had come from overseas with the photographs, these informal meetings increased in number, and the photographs have been circulating informally throughout the community since our first visit to the Reserve in 2001. By the second research trip in the summer of 2002, Brown regularly received phone calls from community members, who had been told about the images by colleagues or relatives, asking to meet up so they could see them as well.[11] It was not uncommon that on her repeat visits people who had been shown or had been given copies of the photographs by relatives who had requested their own copies at an earlier stage would approach her and talk about how much it meant to them to have the chance to see these images and think about the people within them.[12] Perhaps the moment when the social impact of the photographs became most starkly apparent was one afternoon in August 2002 when Andy Blackwater and Brown left some photocopies of the images with one of the residents of the Continuing Care Centre to give him some time to look at and think about them prior to being formally interviewed.[13] Sitting on a bench outside with two other residents, he studied the images carefully, and by the time Brown had reached her car, about thirty metres away, a large group had gathered and the images were being passed around among much animated discussion.

The research hinged on several important elements of our methodology. One of these was our willingness to ask about and to follow cultural protocol for asking for knowledge, while another was our efforts to build trust and to make it clear to Kainai research partners that we cared about what they wanted to happen in the research process and were willing to cooperate with them. As part of this, we tried to communicate and practise our belief that consultation with community members had to be an integral, ongoing process throughout and even beyond this research project: that we were forging lasting relationships with the Kainai community. Once Brown began to do interviews with community members, she made it very clear that each would be sent a copy of the tape and transcript, and that she would come back to ensure that each interviewee approved of both. That she actually did so has been crucial to continued cooperation by Kainai people in the project, and to the depth of Kainai responses in interviews to the photographs.[14] The fact that she knew and had worked with some members of the Kainai community before the beginning of this project, and was known as someone who did follow protocol, was also critical to the speed of the trust-building process and the success of the research. Trust-building proceeded differently across the community: for some, the protocol agreement was important as a formal, written codification of expectations, while for others making sure that every interviewee had the opportunity to control how his or her information would be used was more important. Yet others felt that our initial approach showed that we were respectful in our intentions and this meant much more to them than a written document.[15] Finally, it is important to emphasize once more that all those who assisted us did so for their own reasons, and to benefit future generations of Kainai people in various ways.

In January 2002, following Brown's return to Oxford, work began on transcribing the interviews and sending the transcripts and copies of tapes to the interviewees for their review. Those tapes which contain substantial discussion in Blackfoot were transcribed as fully as possible, with the Blackfoot sections being indicated on the transcripts. At a later stage, parts of these were translated by Andy Blackwater, who also checked the accuracy of the translations with the interviewees. During this period, copies of those photographs which individuals had requested for their family collections were also printed and mailed, and work began on drafting this volume.

The following summer we returned to Canada to report on our progress. Given the insistence of community members that the research facilitate community needs and involve Kainai people in its framing, this trip was an important step in maintaining a collaborative framework for the research: such work is not collaborative for just one part of a project, but must be so throughout its duration. The main purpose of this second visit was to ask for feedback on the work so far and for advice as to how we should structure the book based on our findings, as well as to begin to discuss the community-oriented outcome of the research. It was also essential to consult with those individuals who had been interviewed initially to ensure that they were content with the transcripts of their interviews and that corrections and additions could be made. Interviewees were also formally asked for consent to use their statements as part of the project. Asking the interviewee to read through the transcript in advance was often insufficient, and usually the reviews involved taking the time to sit down with an individual and listen to the interviews in their entirety, making clarifications as necessary.[16] In addition to the review process, we held formal meetings with the Mookaakin Foundation and the Red Crow Community College Elders Advisory Committee, in which we summarized the essential findings from the interviews, asked if we had missed any significant themes that should be explored in the book, and presented a draft of the outline for this book. Several additional interviews were conducted with people who had been unavailable on the first visit. Following comments made at the outset of the project about the errors Blackwood made in her notes about Kainai people, and the problems that such incorrect information can cause in Native communities when it is published, Brown also interviewed several people specifically to explore their views regarding the statements Blackwood recorded in her diary.

Once again it is crucial to emphasize the need to allocate sufficient time for a project of this sort, in order to allow for consultation and for interviewees to feel that they have been granted the opportunity to participate without being rushed or without fully understanding the processes involved. Given the understanding among the participants that the knowledge they shared was for the benefit of all present and future generations of Kainai, it was imperative that they had an opportunity to explain their purpose and intent and to review their statements. Likewise, for us as researchers to fully appreciate what was being shared with us, we had to learn to understand some of the ways in which the community transmits knowledge and some of the protocols which must be followed as part of these processes. Accordingly, though we had initially planned and budgeted for a very short second visit of one week, this would not have been appropriate, nor would it have been practical. In the event, Peers stayed for two weeks, during which time the group meetings were held, and Brown stayed for three months in order to undertake further interviews and to visit with each interviewee individually. This change in plans and budgeting was initially queried by our funding body, the AHRB, and we had to explain to them why these changes and a third visit to the Blood Reserve would be necessary. Happily, our explanations were accepted by the AHRB, which throughout has been very supportive of the project, but we discuss further in chapter 6 the points at which such collaboratively based research does not fit well with standard expectations of academic funding bodies.

The third visit to the community to discuss the manuscript for this volume took place in the late spring of 2003, when we returned together and spent ten days at the community, presenting the manuscript to the Mookaakin Foundation, the Red Crow Elders Advisory Committee, and the people who had been interviewed (see figure 3.3). During the process of writing, we had sent full drafts of the manuscript to representatives from the Mookaakin Foundation and also to Andy Blackwater for review. This had given them an opportunity to summarize the main points of each chapter in Blackfoot in preparation for our final review meetings. During this trip, we discussed with the Mookaakin Foundation the drafts to date and the nature of our continuing relationship with the Foundation and with the broader community. The manuscript was well accepted, but Foundation members noted its draft state and expressed the desire to review the final version of the manuscript just prior to submission for publication. We also met with the Red Crow College Elders Advisory Committee, at which time Andy Blackwater presented a summary of the draft manuscript in Blackfoot. At both meetings we reminded people that the intended audience for the manuscript was museum and archival professionals, and that the purpose of the book was to encourage institutions to consult with First Nations peoples about the meanings and importance of historic materials. We then asked if advisors were happy with the general outline, content, and tone of the manuscript, and whether there were further points they thought should be made. At both meetings, advisors expressed strong support for the project, and optimism about the potential uses of the photographs as resources for community education.

During these and other, individual meetings in people's homes, we showed every person who had been quoted in the manuscript how each of his or her quotations had been adapted from the transcripts and

3.3 Andy Blackwater reviewing book manuscript with Alison Brown, 19 May 2003. (Photograph by Laura Peers)

in what context his or her words had been used. We indexed a copy of the manuscript by the names of persons quoted, and then went through it with each individual. While intensive, this process was crucial in reinforcing the sense of control over the project by Kainai participants, and served to communicate the message that we cared about the relationship of trust we were all working to maintain.

At the end of the visit we formally presented copies of the research materials to the Kainai Nation at an evening celebration at Red Crow Community College.[17] We invited to this event everyone who had participated and helped with the project – people who had been interviewed, people who had mentored and advised us. Following prayers and a wonderful meal cooked for us by Myrna Chief Moon and her team, and speeches in Blackfoot by Andy Blackwater and Frank Weasel Head, we handed over to Anita Singer, Red Crow Community College Vice-President (Administration and Finance), a volume of copies of the photographs, laminated and bound for preservation, together with a bound volume of all the interview transcripts, for deposit in the college library and for the use of community members. We also created 'Educator Packs,' each with a CD-ROM containing jpeg files of all Blackwood's Kainai photographs; the names of the individuals depicted in them; and some information on Blackwood and contacts for the Pitt Rivers Museum. We hope these kits will encourage the use of Blackwood's photographs within the community, and gave them to a representative of the Kainai Board of Education at the handover event.

Brown was able to make a brief fourth trip to the Reserve in June 2004 during which she met with the Mookakin Foundation and Andy Blackwater to discuss suggestions for the cover image and the use of the Blackfoot language in the text, and to ask how they wanted to proceed with commenting on the final version of the manuscript. We anticipate one further trip in connection with the book that will take place on publication, when we will visit the community to present copies to the schools, Red Crow Community College, and project participants. We cannot express enough how crucial these return visits have been to the success of the project. The process of providing feedback and seeking advice on each stage of the project has been extremely important, not only to ensure that we have 'got things right' as best we could, but also so that the community could monitor our progress and contribute advice and knowledge throughout, resulting, we hope, in a much more comprehensive book.

Photo-Elicitation and Visual Repatriation: Changing Histories

> ... as I circulated them [photographs], I began to witness their impact on present lives, and to participate in the experience of recovering identities of younger selves and relatives, to observe the tracing of both kin connections and association with place, and the scrutiny of other cultural details. (Poignant 1996: 8)

Working with indigenous communities in this way – agreeing to act under their guidance, and working for their goals rather than just the researchers' – is a relatively new phenomenon. This is especially so in Britain, where, until the past few years, there have been fewer opportunities to work with indigenous peoples. There is, however, a body of existing work within scholarly publishing which has provided guidance for us and has encouraged us to work with Kainai people in the way we have. Despite the problematic history and dynamics of photography of non-European peoples, historic photographs are important to

First Nations communities today as links to the past, and much productive work has been done bringing them together with community members.

The nature of this work has shifted over the past few decades. Initially, projects involving photographs were conducted within a very traditional social science framework in which they were used to increase the amount of data collected by the researcher. They have been used as memory aids after leaving the research site; as ways of stopping action to facilitate analysis; as ways of capturing a wide range of detailed visual data which cannot simply be described on the spot; as ways of supplementing other forms of data; and (with older photographs) as ways of documenting elements of daily life – clothing, architecture, decorative techniques – that might not otherwise be recorded. They have also been used to increase the amount of information one can retrieve from interviewees. The technique of photo-elicitation involves the use of photographs of people, of places, and of museum collections in interviews to expand the range of data informants are willing and able to speak about: the photographs are intended to provide a trigger for memory and thus allow more data to be transferred to outside research institutions and scholars. On the almost magical effect of family photograph albums in transforming the nature and depth of an informant's responses to his questions, Yannick Geffroy recalled, 'family photographs, by helping her [informant's] memory to recall events and their contexts, allowed us to glean more data and facts from the emotions she was reliving' (Geffroy 1990: 374).[18] Photo-elicitation has also been used in the history of academic studies of the Blackfeet; John Ewers used photographs to 'gain both rapport and cultural information' (Werner 1961: 57, 76 cited in Scherer 1992: 36) during fieldwork with the Blackfeet from the 1940s onwards, and in fact anthropologists have been using this technique at least since the late nineteenth century, when Franz Boas used photographs of objects in museum collections to elicit cultural information from Haida people of the Queen Charlotte Islands (Haida Gwaii) (Brown, Coote and Gosden 2000: 266–7).

Clearly, photo-elicitation is an extremely useful technique: the photographs serve both to evoke memories and information that might not otherwise emerge and, because attention is focused on the image rather than just on the conversation with the researcher, to put the interviewee at ease. The technique has been used by social science researchers in many areas of academia around the world, and has contributed significantly to numerous research projects; it continues to be a standard tool in the range of anthropological research techniques. As Elizabeth Edwards notes, however:

> ... photo-elicitation emerged from the classic power relations of anthropology, its methods and goals, and was developed as a methodological tool to trigger memories and glean cultural information. Despite the acknowledgement of some dialogic quality to such encounters – they 'sharpen the memory' and give a 'gratifying sense of self-expression' (Collier 1967: 48) – the concern was largely a one-way flow from informant to ethnographer. This is clearly, but inadvertently, articulated by Collier: 'questioning the native [with] the photograph can help *us* gather data and enhance *our* understanding' (ibid: 46, added emphasis). (Edwards 2003: 87)

The dynamics of photo-elicitation have therefore emerged as increasingly problematic as the relationship between social science researchers and indigenous communities has shifted since the 1960s, and First Nations peoples have claimed rights to ownership and control over research and its products. During this time, the use of photographs has shifted, as has the role of the outside researcher: the data gathered is expected by First Nations people to enhance their understanding of their own histories, not to benefit academics.

As part of this process of redirecting research, First Nations communities have actively begun to seek out and acquire copies of relevant historic photographs for their own use in telling histories to themselves and their children, and many have founded archives for this purpose, for which they collect copies of images and associated documentation from all the sources they can find (Marr 1996: 62). Some Native communities use less directed forms of photo-elicitation to recover community-based information, for instance publishing historic images in newsletters with requests for help in identifying people or places. Likewise, museums that offer programs aimed specifically at indigenous communities operate similar identification schemes, with the intention of improving museum records as well as increasing community use of the collections. The Berndt Museum of Anthropology at the University of Western Australia, for instance, publishes an image from its photographic collections in each issue of its newsletter with a plea to readers who may recognize the individuals portrayed to contact Museum staff (Berndt Museum of Anthropology 1997: 2). First Nations community historians are generally familiar with the location and nature of basic collections of historic photographs of their community, especially when these are located within the vicinity; when we began discussing this project with Kainai people, one of the first things that emerged was that they were eager to exchange information about comparable photographic collections, their institutional locations, the names of photographers, and their relationships to the community. They were also very knowledgeable about the kinds of bias that outsiders brought to their composition of images, and gave searing critiques of the problematic dynamics of photography of Native peoples:

> Alison Brown: How do you think her [Blackwood's] background affected what she was taking?
> Shirley Bruised Head: I think it really affected them because these photographs, just a couple, as I said, are not really sympathetic to her subject. I think she had a preconceived idea and she was looking to fulfil that idea. And she looked at these guys as objects and this was an idea that she had and here was the evidence for her. (Bruised Head 28 November 2001)

For many First Nations people, their real frame of reference for assessing images, though, is how useful they are for understanding the past and for knowing their ancestors. Photographs in which subjects were dressed up as romantic Noble Savages are useful at some levels because the subjects were known individuals, and the image would thus recall stories about that person, but were also wasted opportunities to understand what life was really like in the past. Thus, where copies of Edward Curtis's and other romanticized images are hung on the wall in First Nations homes, it is not for the same reason as they might be hung on the wall of a non-Native home or gallery, for their iconic meanings, but rather as lovely formal portraits of grandparents and great-grandparents, hung alongside snapshots of children and grandchildren.

In contrast to such readily available photographs, Blackwood's images of people mostly in ordinary working clothes were appreciated for their contribution to the total range of knowledge about the past and for their ability to evoke stories that other kinds of images do not. The images in Blackwood's series of girls at a boarding school and of people in their dress clothes around a tipi also evoke stories and themes of community history in the early decades of the twentieth century, a period which has been little studied by historians. When Brown interviewed community members about the photographs, however, it became immediately apparent that the responses to them went far beyond comment on the surface content and were fitted into Blackfoot ways of talking about culture and the past. In this context of community use, photographs: 'are interlocutors in the process of telling histories. This dynamic model constitutes photographs not as passive images in which communities merely recognise an ancestor or a now deserted settlement. It is more than simply responding to images through a sharpened memory. Photographs are active in the dialogue, become social actors, impressing, articulating and constructing fields of social actions and relations ... powerful stimuli for the maintenance of indigenous knowledge ... Photographs allow people to articulate histories in ways which would not have emerged in that particular figuration if photographs had not existed' (Edwards 2003: 87–8).

Blackwood's photographs are thus potentially crucial for Kainai people in promoting the telling of stories and the transfer of cultural knowledge across generations, something which might not happen if such triggers were not introduced into the community. This is a far cry from the original anthropological use of photo-elicitation, and suggests the range of potential benefits that institutions stand to set in motion by working with source communities. These processes can involve startling shifts and (re)appropriations of meanings: 'photographs that were created as colonial documents, and which became "ethnographic" records through their entanglements within specific institutional structures, become family history, clan history or community history' (Edwards 2003: 85).

Two powerful models of this way of using historic photographs have been provided by Roslyn Poignant (1996) with Aboriginal people in Australia, and by Judith Binney and Gillian Chaplin (1991) with Maori in New Zealand. Both took a keen interest in the scholarly and local contexts in which the photographs were produced, as well as in the effects that returning them had on the particular communities involved. Poignant's project, which we described in the Introduction, was focused on the return of photographs taken by her husband, the late documentary photographer Axel Poignant, in the 1950s, and discusses very thoughtfully community perspectives and concerns with these photographs and the memories they revived. Binney and Chaplin's project uncovered local narratives about a politically oppressive event in the past that had been long denied by dominant-society institutions, and used the photographs to prove oral histories which contested such denials.

This deeper way of using photographs, and the intention of using them to benefit source communities, combines with recent, strong demands by community members that researchers reorient their work to facilitate such aims and to allow community input into research design and the research process itself. A new philosophy and way of doing research, known as community-based, co-managed, collaborative, or participatory action research, has emerged out of these needs and demands. These new ways of working begin with the acknowledgment that dominant-society heritage professionals are not the only ones who know about, own, and control heritage resources: that local communities have rights in their culture and heritage and in its representation and dissemination. While to some extent this approach might be seen as a pragmatic way of 'continuing field research in politicized situations,' it also embraces 'a new ethics of scientific knowledge' (Clifford 2004:22). It also proceeds from the assumption that research should benefit the community as well as the researcher, and thus that the community should participate in deciding the research agenda and methodology (Hall 1979; Warry 1998, 1990; Ryan and Robinson 1990, 1996; Robinson 1996; Krupnik and Jolly 2002; Schneider 2002: 149–60; Phillips 2003; National Science Foundation Office of Polar Programs et al. 2004).

We have drawn on such new praxis over the course of the Kainai-Oxford Photographic Histories Project. As a result, we feel it appropriate not simply to speak of photo-elicitation as the methodological core of the research (although that technique was central to our interviews), but to give it and the attitudes in which we set our research techniques a different name: visual repatriation. This term is now coming to be widely used, along with variants such as 'knowledge repatriation' or 'repatriation of knowledge,' by many scholars working with indigenous and formerly colonized peoples. As defined by anthropologist Ann Fienup-Riordan (1998), visual repatriation involves recovering knowledge from museum and archival collections for community use, and we discuss Fienup-Riordan's pioneering visual repatriation projects below. Other authors (e.g., Wareham 2002: 206) extend the idea to imply the need for a realigning of relationships between museums and the communities drawing on their collections: 'The re-engagements considered here are very differently premised, for the relationships, goals and outcomes of such encounters have changed radically. The emphasis now is on shared approaches, the acknowledgement of sensitivities, an access defined by source communities and the recognition of boundaries– that in such exercises photographs will be reabsorbed into social spaces where the ethnographer cannot and should not go' (Edwards

2003: 87). In this, photographs are used not solely for the benefit of the researcher but primarily for community members, and copies are left with the community for future use. The knowledge that images encode, the memories they trigger, are intended to consolidate traditional knowledge within the community and across generations (and see Poignant 1996: 9), for community purposes. Intriguingly, however, we have found that this does not lead to any impoverishment in the data which we as outside researchers feel is appropriate to analyse or to publish. Rather, we have found just the opposite: this is a way to open multiple cultural readings, to critique former one-sided meanings, and to create a more just and excitingly productive way of working in cross-cultural settings.

Other than Poignant's and Binney and Chaplin's projects, we have found few models of visual repatriation projects which rely on collections of historic photographs. There have been many visual repatriation projects, however, which work with either artefact collections or photographs of these. These projects have done much to set out the dynamics of such cross-cultural work, and the potential benefits of working in this way and with historic artefacts. They also provide a very useful model for research projects when community and collections are separated by great geographical distance.

Taking photographs of artefacts to source communities has proven to be a way of providing community members with records of their material heritage held in distant museums, as well as beginning to understand their perspectives on such artefacts (Niessen 1991; Brown 2000). In one such project, Cath Oberholtzer took her research photographs of Cree clothing from collections in many museums in Canada and Europe to James Bay Cree communities. The Cree provided 'insightful – and at times, unexpected – reactions [to] and identification' of the objects, and discussed in detail their own 'criteria for identifying local variations in forms and motifs' as well as asserting which items were 'ours,' local, and which were not (Oberholtzer 1996: 59). Similarly, Barbara Hail and Kate Duncan used colour slides of nineteenth-century Athapaskan beadwork in a project to better document and understand the subarctic collections of the Haffenreffer Museum of Anthropology and to learn about styles and techniques which were still being used by seamstresses in the region (Hail and Duncan 1989: 13). In another example, Ann Fienup-Riordan and Yup'ik Eskimo linguistic specialist Marie Meade worked with Yup'ik elders and community members to create *Agayuliyararput*, a travelling exhibition of Yup'ik masks which has led to several additional projects bringing Yup'ik people and museums closer together (Fienup-Riordan 1996a; 1996b; 1998; 1999). A central element of the project involved Meade using photographs taken by Fienup-Riordan of masks in museum collections in Europe and North America in interviews with community elders. For Fienup-Riordan the generous response of the elders was tremendously exciting and unprecedented and allowed for the assertion of Yup'ik ownership of the knowledge that was being shared: 'This active interest in remembering accounts for both the quantity and quality of information elders shared. Sitting with her Sony tape recorder at their kitchen tables, Marie rarely interrupted with questions. She showed pictures, then let them talk, and she learned what they wanted to say ... These accounts were partial, emphasizing positive rather than negative characteristics, and as such were not so much facts about the past as keys to how this past is presently remembered' (Fienup-Riordan 1999: 342).

Important as such projects are for increasing a museum's documentation of the objects in its care, as the examples above indicate, it is the possibility for using photographs of objects as a means of reconnecting with cultural heritage that is regarded as of prime importance to indigenous communities. This is particularly the case for those communities who are developing projects of cultural regeneration through the production of traditional forms of clothing and art for which access to historic museum collections is crucial (for examples of such projects see Thompson et al. 2001). Fienup-Riordan also took a group of Yup'ik elders to study a collection in Germany (1998), and as James Clifford notes (2004:13): 'The goal was not the return of traditional artefacts ... The [elders] were primarily interested in the return of important stories and knowledge renewed through the encounter with the old masks, spears, and bows. What mattered was not the reified objects but what they could communicate for a Yup'ik future.'

Understanding that photographs can communicate important messages for indigenous futures has been a very new way of thinking within academia, as has the critical analysis of the history and dynamics of anthropological photography. Some of the most important work on these topics has been written by visual historian and anthropologist Elizabeth Edwards, who is also Curator of Photographs and Manuscripts at the Pitt Rivers Museum (see Edwards 1992, 2001, 2003). Edwards's work has been crucial to understanding one set of meanings Blackwood's photographs carry with them, derived from the traditions of outsider photography of Native people and of anthropological photography in particular. Her approach to curating historic photographs –

as artefacts in themselves, with biographies and as embodying cross-cultural relationships – links her work with other visual repatriation projects such as those described above. It has allowed her to understand the importance of photographs to source communities today, as well as the need to renegotiate the relationships surrounding images such as Blackwood's.

Indigenous peoples themselves have created an intellectual space within which anthropological photography can be critiqued and the meanings of images rethought (e.g., essays in Lippard 1992; Clifford 1997: 127–9; essays in Johnson 1998; Tsinhnahjinnie 1998; J. Thomas n.d.; Thomas and Hudson 2002). The descendants of people photographed by Edward Curtis, for example, interviewed by Anne Makepeace for her film *Coming to Light*, and who included several Blackfoot, vocalized the potential of historical photographs to engender parallel narratives that stripped away the charges of romanticization, allowing genealogical connections to be brought to the fore (Makepeace 2000).[19] Moreover, in response to its colonial associations, some indigenous people have turned to photography themselves, creating works which address and shatter stereotyped images and which creatively articulate their own sense of identity and reality (P. Taylor 1988; Lippard 1992; Tsinhnahjinnie 1998; Passalacqua 2003). Together, these new perspectives and projects have made it possible to think about ways of reclaiming photographs for use in and by source communities: of taking them home, assigning new meanings, and attaching names. Pinney (2003: 4) writes of this process as one of 'particularization, the enclosing in a new space of domesticity and affection of images formerly lost in the public wilderness of the archive.'

Such indigenous critique and reappropriation of colonial genres has been part of a much broader shift within scholarship which has acknowledged the cultural construction of texts as well as of photographs, and has sought to better understand indigenous perspectives on the past, on colonialism, and on the narration of history itself. We have been fortunate to be working at a time when many others have been attempting to understand the past from the dual, but very different, perspectives of colonized as well as colonizers. As researchers have begun to consider the sources and narrative structures they have used to create historical meaning, and to more fully understand and incorporate other cultural perspectives into recording and writing histories (e.g., Schmidt and Patterson 1995; Cruikshank 1998; Schneider 2002; Brown and Vibert 2003), they have also begun to read these documents in ways that try to better understand the cultures described within, and to write in ways that provide a more relevant and effective fit for community voices. Accordingly, they explore the responses of people to circumstances in the past in ways that situate their intent, agency, and actions within their own worldview.

Accessing the 'voices' of ancestors and bringing them together with those of descendants has been a recent emphasis within both scholarly and public-oriented accounts of the past. Multivocality, the idea that there are many simultaneous expressions of differing experiences, has been an especially important theme in recent social science and humanities scholarship as well as in museum theory. The kinds of information embodied within historic photographs and artefacts have been important sources for reconstructing the very different historical experiences of indigenous peoples and thus the multi-perspectival nature of the past, and of our understanding of it. This approach has been most vividly marked in situations involving relations between indigenous and European settler communities (see, for example Phillips 1998; Henare 2005). Studies such as Nicholas Thomas's *Entangled Objects* (1991), which looks at the dual Native and settler histories of the Pacific using material culture as a focus, have been extremely useful in thinking about the different ways that peoples in entangled colonial histories have perceived each other, and how such different perceptions might be 'read' from the materials which survive from such encounters. These materials include photographs, and by 'reading' them, we mean undertaking visual analysis of their content and context (including layers of information added by culture, scholarly perspective, and time), to create meaning for the reader. In the scholarly world, many visual analysis techniques treat images (or objects, or exhibitions) as texts, and rely on literary techniques such as 'close reading' – a careful, detailed analysis of all levels of the writing, moving from the elements of language to the relationship of elements within the text to the relationship between the text and its context – to understand the totality of meanings of an image. This is a fairly logical process, although in practice it tends to work in a less linear fashion, with viewers often beginning with the overall image, moving to consider its very detailed ('forensic,' in Edwards's term) aspects, and then considering how the image was shaped by broader cultural, political, and historical forces.[20]

In wanting to understand how photographs are involved in such 'entangled' but quite different histories, we note that they can be 'linking objects between past and present, between visible and invisible and active in cross-cultural negotiation' (Edwards 2001: 4) precisely because the same image can mean different things to different people. They can also be linking objects between people. One recent idea about artefacts which has been developing within the Pitt Rivers Museum is that they embody the social relations which produced them and led to their transfer to the Museum, and that they can lead back to their original communities as well as outwards in other directions from the Museum, to the scholarly research community and the visiting public (see, for instance, Gosden and Knowles 2001: 17–24). In this view, Blackwood's photographs can be seen as sets of relationships – some historical, some cross-cultural, some being activated in the present through the protocol agreement negotiated during this research project.

That photographs can link eras, meanings, and people has been made clear to us across this project, and understanding the Blackfoot scholarly contexts for our work has highlighted the importance of the ideas discussed above. The Blackfoot Nations have a deep interest in the past, and a comparatively high rate of language retention as well as of cultural knowledge. They also have a number of dedicated and talented historians, who are involved in developing historical resources on the reserves, such as the Siksika Nation Museum, which is currently undergoing a major refurbishment, and the Keep Our Circle Strong project at the Piikani Nation (Crowshoe 1996; Ross and Crowshoe 1999). At the Kainai Nation, concern about the lack of suitable resources for teaching and the need for creating ownership of locally based materials prompted a long-term project coordinated by the Kainai Board of Education to produce quality curriculum materials written in Blackfoot and English. Beginning in 1992, a writing team has interviewed over two hundred elders, and has produced video footage and four volumes of elders' stories about their lives and families, as well as a teachers' pack (Zaharia and Fox 1995a,b,c; Zaharia, Fox and Fox 2003). Subsequent published curriculum materials draw on the volumes (Fox 2001), which are regarded by Kainai people as a deeply valued record of their community's collective history, as well as a treasured source of genealogical information for individual families.

This interest in history and historical materials within the Blackfoot communities led to an important project which preceded our own work and has been an valuable example both for us and for the Kainai: a photographic exhibition entitled *Lost Identities: A Journey of Rediscovery*, which was developed by staff from Head Smashed In Buffalo Jump Interpretative Centre, the Provincial Archives of Alberta, and Community Development and Historic Sites. Since 1999, the exhibition has travelled primarily to reserves throughout southern Alberta and Montana as well as to non-Native locations. Unidentified images taken in the Treaty 7 area from the 1870s to the 1950s are displayed alongside tracings of the photographs upon which visitors are invited to write the names of friends and family members they can identify. Although viewers have shared biographical and historical information as they interact with the images, the primary aim of the exhibition has been to identify the people depicted. Shirley Bruised Head, the Education Officer at Head Smashed In Buffalo Jump Interpretative Centre and member of the project team, has explained that restoring the names takes the photographs 'from being just images and makes them people – people who made a mark while they were here' (quoted in Salkeld 1999: 6). The exhibition has prompted a range of educational activities within Native and non-Native communities and has encouraged visitors to talk and think about the past and how it has been visually represented.

The experience of viewing *Lost Identities*, together with the historical expertise within the Kainai community, our own background working with First Nations peoples, and Kainai desires to further develop historical knowledge while also controlling the nature of research to serve community needs, all came together when we brought Blackwood's photographs back to the Kainai Nation.

CHAPTER FOUR

Reading the Photographs

All the people here on the Blood Reserve, those who are elders, the younger people, even children, we take great pride in our past and looking at these pictures brings [out] all that pride and identification and stories, legends. There is so much that goes with these pictures. It's not just a person, there's a whole life history that they bring forth.

Louis Soop, 30 November 2001

Throughout the course of the Kainai-Oxford Photographic Histories Project we have learned that using historical photographs can facilitate the recovery of specific historical and cultural information but can also encourage a greater understanding of how people from different cultural backgrounds think about the past and the sources that are used today to make histories and structure knowledge. The project has also allowed us to learn about the agendas people bring to these discussions and the kind of histories that are important to communities who are working to reinvigorate their collective history in the wake of colonial disruption. We have learned about the different kinds of histories that documents such as photographs evoke, and how photographs intersect with these different ways of telling history. We have also been taught to think about whose needs these histories can best serve. What we have learned has encouraged us to explore ways of presenting the past that utilize more inclusive methodologies and allow different voices and perspectives to be heard. This book and our continuing links with the Kainai are some of the outcomes.

At the beginning of the project we developed a number of questions concerning the use of historical photographs in exploring cross-cultural encounters which were then used to frame interviews. We wanted to learn how Kainai people would read and respond to the photographs and we wondered what narratives they would evoke about community experiences in the past. We knew from our own readings of the images that they could be used to discuss many aspects of life on the Reserve in the 1920s and we also knew that the links between these photographs and scientific inquiry might raise issues concerning Kainai responses to external researchers in the past and the present. Furthermore, because the majority of the images are portraits, whether of individuals or of groups, we knew that people might choose to talk about the individuals depicted, yet we felt strongly that our role should not be to collect specific biographies and family histories unless requested, but to learn about how the lives of those photographed reflected the variety of experiences of Kainai people in the 1920s and how community members today felt that knowledge could best be used. These concerns were discussed with the people who were interviewed as part of the project, and it was agreed that any stories that were related about individuals were shared primarily for the community's use. In the event, a number of people told short anecdotes about those ancestors in the photographs, and these stories are contained in the transcripts of interviews that are available to the community at Red Crow Community College.

In addition to our interest in how Kainai people viewed the content of the images, we also hoped to learn about their potential as community-based historical documents, which might be used to contribute to the cross-cultural and intergenerational transmission of history. This related to the use of archival photographs more broadly in creating histories, both positive and negative in tone, and in helping younger generations come to terms with the past and work towards creating a strong community for the future. Many Kainai people suggested that the knowledge embedded in historical images is a dynamic force which can be utilized to pass on cultural information as well as historical knowledge, and they felt that these particular photographs offered lessons to be learned about the strength of Kainai identity, traditional values, and cultural pride. In effect, the range of readings which people brought to the images has demonstrated the fluidity of meanings which archival photographs can encompass when source community members engage with them.

In this chapter we discuss the most prominent themes that emerged in the interviews and informal discussions and how they attest to the ways in which Kainai people viewed Blackwood's images. We acknowledge that the extraction of themes from the narratives is somewhat problematic, given the emphasis on balance and interrelatedness of processes and relationships that shapes Kainai worldview. Compartmentalizing the narratives that viewers read in the images and built around them for the purposes of an academic text in some ways diminishes how Kainai people approach the past, present, and future by obscuring the connections between and within them and diluting their complexity. Nonetheless there was such a consistency in the topics of discussion elicited by the photographs and shared in interviews that it is important to discuss these to indicate some of the means through which people from this community related to these photographs, and to underscore the importance such documents have to source communities who are in the process of strengthening their history. The multilayered nature of the discussion that emerged partly dictates the themes chosen for consideration here and the ways in which they are addressed; however, we hope that the discussion provides a representative selection of the responses of the community to the images and to their possible use. Furthermore, it should also be remembered that this book is based largely on dialogue that was held in English, and that during the course of interviews, a number of people preferred to express themselves wholly or in part in Blackfoot. While some of the comments in Blackfoot have been translated and have been used here, others relate to information that is intended to be shared with the community rather than a broader audience and has therefore been excluded from this volume.

Names as History

> The complaint that we had was that pictures were taken of our people and the captions would read, 'Indian' or 'Blood Indian' or 'Peigan' or 'warrior standing next to' and they would give the white person's full name and title, and that says a lot about the thinking [of] people back then. (Blood 6 December 2001)

So many photographs of Native peoples now rest in archives throughout the world and so many of them are unidentified. At some point during the process of becoming historical records and part of a catalogued assemblage of other historical resources, these images become 'locked in the archive' (Edwards 2003), and have largely been separated from the names, the histories, the lives they portray. For many Native people such unidentified photographs are 'a sad reminder of how their ancestors were treated' (Marr 1996: 62) and speak of attempts by the dominant society to categorize them according to tribe or physical type. Shirley Bruised Head, Education Officer at Head Smashed In Buffalo Jump Interpretative Centre in southern Alberta, and member of the Piikani Nation, is scathing about the implied messages projected by the mass of published unidentified images of Native peoples:

> I really didn't like the idea that when I opened a book and I saw a picture of a Native person, they would either have 'Indian' [or] 'Native.' It was very general; there was *no* identification ... When I look at that and I think of these people in these photographs, they're objects. And that's how Native people have been treated. They're objects. You objectify people and you can do anything you want with them. (Bruised Head 28 November 2001)

Bruised Head's concerns led to her involvement in the *Lost Identities* project described in chapter 3. As she has observed, putting names to faces aids the recovery of a Native history and helps to restore the dignity of those who have been photographed, but it is also part of a much wider process which contributes to the continuity of a Native past in the present using names as a focus. Within Kainai society, as in many societies throughout the world, names are more than markers of an individual's identity but are often inextricably linked with kinship and with cultural histories, and have the capacity to carry past events into the present and future (Bodenhorn 2000). Blackfoot names are given and received at naming ceremonies and can be transferred across generations. They are given to the spirit, not to the body, and they can be called upon by the owner for assistance, who, by so doing, draws upon the strength of previous holders of the name. Whereas most women retain the name they are given as infants and only on rare occasions take on a new one, men may change their names several times, through receiving honour names at significant stages in their lives – for example, when joining sacred societies (Standing Alone 27 November 2001). On receiving a new name, the holder's previous name can then be given to another person, though it may be some years before this occurs. Names are often associated with important events in the family history or personal experience of the spiritual advisor giving the name or of the receiver's own ancestry, such as a warrior's victory or circumstances at the time the person being named was born; a name might describe a personal characteristic or physical feature; or it may relate to a way of behaving or doing things.[1] Names are not family property, and though the same name might be held by more than one person at any one time, the stories which were used to explain that name would be different (Frank Weasel Head and Duane Mistaken Chief to Brown, pers. comm. 7 July 2003). A name may carry moral overtones, in that the holder may adopt the persona suggested by it, and if the new owner of a name does not live up to the standards set by previous holders or by what is implied in the name, he or she will face criticism within the community and the name may not 'stick' (F. Taylor 1989: 230; Standing Alone 27 November 2001); conversely, names can 'motivate' people 'to look at their background' and 'follow their role' (Whiteman Left 7 December 2001).

The associated language loss following social and cultural upheaval on the Reserve in the post-Treaty era led to a period when some Kainai names became 'lost' because they were being used less in everyday conversation and ceremonial transfers of names took place less frequently:

> The reason why we lose names is because ... it's not being used. Not being practised. Anything you continue, you'll keep it in mind ... When a person is gone and that name is not mentioned, it dies out with the person unless one of the younger people ... like, see, I'll use that name, the Blackfoot name – our real name. (Crow Chief 20 November 2001)

Furthermore, errors were made when Blackfoot names were translated into English following the signing of Treaty 7 when the Department of Indian Affairs began to maintain extensive administrative records such as Treaty pay lists. The English language is inadequate to allow full translations of Blackfoot words and concepts; consequently, though interpreters would offer what they thought were the best translations, these did not necessarily encapsulate the meaning of Blackfoot names, or were abbreviations. As an example, Pete Standing Alone and *Omahkokomi* (Charlie Crow Chief) commented on the commonly used translation of *Isstsstsiimi*, whom Blackwood photographed during her visit in two group compositions (figs. 18–20; fig. 26). Though his name has usually been translated as 'Rough Hair,' both clarified this translation by stating that the name *Isstsstsiimi* was 'something like a porcupine' (Crow Chief 20 November 2001) and that the hair was rough and 'all over the body' (Standing Alone 27 November 2001). In addition to mistranslating some names, government officials often had difficulties in pronouncing and understanding Blackfoot words, and would record what they thought they heard rather than the actual name of a person, and some of these mistranslations have stuck. When Kainai children started to attend school they acquired a Christian name, which would be used in combination with an English translation of the Blackfoot name of another family member, usually the father or an older brother, though, as *Tanataakii* (Angeline Eagle Bear) explained:

> See, there's some Indians that didn't go to school. They go with their Blackfoot names and when they get their Treaty, their Treaty card is translated with their Blackfoot name. (Eagle Bear 3 December 2001)

The custom of having a surname was alien to the Blackfoot; however, people did and still do identify themselves according to their clan, the name of which played a similar identifying function as the concept of a surname (Heavy Head 8 September 2002). Oral histories recount how Christian names and nicknames were somewhat indiscriminately applied, resulting in people sometimes using the 'wrong' Christian name for many years (Blackwater 20 November 2001). With the ceremonial and cultural revival that has been taking place in recent decades, the proper transfer of ancestors' names throughout the Kainai community is now practised much more frequently and, when speaking in Blackfoot, people address one another using their Kainai name rather than their English one, both in everyday conversation and especially during ceremonial occasions (Whiteman Left 7 December 2001; Blackwater 7 December 2001). It is within this context of loss and recovery of names and their associated histories that a number of people commented on the value of archival images and the importance of identifying ancestors in them with both their Blackfoot and their English names. Unless both these names are available, the identity of those people photographed remains incomplete.

Blackwood's comments in her fieldnotes relating to the personal names used by Kainai people suggest that she was unaware that an individual could carry different names over a lifetime, though she clearly recognized that naming practices were changing and identified some of the factors involved. She seemingly understood that names were connected to stories and also appears to have recognized their importance in kinship relationships, reflecting anthropological theoretical preoccupations of the time, but also hinting at reasons why these relationships have since become somewhat blurred:

> They all have Indian names. A child will not bear his father's name, but each member of a family might have a different name, e.g. 'Chief Moon,' 'Many Bears,' 'Don't Tie His Shoes' etc. This, added to the practice of adoption, makes it difficult to trace relationships and it is not improbable that there is a good deal of consanguineous marriage, though this is not allowed when it is known. The children, however, are now given an English Christian name, and their father's name, the Agent sees to this when paying Treaty, and is frequently asked to choose the Christian name. (Blackwood Papers, Related Documents, Fieldnotes BB.A3.46–75: 4–5)

It seems likely that Blackwood had always intended using her field-work photographs as teaching and research materials. The nature of her scholarly interests meant that individuals' names were less important to her than information on their physical make-up. Identifying these people, however, was viewed by Kainai community members as being of the utmost importance and as the first stage in using the images to record more detailed histories that recall life on the reserve in the 1920s. The very fact that Blackwood used English translations of names related to the wider experience of Kainai people during the years following Treaty 7, and community members discussed it in connection with how people at that time were dealing with this transitional period in their history. Others, however, viewed the recovery of the names as being more than just an opportunity to associate names with faces and considered the Kainai names *themselves* to be history, since cultural knowledge directly connected with events and individuals in historical time or in traditional stories is encoded in them. Literal translations into English of Kainai names can obscure their real meanings and gloss over the associations and guidance that the names can provide, and as they studied Blackwood's photographs, several people explained that younger generations need to hear the stories encompassed within particular names so that they can understand how and why these names originated and what their role can be. The name of Strangling Wolf, for example, refers to a dream involving not the actual animal, the wolf, but the Wolf People, who are associated with the story of *Makoyoohsokoyi*, the Wolf Trail (Crow Chief 30 November 2001; see also Day Rider in Fox 2001: 22–4). Likewise the name *Kiaayo* (Bear) prompted Charlie Crow Chief to share a story about a powerful spirit bear, adding 'these are some of the things I know about bear ... and anybody have the name of bear, it's got something to do with that story, where that bear come from' (Crow Chief 30 November 2001). Another example was provided by *Issokoiyo'maahkaawa* (Bill Heavy Runner), who explained how the name *Aakaokitsii*, or Many Fingers, came about as he looked at the images of *Aakaokitsii* Pete Many Fingers (plates 1–4):

> And this man, his father was warrior. And why they call him Many Fingers ... this man here when they start a fight with the Nakotas and some of them, they already got killed. And he's the only one, his father, was still shooting. And he run out of shells, bullets, and he grabbed the other gun off the one that died, the one that's killed, he grabbed his shooter. And when he emptied that rifle, he took the other gun, and that's why he called himself Many Fingers. Many Fingers, that's *Aakaokitsii*. (Heavy Runner 3 December 2001)

Because some names recall significant events in Kainai history, images have immense value for people who hold those names today: they provide a visible link with the past, with those ancestors who held their names before them, and an opportunity to recall the stories that some names are connected with. Seeing historical images is considered to be particularly important for younger people and for future generations:

> It gives a person an idea as to who that person was and an opportunity to look at that person, how he looked, or how she looked ... looking at these photos, they see that person, their ancestor, at their young age. You know, when they were young. And a lot of cases, they only see them when they are old. (Whiteman Left 7 December 2001, translated by Blackwater)

Given the increasing temporal distance since Blackwood's images were taken, ensuring that photographs are correctly identified so that future generations can engage with their past in this way is seen as vitally important. It is important that all of the names an individual carried be recalled if possible. Furthermore, recalling the names provides an opportunity for those which had been 'lost' to begin to circulate once more. That photographs are used by indigenous people to prompt the recollection of historical narratives that fit with their conceptions of the past is well known (e.g., Binney and Chaplin 1991; Poignant 1996), and, in communities such as the Kainai Nation, where names and their transfer are a primary means through which cultural and historical knowledge is codified, engaging with photographic portraits can add to the processes of transmitting this knowledge, as names are spoken about in connection with those depicted in the photographs, and also in relation to others who have held the name, whether in the past or the present.[2] Accordingly, identifying a person in a photograph permits discussion of the lives of all those who have held that name, not just of the individual in the image. Restoring the Kainai names of the people Blackwood photographed was regarded by some people as a way to ensure that those names continue to be used and, in turn, that the stories connected to them are remembered. The continuity of historical and biographical knowledge demonstrated through the transfer of names was explained by *Piinakoyim* (Rufus Goodstriker), who shared some of the detailed history of his great-great-uncle, *Piinakoyim*, Seen From Afar, a highly respected leader in the nineteenth century:

> Bull Back Fat was his name as a young man and as a warrior. Later on, when he became a great warrior, people had so much respect for him. They saw his camp, either they were Long Knives or they were tribes. When they saw him they said, 'No, let's not bother him.' He was so powerful he fought with any tribe. So they respected him. That's why they gave him the name *Piinakoyim*, Seen From Afar. That's why he got the name after being Bull Back Fat. (R. Goodstriker 19 November 2001)

Mr Goodstriker was named *Piinakoyim* after his ancestor, and he observed that 'it's a good thing that I know a bit about him because I can talk to my children about where I got my name.' He added that he would be very pleased to see an image of his relative: 'There's a painting that I saw, but his real picture, I wouldn't mind if somebody has Buffalo Bull Back Fat. *Stomi'ksaosa'k* is the real name' (R. Goodstriker 19 November 2001).

Names, histories, and kinship are inextricably intertwined within traditional Kainai culture; however, the partial collapse of social and cultural structures as a result of processes of colonialism has had lasting repercussions, and a number of community members talked at length about the sense of social dislocation and lack of identity that some people have experienced as a result. Attendance at residential school for extended periods of time meant that children participated less in family matters, and in cases where a child lost a parent or was orphaned, the situation was often made worse. The breakdown of kinship knowledge in some families has meant that although people know that they are related to one another, they do not necessarily know what the relationship is (Bastien 27 November 2001). *Sowa'tsaakii* (Celina Goodstriker) commented on her own family's experience, while studying photographs taken by Blackwood of her mother and two of her aunties as schoolgirls:

> My Mom never went home because her Mom died at a very young age and she stayed at the residential school. My Mom told me if it wasn't for the nuns and the priests, I don't know ... it would have just been my Mom and her Dad. They were mostly like orphans. And if you ask my Mom anything about the past, she doesn't really know, she was never out. Like yesterday I tried to ask her ... I told her, 'How are you related to Jane Day Chief?' And she said, 'I don't know, but my Mom was very close to her Mom. I don't know how we are related.' (C. Goodstriker 19 November 2001)

In other families, where many traditional adoptions took place, children were raised in different areas and with different families. This, combined with the effects of residential school, has meant that although people know their immediate clan and kin relationships, for some their understanding of their further family history is less clear. The genealogies are, however, beneath the surface, and identifying people in photographs can help those individuals who are searching for their roots begin to reconstruct their lineages through processes that Roslyn Poignant has termed 'making genealogies visible' (Poignant 1996: 95):

> Right now ... a lot of our young people don't know who their relations are from, who their ancestors are. And they can find out where they come from, who they are ... It'll show them, like I said, who they are and where they come from, and, like for me, I don't have hardly any pictures of my grandfather, of those people, my ancestors. And I often wonder what they looked like, who they were, and these pictures can tell a lot of who an individual is. (Weasel Head 28 November 2001)

Expanding on this point in relation to Blackwood's statements in her fieldnotes about kinship relations (see above, page 114), Duane Mistaken Chief has suggested that Blackwood's superficial understanding of Blackfoot concepts of kinship, whereby 'genealogy is not the only determinant of relationships between Kainai people,' meant that these comments were inaccurate. Moreover, the depth of genealogical knowledge varies between families today:

> There are families today that will recite their lineage to anyone that is interested and be very detailed in their recitations. It is the families that have been disconnected with that history and have been severely disrupted by the 'dysfunctions' caused by assimilation policies and 'colonization,' and including residential schools, that have lost that history. Our ancestors had a very good knowledge of their relatives and often erred on the side of caution in that regard ... The complaint, 'How am I supposed to get married when everyone I am interested in is my relative [according to my parents' reckoning] – everyone is my cousin' has been and continues to be heard in many families over successive generations, is a testament to the importance of knowing your genealogy. (Duane Mistaken Chief to Brown, pers. comm. 27 April 2004).

Nonetheless, seeing is important, and a number of people who are too young to have known many of those in Blackwood's photographs remarked upon how much it means to them to see photographs of people they have heard stories about, those members of their family who share the same names with them today, especially if they have only seen a few or no other photographs of them, or if they are only familiar with photographs of them taken when they were elderly. Many times it was noted that showing children images of their ancestors was a productive way to teach them about their own family backgrounds through discussing with them the lives of these relatives. The identification of just one individual in a photograph can be used to relate the wider clan and kinship networks of that person, and the extraction of these layered genealogical histories from photographs can have lasting effects, as *Napia'koisi* Francis (Alphonse) Whiteman Left explained through translator Andy Blackwater:

> Pictures are important to us, and to have access to perhaps all of the pictures. Even though Francis has not recognized all of these photos that are here, he's recognized some of them, and he knows he can elaborate a little into the extended family, their children and all that. And also he knows today, you know, their children, the children of today. And that's why he's indicated that it would be useful, 'cause all of these have offspring, you know? Their families, their kinship are still here today. (Whiteman Left 7 December 2001)

Mr Whiteman Left's comments encapsulated what many people in the community see as being a primary benefit of identifying people in archival photographs and related also to Kainai conceptions of how names and history are interconnected, the transmission of this knowledge, and the potential for these histories that different generations see within the images. While older people articulated the importance of identifying people in order to share clan knowledge and family histories and to promote the understanding of the cultural knowledge embedded in the names, some people from a younger generation suggested that, in addition, the photographs could be used to help reconstruct part of the community's history which has not been passed down and which relates to biographical histories. *Sikapinaakii* (Betty Bastien) observed that the biographies of those people photographed by Blackwood which are well known to those community members whose lifetimes have overlapped with them but which have not been transmitted to succeeding generations can be used to help younger people understand the realities of their ancestors' lives and the importance of the contributions of their former leaders:

> These kinds of pictures give us our connections in terms of the generations. And the history ... about our people and the kind of people they were, their personality, perhaps their accomplishments, what they did for the Tribe ... like Shot Both Sides ... that's a history that we don't have, in terms of our own history of the generations before us. (Bastien 27 November 2001)

Photographs, memories, and histories intersect with one another and, in combination with other ways of articulating perspectives about the past, can prompt 'inside ways of responding to culturally specific actualities, which are not necessarily available to outsiders' (Poignant 1996: 8). The generational responses of Kainai people to Blackwood's photographs echo Poignant's observations, yet as Bastien's remarks demonstrate, there is an acute awareness and concern among some community members that the disruption of the continuity of Kainai historical knowledge has meant that each successive generation has been increasingly cut off from community-focused histories and genealogies, themselves encapsulated in the images. Traditional structures for intergenerational teaching have been severely damaged by the residential school experience, which separated children and grandparents, and have yet to fully recover. In addition, what is history to the young is lived experience to older generations, and the latter's connections with people depicted in photographs are quite different from those of younger people. To an extent, the gaps in community knowledge of the past have meant that in some ways younger generations are like 'outsiders' to their own history, and for those people who care about history, access to archival photographs and to the memories of those people within the community who have direct knowledge of their content is absolutely crucial. It permits the sharing of the 'inside' readings of the images which can then be reincorporated into successive generations' understandings of their community's collective history as well as individual family histories.

Change and the Effects of Change

Look at the cut of the hair. No more braids. Everything was over. The sad part of it was they wanted to do it overnight. That's how there was a lot of resistance to change things over the night.

Charlie Crow Chief, 30 November 2001

Blackwood's photographs were taken during a time when the differences between the experiences and expectations of community members who had grown up on the Reserve and those of people who recalled the pre-Treaty era were becoming starkly apparent. As discussed in chapter 1, the introduction of new systems of education, political organization, religion, and healthcare, combined with new agrarian developments based on the raising of crops as well as livestock, fostered an environment in which Kainai embraced and adapted to these changes at varying levels. As visual indicators of people's responses to their changing circumstances, the forensic details in photographs such as Blackwood's enable them to be read in ways which complement documentary sources and confirm oral histories about life on the Reserve during this era and to be utilized to broaden understanding of a period of Kainai history that has not been subject to extensive research. Until quite recently, the experiences of First Nations people in the 1920s have received far less scholarly attention than the Treaty-signing period and its immediate aftermath. While a number of studies have been made of First Nations communities during the 1920s and the Depression era, some of which have considered Kainai experiences, most of these have for various reasons relied primarily on sources traditionally available to historians trained within the Western academic tradition (Samek 1987; Regular 1999) or were based on short periods of anthropological fieldwork (Goldfrank 1945). In recent years, however, those working with visual sources have realized that photographs have the potential to participate in historical dialogues as active agents rather than as documents with 'too many meanings' (Pinney 1992: 27, cited in Edwards 2001: 5). Indeed it is the instability and multiplicity of photographic meanings, combined with an appreciation of the need to incorporate other voices and perspectives into historical representations, which has enabled projects such as this one to take place. Photographs are beginning to be seen as an untapped source for exploring dimensions of historical experience that have been overlooked, or for re-examining current and accepted historical interpretations. Historians such as William Farr (1984) and J.R. Miller (2003) have written evocatively on the use of visual images in recovering and understanding First Nations histories; where their work differs from this volume is that, following from Elizabeth Edwards, we suggest that photographs can also be read *as* history (Edwards 2001), in that the creation of the documents themselves testifies to the nature of the interactions between Kainai people and non-Natives.

Many Kainai people's initial reactions to Blackwood's images were observations that they were taken during a transitional time in the community's history. They drew attention especially to how the physical appearance of the people in the images related to the changing circumstances the community faced in the post-Treaty era, and they regarded the clothing and hairstyles of those in the photos as the most visible manifestation of people's varied responses to these changes. Blackwood's photographs show men wearing Western trousers and shirts appropriate to their new occupations as ranchers or farmers, and women wearing hand-made cloth dresses of a modest cut, often with a shawl or blanket and a headscarf. Blackwood's own observations of the women was that they 'all wear shawls except some who had European dress' (Blackwood Diary 1924–7, 3 August 1925). Those girls who were photographed with their families wore dresses, the two boys photographed in the field wore work clothes, and the images taken at the school are of girls dressed alike in checked dresses and white aprons, stockings and boots. Though most images show people in everyday clothing inspired to varying degrees by European fashions, Blackwood also took a series of images which provided her with visual evidence for the contrast between 'traditional' and 'modern.' By the 1920s buckskin outfits and other traditional clothing were usually worn only at special events, such as stampedes and parades, and, on occasion, for the camera. In Blackwood's series of images of *Mi'kaníki'soyii* (Red Wing

Bird Woman/Mrs Yellow Shine), *Misaamahkoiyinnimaakii* (Long Time Medicine Pipe Woman/Mrs Shot Both Sides), *Naipisstsaakii* (Cloth Woman), *Isstsstsiimi* (Rough Hair), and Margaret Yellow Shine, *Misaamahkoiyinnimaakii*, *Naipisstsaakii*, and Margaret are resplendent in their finest dresses while *Isstsstsiimi* wears a magnificent Pendleton blanket over his working clothes, though, as noted in chapter 1, it is not at all clear at whose suggestion they wore their best outfits.[3]

The gradual depletion of the vast bison herds – regarded by Kainai historians as a deliberate war move on the part of Euro-Americans (Blood 6 December 2001) – and the reduction of hunting of other game meant that the hides from which all clothing had previously been made had largely been unavailable for some decades and cloth of various kinds – once a rare commodity – had been used instead for many years. Indeed the transition from hide to cloth is apparent in the clothing of *Naipisstsaakii* and Margaret Yellow Shine in the photographs just described, in which elk teeth[4] have been used to decorate cloth dresses that in the past would have been made from hide. Though the basic material may have changed, the style remained essentially the same. In the early part of the twentieth century women made their family's clothes using store-bought fabric instead of hide, as *Immi'tsimaakii* (Annie Bare Shin Bone) and *Tsiinaaki* (Rosie Red Crow), both extremely productive seamstresses themselves, recalled while looking at the photographs:

> That's the way our mothers make our dresses. They're all hand-sewn. The grandmothers used to make dresses like that. When I was at school I had a dress like it ... We had a store, just across the river here, and material comes in rolls and our parents used to buy one roll and they make about ten dresses for the whole family. (A. Bare Shin Bone 27 November 2001)

> [At] that time we were very poor. We can't afford to buy clothes. Mostly we have to make, get the material, and make our own clothes. They had to sew by hand. But round the twenties, my mother had a machine. (Red Crow 21 November 2001)

As the Kainai began to participate in a cash economy and the personal wealth of some individuals increased, there was a gradual shift towards buying ready-made clothes and accessories; other items of European manufacture were donated to the missions and were distributed to those with less money to purchase cloth and who were in need. While the images generated discussion of how change could be seen in the kind of clothing worn, they elicited as much commentary on the extent to which aspects of traditional Kainai appearance were visibly maintained in this period, for instance through wearing certain items of jewellery, and most often through wearing moccasins rather than boots or shoes. Similarly, many of those who viewed the images commented on the universal wearing of shawls or blankets by the women, and remarked that blankets, moccasins, and headscarves are now only worn on ceremonial occasions. Shirley Bruised Head's close reading of the group outside the tipi illustrates this point most clearly:

> I think these are important because if you look at the clothing you can see the introduction of ... like this one is a mixture of the shell and the velvet. It looks like a velvet. But here on the wrist you also see another older object. The earrings are old ... You know, you look closely at the younger women with their dresses and their shoes and it probably means that they have come out of boarding school. And the older woman with her heavily beaded moccasins ... Look at his blanket. Wow! I wouldn't mind one of them! (Bruised Head 28 November 2001)

Comparison of practices 'then' and 'now' was a theme that emerged throughout many of the discussions. The appearance of the younger people in the images was contrasted with that of older generations who would not have attended school, and it was with sadness that many people observed the children in Blackwood's photographs, especially the schoolgirls who, with their uniforms and cropped hair, resembled European children. Unless the parents insisted otherwise, a child's hair would be cut short on entry to school, a practice horrifying to the Kainai and to many other Native people who also experienced the forced cutting of hair at school, and who believed that hair should be cut only for cultural reasons (Heavy Head 16 November 2001). In Blackwood's photographs, only three girls out of the twenty-one who posed wore their hair in braids, and the messages photographs of this genre have for some Kainai people today are painfully clear:

> It's always sad to see young students, our people, you know, our grandparents, when they are all lined up, you know, and they take a picture of them. And what, in retrospect, what they are saying is 'Look. Look at how much we've assimilated [them]. We're doing a very good job.' ... And they were starting to make some of us into something we're not. Not that it was always achieved, you know? (Blood 6 December 2001)

The hairstyles of the men elicited similar comments. *Mamio'kakiin* (Adam Delaney), for example, observed that most of those Blackwood photographed were of middle age or older and would not have been to school. They wore their hair in braids, sometimes tied together across their chests, in contrast to many of the younger men who had been forced to have their hair cut and who usually did not let it grow back on leaving school (Delaney 4 December 2001). Through comparing the physical appearances of those depicted, people used the photographs as a means to explore the gulf between those who did and those who did not attend school, and who accordingly had been exposed to different sets of values and attitudes which affected their subsequent behaviour and generational responses to them:

> In the old days when you see a person dresses neat and always uses the language, the white society's language, and don't use his own background too often, always they would say, 'He's trying to be a white man,' or, 'He's turning into a white man.' (Delaney 4 December 2001)

> I would say they were very hard-working people and they were going into farming, especially the way he's dressed, you know, the straw hat. He's probably been influenced by the residential school. He has his braids so that means that he didn't really take to the ideas that we were being taught at the residential schools. Either that or he did go to a residential school but was allowed to keep his hair, and learned how to farm, and learned how to ranch and learned all of that good stuff that they were teaching at that time. Proud, he looks proud that he worked hard. (Bruised Head 28 November 2001)

These comments and similar remarks made by other viewers give some sense of how the shock of transition and the implications of change for Kainai people were interpreted, both within the community at the time the photographs were taken and since. As previously indicated, the residential school photographs in particular provoked narratives of loss and sadness since they perhaps more than any of the other images symbolized how dramatically the lives of Kainai people had changed in such a short period of time. The facial expressions of the schoolgirls which, with the exception of *Noyiss* (Louise Don't Tie His Shoes), who smiled for the camera, range from nervous to resistant to scared, and the painful associations of residential school for many people today undoubtedly contributed to the often negative readings of these particular images. We make the above statement cautiously, as it can be dangerous to read too much into body language recorded in the split second of exposure; however, the girls' expressions are consistent across the whole series of shots and Kainai readers interpreted them consistently as well.

The more formal photographs, such as those taken at the school and some of the anthropometric images, elicited astute comments relating to colonial perceptions of 'otherness' and ethnographic representation, and an acute sense of the assumptions held by Canadian society during the transitional era:

> I suppose they are trying to say, 'Look, these people are becoming civilized,' I guess, in *their* terms. (G. Fox 5 December 2001)

Many of the other photographs were discussed in relation to changes in the community and the strategies people developed to cope with the conditions they faced. Some photographs depict men in their working clothes, who had taken a break from working in the fields to be photographed by Blackwood. These elicited commentary on the extent to which the roles of men and women had changed in the years between Treaty 7 and the 1920s. The focus of women's lives at this time was still the family and the home; however, the first and second generations of men who grew up on the Reserve experienced considerable shifts in their traditional roles. Men whose fathers and grandfathers had been accustomed to hunting and going to war were now forced to adopt new economic initiatives in order to support their families:

> During this time they were making a transition and tilling the soil was really a woman's job – digging in the soil was a woman's job ... So they had to make that transition from being a warrior to someone who would dig the soil. So I think that's one thing that really comes out. (Heavy Head 16 November 2001)

Though initially there was resistance to adopting a settled lifestyle, oral histories and some documentary sources from this time period describe how quickly and effectively the Kainai learned agricultural skills and began to compete in the farming industry. For many people today these photographs of their ancestors not only reinforce their understanding of how hard they worked in order to survive and to provide for their families, but also serve to contradict the reports of some government officials and other authority figures who claimed that the Kainai were not capable of maintaining their own homesteads. *Iitomomaahkaa* (Dorothy First Rider), for instance, observed how healthy the hay in some of the photographs appears and that the fences and buildings seem well cared for, and she noted that photographs of this nature could be used to challenge statements in the historical record that belittle the achievements of Kainai farmers during this era (First Rider 4 December 2001). First Rider also suggested that looking at the details in the photographs raises questions pertaining to the fulfilment of Treaty promises that had been made fifty years earlier. Why, for example, do some people appear to be living in tents when it had been agreed that houses would be provided (plate 10)? The images provide an opportunity to 'reopen the history' (Binney and Chaplin 1991: 433), and, through looking at the forensic details, consider how these fit both with the versions of their history that Kainai people know and with mainstream interpretations of their past.

Disruption and Loss

> The one that really strikes me of the way she looked, that's Mrs Shot Both Sides' picture. Sitting in the tipi. It really strikes me as a person that's not very happy ... sitting alone, and the image looks like the tipi is so neat, and the bed. Everything. Her best blankets on, and everything which she normally won't have on if she was still living in there. To me she was sad because she was just posing. It wasn't a natural setting, really. A natural setting for her any more, which was about thirty years before this photo was taken, this would have been a natural setting for her ... 'This has been taken away from me, but for a picture they want me to be in a tipi. They want to get rid of this way of life, but for a picture, they want me to be there.' (Weasel Head 28 November 2001)

Blackwood's photographs continually slip between being objects of history and objects as history, a dynamic which results in numerous simultaneous readings of them, even by the same individuals. This small collection of images is a manifestation of larger processes both of colonial will and negative representation and evokes complex responses in which photographic meanings merge together with the realities of cross-cultural encounters as they are remembered within the Kainai Nation, to produce narratives of pride tinged with sorrow at the way in which ancestors had been treated. Comparing the photographs against

Plate 1. *Aakaokitsii* Pete Many Fingers, known also as Six Toed Pete. Photograph by Beatrice Blackwood. (Pitt Rivers Museum, University of Oxford, PRM. BB.A3.48)

Plate 2. *Aakaokitsii* Pete Many Fingers, known also as Six Toed Pete. Photograph by Beatrice Blackwood. (Pitt Rivers Museum, University of Oxford, PRM. BB.A3.49)

Plate 3. *Aakaokitsii* Pete Many Fingers, known also as Six Toed Pete. Photograph by Beatrice Blackwood. (Pitt Rivers Museum, University of Oxford, PRM. BB.A3.50)

Plate 4. *Aakaokitsii* Pete Many Fingers, known also as Six Toed Pete. Photograph by Beatrice Blackwood. (Pitt Rivers Museum, University of Oxford, PRM. BB.A3.20B)

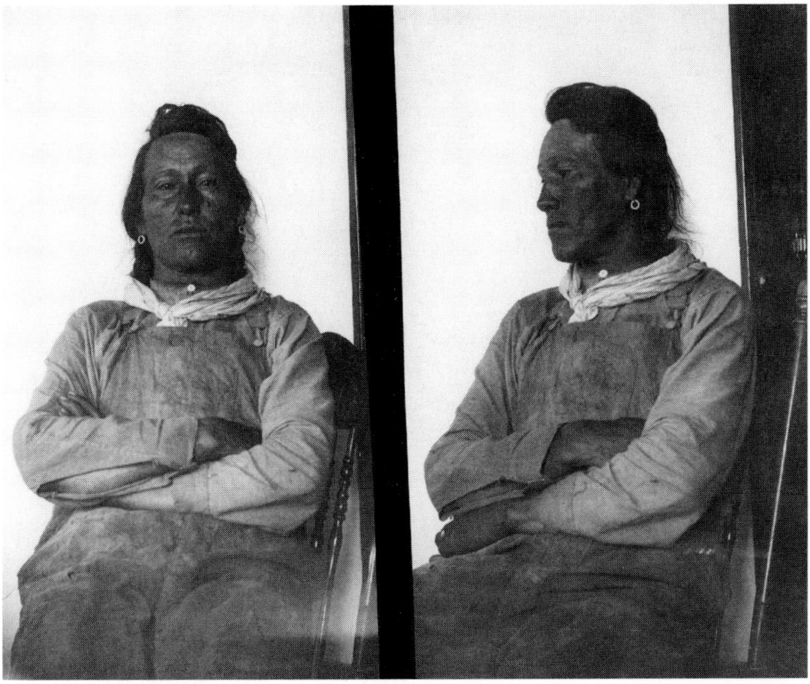

Plate 5. Community members identified this man as *Aiyiisoiisaami* Double Train Headdress. His nickname was *I'kotsiisoiyikkaawa* Red Leggings. Beatrice Blackwood listed him as Charlie Wolf Plume. Photograph by Beatrice Blackwood. (Pitt Rivers Museum, University of Oxford, PRM. BB.A3.20M)

Plate 6. *Aatso'to'aawa* Head Chief Shot Both Sides. Photograph by Beatrice Blackwood. (Pitt Rivers Museum, University of Oxford, PRM. BB.A3.51)

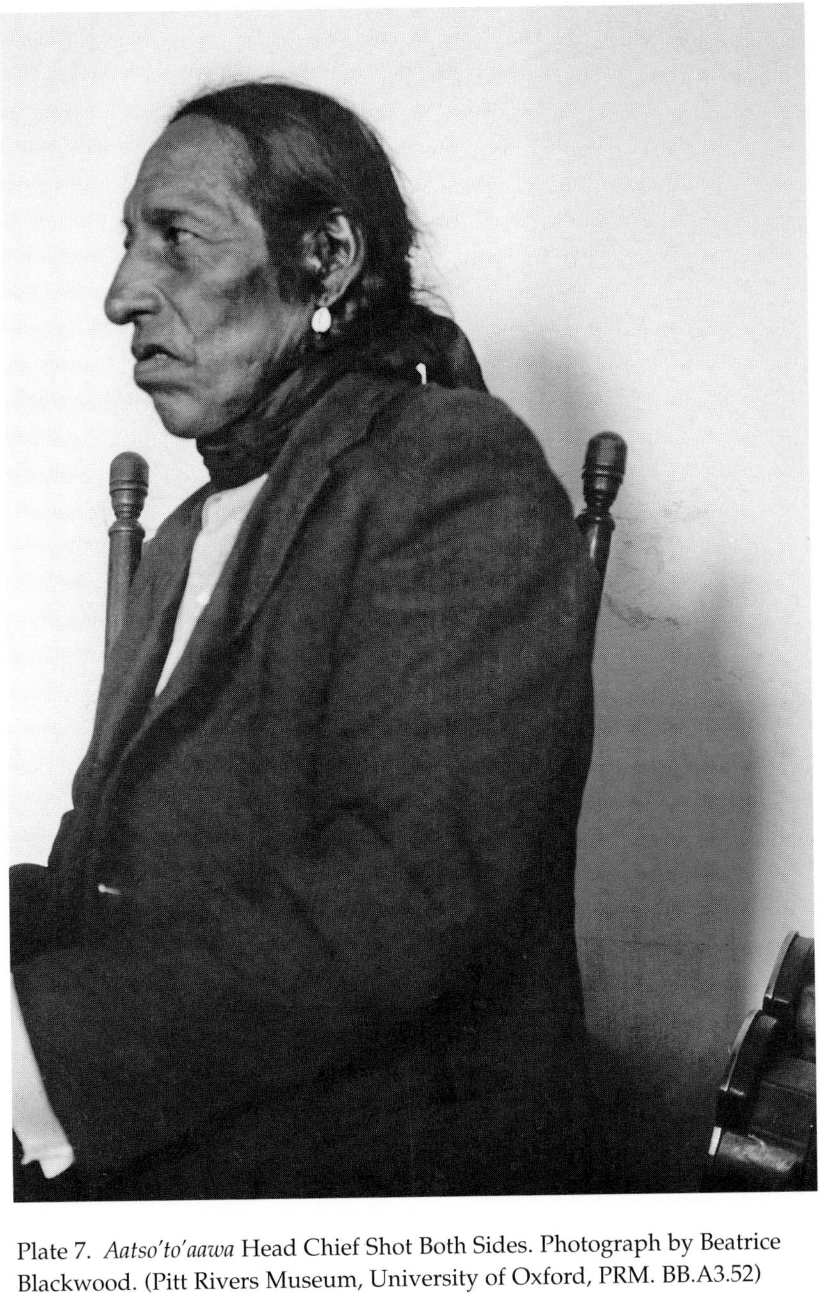

Plate 7. *Aatso'to'aawa* Head Chief Shot Both Sides. Photograph by Beatrice Blackwood. (Pitt Rivers Museum, University of Oxford, PRM. BB.A3.52)

Plate 8. *Pa'nii* Sam Black Plume. Photograph by Beatrice Blackwood. (Pitt Rivers Museum, University of Oxford, PRM. BB.A3.55)

Plate 9. *Pa'nii* Sam Black Plume. Photograph by Beatrice Blackwood. (Pitt Rivers Museum, University of Oxford, PRM. BB.A3.56

Plate 10. *Piaana* Falling over the Cutbank. Photograph by Beatrice Blackwood. (Pitt Rivers Museum, University of Oxford, PRM. BB.A3.57)

Plate 11. *Aatso'toaowa* Shot at from All Sides (Ben Strangling Wolf) with his wife *Kaaksikamo'saaki* Just Stole Woman or Day Steal Woman (Lucy) and their daughter Dolly. Photograph by Beatrice Blackwood. (Pitt Rivers Museum, University of Oxford, PRM. BB.A3.58)

Plate 12. *Aisstaohkomiaakii* Comes Calling Woman (Mrs Ethel Tail Feathers) with Gerald Tailfeathers. Photograph by Beatrice Blackwood. (Pitt Rivers Museum, University of Oxford, PRM. BB.A3.59)

Plate 13. (l–r) *Natoiyisskii* Striking Holy Face or *To'yisskii* Plain Face Woman (Mrs Cougar/Lynx Head) with *Siipiikamo'saakii* Steals at Night, or Stealing at Night (Mary Eva Spotted Bull); *Pissohkomii or Pissohkomiiwa* Calling From the Side (Mrs Jack Burning Fire) also identified as *Iitohtawa* (Mrs Hungry Crow); and *Makaisimii* Young Drinker (Mrs Brown Chief Calf) at the ration house. Photograph by Beatrice Blackwood. (Pitt Rivers Museum, University of Oxford, PRM. BB.A3.60)

Plate 14. (l–r) Unidentified woman and child; *Makaisimii* Young Drinker (Mrs Brown Chief Calf); *Natoiyisskii* Striking Holy Face or *To'yisskii* Plain Face Woman (Mrs Cougar/Lynx Head), with *Siipiikamo'saakii* Steals at Night, or Stealing at Night (Mary Eva Spotted Bull) at the ration house. Photograph by Beatrice Blackwood. (Pitt Rivers Museum, University of Oxford, PRM. BB.A3.61

Plate 15. *Api'saakii* Coyote Woman or *Sikaipisstsaakii* Black Cloth Woman (Mrs Red Leggings). Photograph by Beatrice Blackwood. (Pitt Rivers Museum, University of Oxford, PRM. BB.A3.62)

Plate 16. *Misstomohtsikitstakii* Merry Sacrifice, Good Offering or Double Offering (Mrs Billy Heavy Runner) with two of her children, possibly *Issokoiyo'maahkaawa* Heavy Runner (Bill Heavy Runner Jr) and Lucy. Photograph by Beatrice Blackwood. (Pitt Rivers Museum, University of Oxford, PRM. BB.A3.63)

Plate 17. Another photograph of the same family. Photograph by Beatrice Blackwood. (Pitt Rivers Museum, University of Oxford, PRM. BB.A3.64)

Plate 18. (l–r) *Mi'kaníki'soyii* Red Wing Bird Woman (Mrs Yellow Shine); Margaret Yellow Shine; *Misaamahkoiyinnimaakii* Long Time Medicine Pipe Woman (Mrs Shot on Both Sides); *Naipisstsaakii* Cloth Woman (Mrs Rough Hair); and *Isstsstsiimi* Rough Hair. Photograph by Beatrice Blackwood. (Pitt Rivers Museum, University of Oxford, PRM. BB.A3.65)

Plate 19. (l–r) *Mi'kaníki'soyii* Red Wing Bird Woman (Mrs Yellow Shine); *Misaamahkoiyinnimaakii* Long Time Medicine Pipe Woman (Mrs Shot on Both Sides); Margaret Yellow Shine; *Na'pisstsaakii* Cloth Woman (Mrs Rough Hair); *Isstsstsiimi* Rough Hair. Photograph by Beatrice Blackwood. (Pitt Rivers Museum, University of Oxford, PRM. BB.A3.66)

Plate 20. (l–r) *Mi'kaníki'soyii* Red Wing Bird Woman (Mrs Yellow Shine); *Misaamahkoiyinnimaakii* Long Time Medicine Pipe Woman (Mrs Shot on Both Sides); Margaret Yellow Shine; *Naipisstsaakii* Cloth Woman (Mrs Rough Hair); *Isstsstsiimi* Rough Hair. Photograph by Beatrice Blackwood. (Pitt Rivers Museum, University of Oxford, PRM. BB.A3.67)

Plate 21. *Misaamahkoiyinnimaakii* Long Time Medicine Pipe Woman (Mrs Shot on Both Sides). Photograph by Beatrice Blackwood. (Pitt Rivers Museum, University of Oxford, PRM. BB.A3.68)

Plate 22. *Iikaiyissi'nikki* Killed Before You Did (Mrs Coming Singer) with an unidentified girl. Photograph by Beatrice Blackwood. (Pitt Rivers Museum, University of Oxford, PRM. BB.A3.71)

Plate 23. *Aistainsskii* Coming Singer with *Iikaiyissi'nikki* Killed Before You Did (Mrs Coming Singer). Photograph by Beatrice Blackwood. (Pitt Rivers Museum, University of Oxford, PRM. BB.A3.69)

Plate 24. This couple was identified by some Kainai people as Joe and Clara Heavy Head, though others strongly disagreed. Blackwood identified them as Mr and Mrs Melting Tallow. Photograph by Beatrice Blackwood. (Pitt Rivers Museum, University of Oxford, PRM. BB.A3.72)

Plate 25. The same couple in profile. Photograph by Beatrice Blackwood. (Pitt Rivers Museum, University of Oxford, PRM. BB.A3.73)

Plate 26. (l–r) *Kiaayo* The Bear; *Isstsstsiimi* Rough Hair; *Aatso'to'aawa* Shot on Both Sides; and *Aasainio'tokaani* Crying Head. Photograph by Beatrice Blackwood. (Pitt Rivers Museum, University of Oxford, PRM. BB.A3.74)

Plate 27. Two boys in the fields. They have been identified as possibly (l–r) Bernard Whiteman Left and Albert Vielle (Pitt Rivers Museum, University of Oxford, PRM. BB.A3.75)

Plate 28. Schoolgirls at St Mary's Roman Catholic Indian Residential School. Back row (l–r): *Kimmata'pssii* (Lily Shot Both Sides, later Mrs Bare Shin Bone); *Iinakay* (Annie Good Rider, later Mrs Brewer); Minnie Snake (or Bug) Eater; Rosine Two Flags; Antonia Hairy Bull; *Mini* (Minnie Sun Going up the Hill, later Mrs Joe Shouting). Middle row, l–r: Annette Good Rider (later Mrs Paul Russell); *Sii'pikitstakii* Making Night Offering Woman (Mary Striped Wolf, later Mrs John Many Chiefs); Mary A. Skipper; *Otskapinaakii* Blue Eyed Woman (Jane Blood, later Mrs Pete Bruised Head); Nancy Many Bears; Josette Melting Tallow; Susan Crazy Bull; *No'si* (Rosie Morning Owl, later Mrs Dan Chief Moon); Lizzie Standing Alone; *Noyiss* (Louise Don't Tie His Shoes, later Mrs Iron Shirt). Front row (l–r): Mary MacDonald; *Mini* (Minnie Chief Moon); *Aistaayohtowa* (Eva or Emma Mills); Bibian Sun Dance (later Mrs Mike Wolf Child); Adeline Fox (later Mrs Heavy Shield). Photograph by Beatrice Blackwood. (Pitt Rivers Museum, University of Oxford, PRM. BB.A3.76)

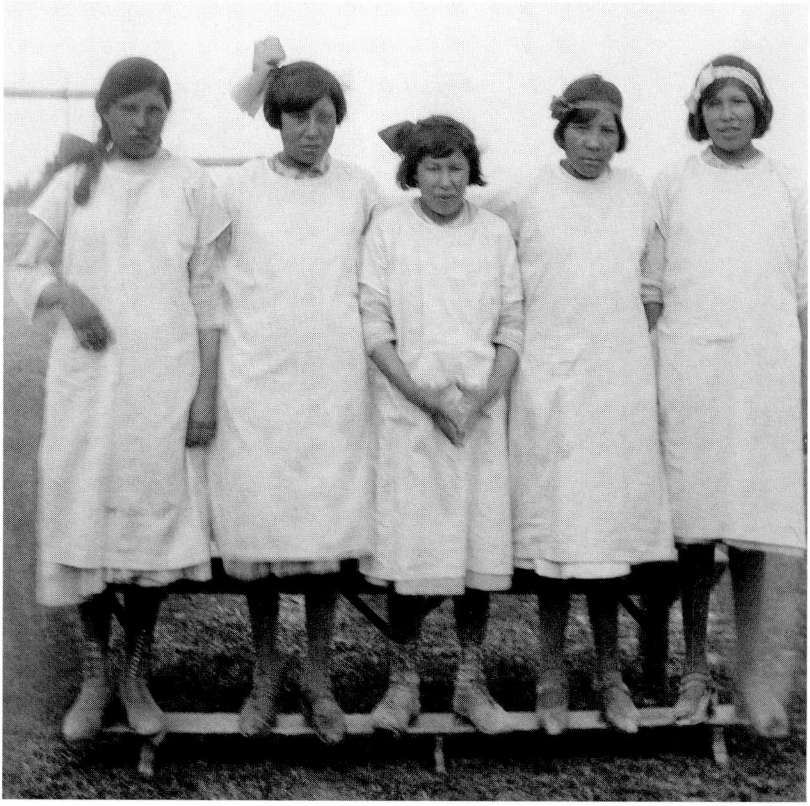

Plate 29. Schoolgirls over the age of fifteen. (l–r) *Otskapinaaki* Blue Eyed Woman (Jane Blood, later Mrs Pete Bruised Head); *Sii'pikitstakii* Making Night Offering Woman (Mary Striped Wolf, later Mrs John Many Chiefs); Annette Good Rider (later Mrs Paul Russell); *No'si* (Rosie Morning Owl, later Mrs Dan Chief Moon); *Noyiss* (Louise Don't Tie His Shoes, later Mrs Iron Shirt). Photograph by Beatrice Blackwood. (Pitt Rivers Museum, University of Oxford, PRM. BB.A3.77)

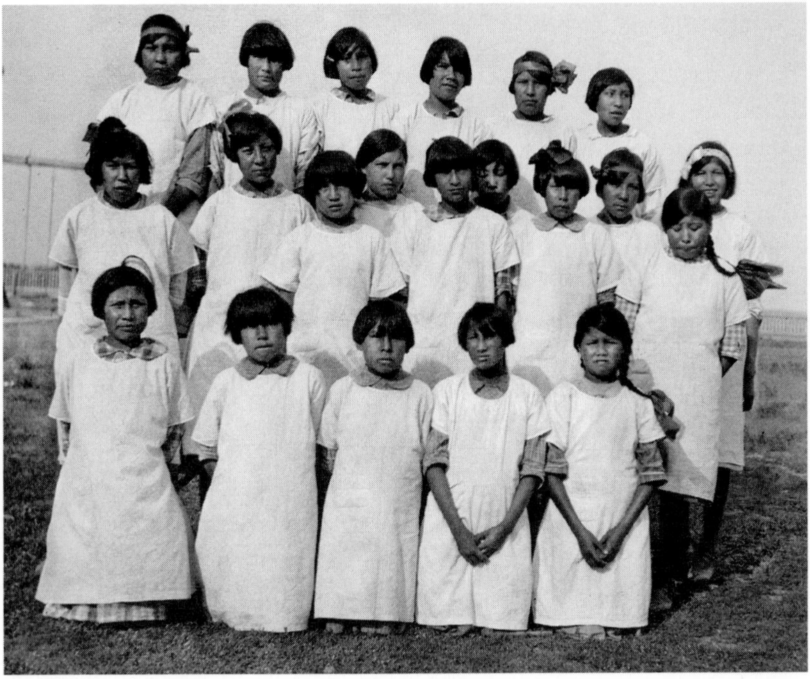

Plate 30. Schoolgirls at St Mary's Roman Catholic Indian Residential School. This image shows the same girls in the same order as in plate 28. Photograph by Beatrice Blackwood. (Pitt Rivers Museum, University of Oxford, PRM. BB.A3.78)

Plate 31. Schoolgirls under the age of fifteen. Back row, l–r: *Kimmata'pssii* (Lily Shot Both Sides, later Mrs Bare Shin Bone); *Iinakay* (Annie Good Rider, later Mrs Brewer); Minnie Snake (or Bug) Eater; Rosine Two Flags; Antonia Hairy Bull; *Mini* (Minnie Sun Going up the Hill, later Mrs Joe Shouting). Front row, l–r: *Aistaayohtowa* (Eva or Emma Mills); *Mini* (Minnie Chief Moon); Josette Melting Tallow; Mary MacDonald; Bibian Sun Dance (later Mrs Mike Wolf Child); Mary A. Skipper; Nancy Many Bears; Susan Crazy Bull; Adeline Fox (later Mrs Heavy Shield); Lizzie Standing Alone. Photograph by Beatrice Blackwood. (Pitt Rivers Museum, University of Oxford, PRM. BB.A3.79)

Plate 32. Landscape, Blood Reserve. Photograph by Beatrice Blackwood. (Pitt Rivers Museum, University of Oxford, PRM BB.A3.46)

each other led some viewers to comment on the asymmetries of power inherent in the encounter between Blackwood and Kainai people in 1925 that are reflected in the photographs and also in their production. The genre of classificatory portraiture favoured by Blackwood has resulted in a series of images through which the scientific concerns of the 1920s are visualized. At the same time, their very existence testifies to the unequal relationship between the photographer and her subjects. Though Kainai readings of the images focused on recontextualizing them in ways which foreground their potential for teaching historical and cultural knowledge from Kainai perspectives, for some people, the narratives of colonialism projected by the content of the images were central to understanding them. Mostly these responses were not explicitly articulated, but were implied during commentary which linked the images to narratives of disruption and its social consequences.

Colonial experiences as they were manifested through photographic representation were alluded to in some comments pertaining to anthropometry, for instance by describing an individual whose portrait Blackwood printed as a composite frontal and side profile (plate 5) as someone who looked as though he were in jail (Bruised Head 28 November 2001). More frequently, however, narratives concerning imbalances of power were expressed speculatively in relation to Blackwood's motives and techniques for securing images, while reflection on the anthropometric nature of so many of the images was minimal. At first it seemed striking that people chose not to comment on the classificatory nature of the photographs unless prompted, as to us this was perhaps the most prominent of the narratives and was inescapable. In part, the lack of commentary was connected with politeness – people did not wish to make negative or disrespectful comments about Blackwood – but in time it became clear that although for some viewers the anthropometric quality was an integral part of their readings of the photographs, it was not the most important. Even though when viewed as a pair, the images fitted into the convention of anthropometric photography, the frontal views stand very well alone as portraits of varying degrees of formality, and any scientific narratives which viewers may have picked up on were often submerged by the stories which they chose to focus on instead; this being an opportunity to voice the kind of histories which were important to them, and which they felt needed to be shared.

That said, the photographs did evoke discussion of negative experiences, both on a personal level and as an indication of the ways in which the Kainai community had suffered during the early decades of the twentieth century and had survived. Though they encapsulated hardship, they also encapsulated Kainai pride:

> [The photographs] help us to realize today that our ancestors tried to make the best of the limited resources they had at that time ... Our ancestors started to experience some of the restrictions that were imposed upon us, such as you can see in the photos. The activities of those of our people, who at that time, were into hay production – even the marketing of that hay was totally controlled and restricted by the government's Indian Agent – especially if we were to sell our products off the Reserve ... It is common knowledge today that they even went as far as forbidding our Sun Dances. The motive, of course, is to assimilate us into the White society. But the strong determination of our ancestors to preserve our way effected a slower transition. They realized it was important that our ways carry on, as this is the only way we would survive to this day and into the future. Our ways are very powerful. (Whiteman Left 9 September 2002, translated by Blackwater)

Visual clues in the appearance, expression, and surroundings of the subjects were indicators of how difficult this period was for the Kainai and supported the stories that people had heard about this period and the words of those who had lived through it. It was frequently explained that younger generations need to learn about this part of their past in order to understand some of the contemporary challenges that face the community, and to understand the choices their leaders had made:

> When you see some of those pictures here, in the 1925 era, that was the time they were just getting into the Hungry Thirties, when there was terrible drought and there was still a lot of tuberculosis. Smallpox has gone by long time, but tuberculosis got us, and malnutrition. Not having enough to eat 'cause they took all the buffalo away. We had no more buffalo to eat. That's why it is so important that we teach our children, we tell our children that we went through hardship in the past. (R. Goodstriker 19 November 2001)

However restricted the lives of the adults Blackwood photographed, it was the images of the schoolgirls which evoked most discussion concerning the social effects of the assimilation policies of the early twentieth century. Having experienced residential school themselves, most viewers commented that they could relate to the experiences of the girls Blackwood photographed and compared the images to those which showed children who were too young to be attending school:

> Dorothy First Rider: The girls in these pictures do not look very happy. Some of them look a little bit scared, especially the one in the middle. They look lost, except the one at the end. They were not very happy. These children were probably in residential school. And all of their hair's short. They've been taken away from their parents. The other women, the other children over here [plate 14], the one with their mother and grandmother, they look quite different from the residential school children.
>
> Alison Brown: It must have been quite an unsettling experience for those girls to have this woman come, and she wanted to take their measurements – she did take their measurements – and then have them stand for a photograph like that.
>
> Dorothy First Rider: None of these children are happy. But it also goes to confirm a lot of these stories that we've heard about residential school. I, as a child, experienced the residential school on a personal basis and can relate to what all these girls ... they look lost and confused. Troubled. That one looks happy having her photograph taken.
>
> Alison Brown: Yes.
>
> Dorothy First Rider: Just the one out of so many girls. (First Rider 4 December 2001)[5]

Dressed in their own clothes, the little girls who were photographed with their mothers and grandmothers were yet to undergo the processes of transformation that would attempt to erase their individuality, which their older sisters and cousins had experienced. Andy Blackwater and Annie Bare Shin Bone described the dehumanizing process that children endured on arrival at school, thereby demonstrating the ability of photographs to participate as intermediaries in discussions about the past:

> Annie Bare Shin Bone: As soon as you get in the school there, your own clothes that you wear, they take them and put them away from you. And you always had to wear uniforms.
>
> Andy Blackwater: They gave you a number.
>
> Annie Bare Shin Bone: Yes. And then we were numbered. I still have my number. Thirteen.

Andy Blackwater: I was fifty-nine. Just like a concentration camp ... They gave you a number rather than use your name.

Following from this exchange, Mrs Bare Shin Bone studied the school photographs even more carefully and stated, with some surprise, that these girls were her classmates and that she should have been photographed with them.

Alison Brown: This was your class?
Annie Bare Shin Bone: Yes, this is it. I don't know why I'm not here.
Andy Blackwater: Sometimes, you run away.
Annie Bare Shin Bone: Yes.
Alison Brown: Did you run away from school?
Annie Bare Shin Bone: No. There were times, too, I was always held back. I was taught music by the Grey Nuns. I played the organ and, yeah, I was always ... Every time these girls go out to play or something, then I have to stay back there. Somebody teach me the organ ... Oh, I should have been in this picture. Why wasn't I? ... Her number was, Lily, that's eleven. Annie Good Rider's seventy-eight. Minnie was eighty-eight. Rosine, Rosine Two Flags, yeah. They were all numbered. You always had a number to go by. (A. Bare Shin Bone 27 November 2001)

These photographs, then, were used at times as prompts to discuss difficult experiences in the past. Some people felt that this added to their value as images which could be used to help people come to terms with the effects of former official policies that are still very much current issues. Through listening to stories shared by their own community members, rather than reading the versions of non-Native scholars, people can use photographic images to restore a sense of balance, reality, and understanding of certain aspects of community history that some of them have had little exposure to. Shirley Bruised Head reinforced this point in her description of the responses of Blackfoot visitors to the residential school photographs included in the *Lost Identities* exhibition:

[The photographs] gave them another perspective on the residential school. How, as they were looking at them, the first thing they would talk about was the nastiness, the meanness, the anger that they had towards residential school. But as they talked, they picked out an individual. 'Oh yeah, this was my friend,' and they started looking at the good times as well as the bad times. (Bruised Head 28 November 2001)

Many of those people who looked at Blackwood's photographs of the schoolgirls responded similarly, and the message that these photographs are needed because of their potential to help explain traumatic experiences was expressed particularly by older people and by educators who, on a daily basis, observe how historical events have shaped their community, and how a secure understanding of the past has been disrupted as a result.[6] Using photographs to help recover perspectives on the past that some community members have avoided or are utterly unaware of is, then, a means of taking responsibility for how that history is recovered and shared. Such actions fit well with how the community is determining its own future in all other areas of its development. Commenting on the community's continued efforts to ensure cultural preservation and regeneration, Narcisse Blood observed the importance of understanding the historical processes which have shaped the community's current experiences:

> I think for the Bloods, we've done okay. We've done a lot better in terms of coping with what has happened to us, but it's an ongoing struggle. It's definitely ... it's hard being Native, being Blood Indian, you know, to survive and get back control of our lives. And you're seeing what we've been able to do. We've still got a ways to go, but also we have to deal with how colonized some of our people have become, you know? It was in these schools, in these residential schools, that a lot of that took place. So, it's important that we teach [about] colonialism, so that people have an idea of what colonization has done. (Blood, 6 December 2001)

The Right Way of Doing Things

> These pictures are like dictionaries and that's what the elders are on the Reserve; they are dictionaries. (Wolf Child 20 November 2001)

Eighty years have elapsed since Blackwood's visit to the Kainai Nation, and the changes in lifestyle within the community since 1925 have been tremendous. In a rapidly changing world, Kainai people today experience different kinds of challenges from their ancestors and operate within a global arena in ways which were never possible for their parents, grandparents, and great-grandparents, who were subject to a deliberate assault on their culture, scathingly described by Andy Blackwater as 'legalized genocide' (Blackwater to Brown, pers. comm. 23 July 2002). As they embrace these challenges and opportunities, many Kainai people continue to regard traditional values as essential to their identity and as inextricably intertwined with their daily activities and social relationships. Others are less traditionally oriented for a range of reasons, including the circumstances in which they were raised, their ability to access cultural and historical knowledge, or their adherence to non-Native spiritual beliefs. Of these, some may actively be seeking to learn more about Kainai culture, while others are less inclined to participate in ceremonial or cultural matters. Notwithstanding the variety of personal beliefs and philosophies held by Kainai people today, the community supports the following of traditional protocol and the incorporation of Kainai perspectives into the way the Nation operates, and, through the development of educational resources or through tackling healthcare issues and social problems according to culturally appropriate means, the Kainai are taking control of their future and are developing ways of ensuring that their culture is strengthened and is passed on to younger generations.[7]

Historical photographs can play a role in these processes because images of the past allow for reflection on what traditional Kainai culture is and how it was practised by previous generations. Such images invariably evoke comparisons between life as it is understood to have been in the past and as it is today, questions about what has changed and why, and which aspects of Kainai society and culture have remained constant. The Kainai Board of Education, for example, has published innovative teaching materials in which historical photographs are used in conjunction with oral narratives concerning growing up and living on the Blood Reserve and traditional stories and advice from elders about Kainai values, in an effort to teach students about the roots of drug and alcohol abuse and encourage them to seek out and understand traditional solutions for problems (Fox 2001). Blackwood's photographs, particularly her more informal compositions, can similarly contribute to narratives of change and continuity and were often discussed in relation to traditional values and how these were maintained through the transitional era. Connected with their observations that this collection of photographs is a visual record of their community at this time, many people also remarked upon the extent to which traditional values and behaviour considered natural and 'correct,' which they saw in the images, are still current. In this respect, the photographs were viewed as having a dual purpose in that they illustrated values and behavioural codes in action and also could be used to teach younger generations about proper ways of doing things according to Kainai protocol. Some viewers expressed concern that the separation from and lack of access to information about traditional culture meant that younger generations often are unaware of the correct ways of being and behaving, and suggested that historical photographs, which show how ancestors lived, can be immensely valuable in educating people today about such matters.

In order to explain this point, several people chose to use the image of *Misaamahkoiyinnimaakii* (Long Time Medicine Pipe Woman/Mrs Shot Both Sides) seated in the tipi (plate 21). In addition to pointing out how well kept this tipi appears, commenting on the designs of the tipi liners, and explaining the seating arrangements, a number of viewers noted how *Misaamahkoiyinnimaakii* was sitting; her knees bent and her legs to one side:

> That's what you call *awaakiyopi*. That is the way ladies sit. This way ... Not in front. Not crossed like that, but sideways like that. Then you look at it and they wear the hairstyle very simple, but very graceful. And when the young people see that and you explain to them the designs and why our ladies sit like that – traditional female sitting position – then they know. They begin to understand that everything has a purpose and it's not random. (Blackwater 26 November 2001)

This, the proper way of sitting, is not always practised by women today, who, it was observed, sometimes sit like men at ceremonial events for want of knowing otherwise (Delaney 4 December 2001). Strict codes of behaviour are observed within traditional Kainai culture and actions are noted and checked. It was observed that, as many younger people are trying to go back to following the ways of their ancestors, they need help to ensure that they are not making mistakes and mixing things up. The gaps between the lifestyles of people today and previous generations are so great that it is sometimes difficult to explain to a younger person about certain concepts or ways of behaving. Visual images which depict aspects of traditional culture are therefore seen as educational aids, which allow the young to appreciate what is being described by their elders. For Kainai people, these photographs do much more than illustrate how to do things correctly, however, be it how to wear a shawl, or how men's braids should be worn – two examples derived from Blackwood's photographs that were picked up on by several viewers because of their particular cultural meanings. These images show the connections which those people depicted still had with their traditional culture and worldview, even though the community had been confined to a reserve for fifty years; connections that are not always understood by people today, who sometimes do things in particular ways because they know they should, not because they necessarily know why (Bastien 27 November 2001). As a result, the images can be read as poignant reminders of how much has changed within the community and how much has since been lost over a very short span of time, as well as being a focus for recovering cultural information.

The images were used by some viewers to draw attention to aspects of Kainai culture that are implicit and behavioural, though not always visual. These were observed in the photographic details or were explored in connection with stories about the individuals Blackwood encountered. Such readings are not at all obvious to people unfamiliar with Kainai culture, and added layers of meaning to the images that situated them within Kainai worldview and understandings of the connections between all people and things. Martin Heavy Head described a photograph with which he was familiar that showed very clearly how the centrality of Kainai cultural protocol to all aspects of life could be read within historical images by those cognizant of these rules:

> There was a picture here, and I think it's still around some place, of Blood Indians gathered at residential school and there was a head chief, and of course, the head chief is recognized by Indian Affairs, by school officials, by the Church, and so on and so forth. So he was given a place of honour, you know, he sat right in the middle of the picture. But beside him there was another person, and then there was a long line of people off to this side. And then off to the right there's just a crowd. But I don't think the people that took the picture had any idea of what the significance was. But the person standing beside him was the leader of the Horn Society, and the people standing on each side were the members of the Horn Society. So we know that, but I don't think the person taking the picture or the school officials knew what was going on. They had absolutely no idea what was going on, and of course, the Priest was standing behind the chief and all of that. But I think we, as you know, being from the community, we'll look at a picture and know what's going on and derive a lot more meaning from that picture than somebody else would. (Heavy Head 16 November 2001)

Photographs are consequently seen as having the potential to contain histories and culture within the tracings on the paper, but also to foster the sharing of knowledge and values associated with the narratives that emerge from the images, rather than just in the internal details. While this was especially apparent when names and naming practices were being discussed, it also resonated through to discussions of other themes central to Kainai culture, such as sharing, respect, and family values.

Those people who commented on traditional Kainai values and how they could be viewed in the photographs discussed them in terms of their continuity and how they have been affected by historical circumstances. The closeness between grandparents and grandchildren, for example, was remarked upon when those images in which women stand holding their granddaughters to them were studied (plates 13–14, 18–20, and 22) and were discussed in connection with the effects that residential schools have had on the strength of this relationship, on the intergenerational transmission of knowledge, and on child-raising practices more broadly. In other cases, the photographs led to discussion of how the essential values of Kainai culture have been maintained in spite of such tremendous upheaval:

> But during the time as it has changed, we still continue the same as we are living. Some might be, let's say, wild, extravagant, and everything they have in their home, but the same methods still going on. People still sharing. They don't just stockpile. They share. And some of the older people like me, we still practise much of that. I still practise what I had known way back then. It was to continue exercising what I had learned from the people back there in early years. I still exercise what they had taught me. And today I'm very fortunate that I am still doing it. The biggest part is respect. To honour. And to have that patience, the patience, no matter what the rush is. (Crow Chief 20 November 2001)

As they discussed how values are manifested in the present, many people commented on how concepts such as materialism have affected people today. Several observers suggested that though the people in the photographs may appear not to have had much in the way of material goods (to non-Native eyes), they were rich in other ways, such as in their cultural knowledge and their connection with their spirituality (Blackwater 26 November 2001). Some people saw contentment in the faces of the individuals and reflected upon this in comparison to people today:

> These people may have been poor in those days, they may have suffered a lot, they didn't have very much, but they had what they needed to get by. And it may have been such a struggle just to do that but you can tell they

> were very happy. You get a sense of accomplishment, a sense of contentment, a sense of happiness from these pictures. And like I said, that's something that is lacking today. And it leads to a lot of questions. What is missing today that people had in those days, those people who didn't have very much? We have a lot more today but why do people seem to have been so much happier yesterday? (First Rider 4 December 2001)

Surviving and Learning

> Them days, some of these pictures, well those were hard times way back then in the twenties, thirties. In that time there was no welfare, nothing for the people. But the students here, like today, there's a lot of difference, eh? It's easier, but them days ... yet the people survived.
>
> Allan Prairie Chicken, 5 December 2001

Of all the narratives that emerged from the many different readings of the photographs, those which were most constant concerned the theme of survival, and, as they discussed the transitions that their ancestors had experienced, many individuals commented on the ability of the Kainai people to survive and maintain their identity as Kainai, despite extreme hardships and the destructive impact of colonial rule. This sense of survival and pride in identity and in history, which so many read in the faces of those photographed, was remarked upon with great admiration and respect. Even though the images held so many mixed messages for viewers – sadness in the realities of the circumstances of the lives of those depicted and of the circumstances of the production of the photographs; respect for the people's dedication and ability to continue to exercise Kainai beliefs in spite of repression; humour when recalling stories about individuals – the theme of survival and awe of what their ancestors endured for the benefit of their children and grandchildren was articulated again and again, and in terms that emphasized the importance of understanding their struggles and experiences:

> We need to see them [the photographs]. There's that sadness in their eyes, but yet, they're telling me, 'Yes, I'm sad, but I'm still proud. I will not be broken. I will not be broken ... My spirit will not be broken.' There's a difference between being sad and there's a difference between pride. You can be both sad and be proud at the same time ... Like this picture [plate 10], yes, that picture compared to in the twenties or whenever, whenever it was taken, and you get a white man besides and you see the difference

in dress, yet he's not ashamed, because that's what he had. He was proud to have those clothes. He was satisfied with them. He didn't need to go put a necktie or anything on. (Weasel Head 28 November 2001)

As with so many other narratives concerning the images, viewers contrasted their ancestors' ability to adapt and survive with people's lives today, and many remarked upon how easy life is today in comparison with life in the 1920s, even though people have different sorts of problems. These comments were expressed in connection with discourse concerning values and traditions, as described above, and many commented on how hard people had worked to ensure that these values were maintained, without the benefits that are available today. Several people remarked upon the contentment and confidence they saw in the images and reflected on what has changed in the years since that has resulted in some of that pride and confidence no longer being so strong (First Rider 4 December 2001). Numerous people were also drawn to what they viewed as the 'healthiness' of the individuals in the photographs, which was connected with the sense of pride that many felt emanated from the images. The outdoor lifestyle which people enjoyed in those years is no longer common today, and it was frequently observed how physically healthy the people in the images appeared. In spite of external pressures, the expressions of contentment and pride, combined with the physical presence recorded by Blackwood's camera, project a sense of well-being which contributes to the record she made of a strong community in transition. When voicing these thoughts, viewers suggested that the photographs could be educational tools to teach people about the persistence and strength of individuals and community members and, accordingly, provide guidance in maintaining that sense of strength and in developing confidence within the community today.

The theme of survival informed almost all responses to the photographs in some form. It was explicitly expressed in the discussion of daily life based on the memories of older people who had grown up in the years immediately before and after the images were taken and also in the stories younger generations had heard from their elders about life in those days and about the struggles that many families had experienced. It was also alluded to in discussion of the importance of identity and spirituality, whether in relation to historical circumstances, such as fighting for the right to exercise ceremonial beliefs, or in more abstract terms in relation to what it means to be Kainai. In this regard the images prompted commentary about the persistence and strength of the individuals in the photographs in ensuring that their traditional knowledge was passed on and in being secure in who they were, as Kainai individuals and as leaders:

> In some ways, for our survival, we had to give almost the pretence that we were almost obliging the assimilation by wearing the clothes, cutting our hair, so that they'd leave us alone a little bit. It was what's in your mind that counts the most. (Blood 6 December 2001)

Conclusion

Narratives of hardship, adaptation, and, most of all, survival are so closely interlinked when Kainai people talk about these photographs that almost all of the statements made in connection to the difficulties of the 1920s were followed by a further comment emphasizing the ability of the Kainai to regain control of their lives. As discussions progressed, it became apparent that while Blackwood's photographs portray the visible elements of a society undergoing rapid change, it is only when they are contextualized by Kainai readings of them that the human response to these processes of change can be fully appreciated. These readings emphasize the flexibility of a people who have a long history of making adjustments to fit with their situation and in determining positive responses to their circumstances. The readings are culturally grounded, and underscore the values and priorities of Kainai people that contributed to the sense of contentment which so many viewers observed in the expressions of their ancestors:

> [This] was perhaps almost the lowest point in our history. When the buffalo were all gone. Not having the kind of industrial skills and farming, ranching ... And it's reflected even in the faces of the pictures. But being a First Nation people, your priorities are different. Of course we joke about ourselves, character-wise, but the richness of our people is on the inside rather than on the outside. And you look at these pictures and even though they are going through some hardship, you can see people are somewhat content. Still content. Some are able to laugh. They are not completely succumbed to the outside forces. Still have their liberty, freedom at least to facial and other expressions. But a lot of it has ... well it shows the diversity and the ability to adapt to new situations. We are very adaptable. (Blackwater 26 November 2001)

Considering Kainai perspectives on Beatrice Blackwood's photographs allows them to be read in ways which subvert the photographer's original intentions. Kainai views enrich the images by adding cultural and biographical layers of meaning to portraits that otherwise would have been starkly classificatory in nature. By absorbing the messages of the images into Kainai systems of knowledge and teaching, the photographs can become part of a process of reviving and affirming family and community-based histories. As we discuss in the following chapter, through listening to these same messages and the ways in which Kainai people express them, researchers can respond to Kainai concerns and can begin to learn how they can enrich their own perspectives on the past and its place in the present.

CHAPTER FIVE

The Past in the Present: Community Conclusions

Sinaakssiiksi aohtsimaahpihkookiyaawa. The translation of that is: photos tell us stories or images or messages. Pictures provide us with messages; they portray messages for us.

Andy Blackwater, 3 September 2002

Having placed Blackwood's photographs of the Kainai squarely – and uneasily – between the history of anthropological photography and Kainai readings of the past, we consider in this and the following chapter the lessons to be learned from the project, and the implications of the tensions of meaning which exist between Kainai and anthropological understandings of the past as manifested in these images. These lessons seem to fall into two sets, those with implications for the Kainai community itself, as well as for outside scholars interested in its heritage, which we consider in this chapter, and those which potentially affect heritage institutions such as museums and archives, which we consider in chapter 6.

Despite our knowledge of the importance of other visual repatriation projects to their source communities, we have been surprised at the range and depth of ways in which these thirty-three photographs from the 1920s have been reincorporated into the Kainai community, and at the potential these images have for achieving Kainai goals of transmitting cultural and historical knowledge across generations. This became especially clear to us when Brown taped statements of consent from Kainai people for the inclusion of their words in this book and the depositing of tapes and transcripts at Red Crow Community College. In these statements, a number of interviewees spoke not to us, but to their children, grandchildren, and unborn generations of kin, emphasizing the potential of these materials for keeping Kainai culture alive. In other ways, across the project, Kainai people showed us how these photographs allowed them to voice their own perspectives on the past, to be able to speak about family members, and to consider how to carry elements of the past into the future. As we began to understand these responses, we also realized that they had implications – messages, if you will – for how outside scholars have perceived and tried to understand Kainai culture.

Voices, Perspectives, Knowledge

This was reality. A lot of our history has been romanticized, unfortunately, and people in Europe who have never been introduced to Native culture, have never interacted with Native people ... what they have read in books or seen in the movies ... they would be completely shocked. They wouldn't get the same appreciation today of Native people as they would with these photographs.

Dorothy First Rider, 4 December 2001

The Kainai-Oxford Photographic Histories Project has been as much an inquiry into learning about the different forms histories can take as an appreciation of how the roles of history are culturally conceptualized. Through talking about the role of stories and biographies, particularly in relation to names, Kainai participants in this project have demonstrated that, for them, events in the past can provide very clear guidance for the present. Furthermore, the discussions emanating from the images provided information on a wealth of topics within the recent past that can be used to contribute to the more formalized teaching of history within the community, most specifically concerning how colonialism has affected the Kainai Nation and how its members can respond to it.

The Kainai-Oxford Photographic Histories Project also concerns how museums can mediate these different forms of history and can participate in them. It has involved learning about the multiplicity of voices that contribute to historical narratives and about how visual records can be 'excavated' (Katakis 1998) to uncover layers of historical meaning that are then open to new and changing interpretations by Kainai and others. The narratives that emerged within the interviews encompass biographical and cultural information that can enliven the voices of ancestors and also contemporary reflections on how the past can be relevant today. As this study of the community meanings of Beatrice Blackwood's images has shown, when the voices of ancestors and descendants are brought together, the stories and knowledge contained within the images become interwoven and reworked to create vibrant and continuing messages of cultural survival in changing times.

Photographs, especially anthropological photographs, are particularly complex visual resources. As we have noted, Blackwood's images were constructed to be meaningful within a pre-existing set of anthropological categories, and yet they are also representations of Kainai lives and histories. Perhaps the most important theoretical realization to emerge from this project has been the understanding of the extent to which photographs can be sites of 'intersecting histories' (Edwards 2001: 83), the cross-cultural analysis of which can reveal entire bodies of knowledge and narratives of history which might not otherwise be recorded. After speaking to Kainai people about what the photographs mean to them, we see that without these Kainai interpretations, the Blackwood photos would seem flat and one-sided – very like the scholarly conversation in which they have been embedded until this project. Indeed, one of the most interesting aspects of what happened when the photographs were reintroduced to the Kainai community was the way the nature of the conversation shifted: instead of scholarly voices, the voices became Kainai, the language was often Blackfoot, and many older people spoke about the images in ways which derive from the patterns of Kainai oral history and oral narrative. The manner in which a speaker carefully gave the source for his or her information, like an oral version of a scholarly footnote; certain rhythms and figures of speech; particular ways in which stories were structured, were all very much Kainai ways of speaking. Photographs are for talking about as well as for looking at, and the ways in which they are spoken of are important.

If this project has been about voices and the processes used to recover and make them audible, it has also been about silences, and how they have contributed to an unevenness of historical understanding concerning relationships between Native and non-Native people which has had lasting implications and has caused misunderstandings across cultures. It is said that photographs 'can speak. They can whisper or shout. They can lie' (Historic Sites Service and Alberta Community Development n.d.: 2). More often, of course, voices have been silenced in the one-sided conversations in which non-Native scholars say a great deal, and Native voices and perspectives are not heard at all. Kainai community members know very well how deep these silences (and misunderstandings) can be if their own readings of the photographs are not heard, as *Niipomaakii* (Georgette Fox) observed:

> It's not only these photographs, but other photographs that I've seen of our people. They always, most of them, there's such a blank look in their eye and they look so serious, and it makes me feel sad because that's not how we are. We're a real happy people. (G. Fox 27, August 2002)

> They started taking more photos of us during the worst time in our history. That was when we really went down because of the whisky ... The buffalo were gone and we almost resorted to begging for food ... And these people, like this one here [plate 10], in England, if you put this out on public display, they'd be like, 'Holy! Those Indians must have been extremely poor.' But we were very rich before *napiikowaiksi* [White people came]. (Blackwater 9 September 2002)

> [The photographs] really [don't] say what was going on in the community. It's just an image. Why were all these people there? Like the images of these people are taking priority over their surroundings. So you have that clear image, but there's no information to go with it, except for what you can read out of the photographs. This one [plate 10] has a little bit of the tent at the back. The guy probably said, 'I'm not standing over there!' ... These are just images of individuals that are actually objects. They are objects. It's almost like a statue. You know? Like a statue up in the garden some place. (Bruised Head 28 November 2001).

Left in the archives, perceived solely within anthropological traditions of thought, Blackwood's photographs have less than half their meanings attached to them, and these are shallow understandings of Native culture and history. The narratives that emerged while discussing the images with Kainai people barely touched upon the anthropological messages of the photographs. This may, in part, have been because we showed these photographs in Kainai spaces, rather than in an archival setting, and in a format that contrasted to how they would have been viewed within the archives: we presented single images rather than pairs (as they had been printed and stored within the Pitt Rivers Museum collections), and with one exception, did not join pairs together or print them on the same page.

While the presentation of the photographs within Kainai cultural spaces did indeed contribute to the submerging of the original anthropological meanings as well as of those they had assumed through being part of a research archive in the Pitt Rivers Museum, equally important was that Kainai people did not wish to seem overly critical of Blackwood. Moreover, they were far more interested in discussing their ancestors and how the images could be productively used today than in considering Blackwood's own interpretations of and uses for the photographs. As a result, biographies, family histories, and the distinct themes of loss, survival, and the transitional era – with their attendant chronologies and narratives – dominated the interviews. As Edwards has cautioned, these sets of different cultural meanings are not even, at some levels, tied to the same events or chronologies that outside scholars might bring to them (Edwards 2001: 93). They are certainly not tied to the same understandings or concerns. The contrast between Blackwood's portraits of Shot Both Sides and her terse comments on him ('Another man, full face and profile. Close up' and '*Shot on Both Sides. Head Chief of the Bloods. Full Blood*'), and the rich oral accounts by community members of his leadership and his challenging of government intrusion, stands as an important testimony to the very different emphases of these sets of meanings, as well as to the impoverishment of the images without the Kainai knowledge in which they sit. As Duane Mistaken Chief observed, photographs such as those taken by Blackwood:

> did much to objectify *Niitsitapiiwa* in the minds of others. Without the information that gave them life, it was much easier to look at them as 'others' and even [as] less than human. Knowing their stories suddenly instigates compassion and human fellowship and empathy. (Duane Mistaken Chief to Brown, pers. comm. 8 September 2004)

Such reactions to anthropologists' photographs of First Nations people are not uncommon, as artist and curator Jeff Thomas has described in connection with his own experiences of looking at photographs in the Canadian Museum of Civilization, taken on the Six Nations Reserve where he spent part of his childhood: 'My CMC discovery was like finding a forgotten family photograph album tucked away in the attic. Turning its pages revealed people I had only heard stories about. My experience of the photographs began to change from a detachment generated by static anthropological documents to excitement at finding and reclaiming a lost community history' (Thomas and Hudson 2002: 138). Similarly, for Kainai people, Blackwood's photographs depict

Kainai lives, ancestors, and history, albeit seen through the eyes of someone who passed through the community in two days with firm preconceptions. Indeed, the fact that the photographs are so obviously 'framed' by one set of cultural assumptions makes what is out of frame – the corresponding Kainai set of cultural assumptions – equally obvious (when one thinks to look for it). The stains below the windowsill of the ration house where grease or washwater was thrown out, and where Blackwood photographed the women (plate 14); the expressions on the faces of those in the images; the reins of a horse, held by *Aasainio'tokaani* (Crying Head), which disappear off-frame (plate 26); the details (sometimes barely visible) of shoes and hairstyles and clothing, as read by Kainai people, signal Kainai meanings and realities just as the paired poses signalled anthropometric ones for Blackwood (see also Geffroy 1990: 407 for discussion of similar responses in his analysis of French family photographs).

Others who have worked with indigenous communities on photographic projects have observed similar responses. Aird has noted of photographs of Australian Aboriginals taken within scientific frames of reference:

> Photographs taken by professional photographers or government officials have proved to be extremely valuable to Aboriginal people as historical documents, even though they are often heavily influenced by the artistic or political intentions of the photographer and misguided and racist beliefs resulting in the portrayal of Aboriginal people as savages, beggars, or as the last of a dying race.
>
> I have, however, often seen Aboriginal people look past the stereotypical way in which their relatives and ancestors have been portrayed, because they are just happy to be able to see photographs of people who play a part in their family's history. (Aird 2003: 24–5)

In the case of the Kainai-Oxford Photographic Histories Project, the interviews and informal chats were an opportunity to discuss the photographs in terms that were important to the viewers, as family photographs, and not as anthropological portraiture.

The Colonial Gaze – and Gazing Back

This turning-around of anthropological intentions and perspectives leads us to another implication of this project, which has been to challenge theory about the dominant society's 'gaze' on indigenous peoples. This 'gaze' is the way in which whites have seen other peoples through ethnocentric lenses, and has been part of the way that indigenous peoples have been controlled. The idea of the 'gaze' has been explored extensively by Foucault (1970, 1976) regarding controlling structures within Western society such as prisons, and has been usefully applied to cross-cultural situations, particularly involving tourism and the way that Western tourists see non-Western peoples. In this sense, dominant-society Western tourists are said to have a certain rigidly defined set of expectations of non-Western peoples, who occupy 'imaginative spaces' (Lutz and Collins 1993: 2) in Western culture – so that First Nations people, for example, come to signify 'noble' or 'traditional' in the minds of Western viewers, who also occupy positions of power in relation to non-Western peoples (Said 1978; Lutz and Collins 1993; Urry 2002).

Blackwood worked very much in this tradition. As she looked at Kainai people, she saw not complex individuals, but 'pure-blood,' 'hybrid,' 'mixed blood,' 'traditional,' or 'modern': cues in the shape of people's bodies and faces, and in their clothing and community environment, which meant something to her on the basis of the intellectual categories she brought with her from academia. Frank Weasel Head understood these dynamics:

> Frank Weasel Head: I read a little about what she wrote about us, getting the side of the face – like she said we had big noses – to show the features, instead of showing what the individual was, who was the individual. Nothing was said too much about the individuals in her writing ... Some of them [the people in the photographs] are natural, some of them are natural looking, I think, and some of them are not really a natural look. The one that really strikes me of the way she looked, that's Mrs Shot Both Sides' picture. Sitting in the tipi [plate 21]. It really strikes me as a person that's not very happy ... because she's, like she's sitting in a tipi, which was a natural setting years before these pictures were taken and which wasn't a natural setting any more.
>
> Alison Brown: Yeah, she's sitting alone, as well.
>
> Frank Weasel Head: Yes, sitting alone, and the image looks like the tipi is so neat, and the bed. Everything. Her best blankets on, and everything which she normally won't have on if she was still living in there. To me she was sad because she was just posing. It wasn't a natural setting, really. A natural setting for her any more, which was about thirty years before this photo was taken, this would have been a natural setting for her. So

> now to me it's almost like that picture – stereotyping. And the next one with her husband, just to show his features, so she could validate her statements ... They're good. They're nice to have. It shows our people that we adapted and changed, but a lot of them to me ... I look at them and to some extent I see a sadness of our people being forced to do things. And like she wrote at the beginning, the Indian Agent took them out and probably the Indian Agent told them, 'You have to do this.' (Weasel Head 28 November 2001)

Alongside these meanings, however, are the equally valid ones that the photographs have for Kainai people today, and which are strengthened by the intellectual categories within Kainai culture which reappropriate the images: the contemporary Kainai gaze. There is not just one, controlling, dominant-society gaze, then. There is another: that of those Kainai individuals whom Blackwood photographed, who continue to gaze back at Blackwood, and of their descendants who look at these images decades later.[1] The force of the expressions in the eyes of people whom Blackwood photographed conveys this response very clearly. While remaining dignified, and not obviously angry, there is such uncertainty, reserve, stiff submission, and sometimes contempt in some faces that one wonders Blackwood never commented on it.

None of the Kainai responses to Blackwood's work, either at the time the photographs were taken or during our interviews, shows an acceptance of the intentions of her anthropological gaze. As Frank Weasel Head notes:

> When I look at these pictures and I look deeply into their faces, into their eyes, they're sad. You can see the sorrow in their eyes, the way they go, and yet, they were proud. They were not broken. Our young people can learn from that ... I think that's why they have such a sad face. Another photographer coming out to study us, to see what we are. 'But I can't really say who I am because I am being told what to do. How to pose. What to wear.' That's like I say, that's my personal ... others have different [views]. I think to me, I don't know if I'm the first one, but others are just looking superficially at the photographs, but are not looking, you might say, deep into their eyes. When I see old paintings or photographs of my ancestors I try and look at the past, at what's in their eyes. I try to look at the eyes. Although, I guess that's part of their belief, their spirit, part of their spirit being taken away from them. I can look into their eyes and their spirit lives through them ...
>
> There's that sadness in their eyes, but yet, to me they're telling me, 'Yes,

I'm sad, but I'm still proud. I will not be broken. I will not be broken.' (Weasel Head 28 November 2001)

If Beatrice Blackwood used an anthropological and dominant-society 'gaze' in creating her images of Kainai people and imbuing them with meaning, Kainai people are well able to deconstruct these meanings and to gaze back, very forcefully, at Blackwood.

Reading the Photographs: Surface and Depth

'The gaze,' as analysed by academics, is often about surface details of images and how these are understood within the preconceived and objectifying (and thus controlling) categories of outsiders. Kainai perspectives took us further. Though many of the comments people made in response to the photographs focused on surface details – how people were dressed, how they wore their hair – it would be a mistake to assume that these were superficial observations. As has happened during other visual repatriation projects, Kainai people conducted very careful readings of surface detail which linked to and revealed much deeper interpretations of history and of the location of these photographs and the people they depict. Edwards, discussing the return of some of Diamond Jenness's Pacific photographs to the D'Entrecasteaux Islands notes that Islanders' responses to these were 'forensic,' focused on close readings of surface details, but that their readings of these details linked to much deeper cultural and historical knowledge and activated deep memories (Edwards 2001: 95). Similarly, Poignant was greeted by Aboriginal people at Nagalarramba when she brought photographs back to them with the question, 'Are you the lady with our memories?' Her wise interpretation of this startling question, which equated photographs with memories, was that community members expected the images to function within family and local historical knowledge and assumed that the surface reality of the photographs linked to these deeper structures of knowledge (Poignant 1996: 7).

Kainai responses to Blackwood's photographs have taught us much about the nature of these structures, through which Kainai people have experienced history. Where non-Native scholars working on Native histories have focused on 'the tribe,' Kainai responses to the photographs emphasize the extended family and clan first, and the broader community and nation second. Roslyn Poignant's visual repatriation project also generated a focus on family structures of knowledge from

Aboriginal respondents, and reflected on what she understood to be 'genealogical constructions of history,' noting that 'the recollection of genealogical histories *through* the photographs also coexisted with other ways of articulating them, so that the experiences gained in these sessions focused my attention on the different ways in which the photographs, memory and history connected with one another – within the community' (Poignant 1996: 8). Through this research it has become very clear that for Kainai people the clan and the local community are the focus of history, and are the social structures through which one experiences and understands history. Biography is also an important focus for historical narrative, as a means of exemplifying appropriate courses of action and moral behaviour. This is a very different structure from dominant-society scholarly ways of understanding the past, which focus either on influential individuals (although less as role models) or on the broader categories of the social, political, and economic contexts in which they lived. Within academia, there has long been a rigid division between family or community history (often referred to as 'local history' or genealogy and often carried out by amateurs) and what is seen as 'real' history, which privileges the analysis of historical events and phenomena, and the forces behind these, instead of detailing what are seen as the concrete manifestations of those forces: institutions, families, communities. Traditionally, there has been a hierarchical division within the heritage profession involving status and access to funding for research and publication projects. Social history and material history have bridged these divisions, but still do not equate with Kainai and other indigenous conceptions of kinship-based history. The categories within which we seek, privilege, and synthesize historical information need to be rethought if scholars are not simply to impose ethnocentric models when attempting to do revisionist histories, reworkings of history that are still held to be problematic. Indeed, scholars might usefully focus on the problematic dynamics of reconciling (or not) multiperspectival narratives of the past. They might also explore greater inclusion of indigenous narratives of historical experience within broader regional and national histories, within which even 'new' indigenous histories tend to be presented as sidebars to a main narrative of settler experience. As McMaster has asked, 'what ... is the potential, or latitude, for Native perspectives on history in the face of the prevailing disregard with which revisionist histories are greeted, even when they are written by white people?' (McMaster 1992: 78).

For Native community historians, family and community form the points of reference that locate individuals in the world. The care and concern expressed by all of the Kainai people who were interviewed to reattach names to the individuals in Blackwood's photographs were not, therefore, simply an interest in what some professional historians might see as unimportant surface detail: they were very deeply felt needs to reattach both the individuals in the images to their kin, and the interviewees to the people in the photographs, and thus to repair and preserve part of the knowledge structure which is necessary for understanding who one is in relation to past, present, and future. Similarly, the biographical information offered about the people in the photographs pertained specifically to those individuals and also to the values, traditions, beliefs, knowledge, and relationships which are at the heart of Kainai culture, and to the experiences which have been the stuff of Kainai history: people shared biographies of ancestors, but by so doing, they were relating Kainai lives much more broadly. Academic historians, even those trying to do new kinds of histories of First Nations communities, have often not taken such cultural perceptions and structures seriously enough, nor have they even understood them very well. Working with these photographs has pointed to a different way of understanding Native histories, and one that would not be so distanced from the communities we seek to understand.

Photographs and Kainai Structures of Historical Knowledge

Indeed, as well as pointing to different structures through which history is understood in the Kainai community, the responses to the photographs suggest broader Kainai systems of thought about heritage and about the transmitting of historical and cultural knowledge. These concepts have implications for the processes of writing cross-cultural histories and suggest limitations to texts written by non-indigenous scholars.

In order to understand Kainai historical perspectives as they are expressed today it is important to appreciate that they are informed both by oral traditions which focus on the intervention of supernatural forces in human life (DeMallie and Parks 2001: 1062) and by those forms of historical evaluation commonly associated with Euro-Canadian historical analyses. As Wilton Goodstriker has observed: 'Our people's memory goes back to the beginning of time and in some respects beyond. Our story has come through seven ages, the last one being referred to as *i'kookaiksi* (the age when the people used tipi designs). We are still in this age and will be for as long as the people use the tipi design. This era dates back some five hundred years ... it is an era that saw the coming of the horse, of the immigrant nations to our land, and of new ways to a people' (Goodstriker 1996: 7).

Like all other peoples, the Blackfoot have always kept an accurate record of significant events in their history, which have been remembered in many forms.[2] Knowledge of the past is embedded in the landscape, but also in the songs and stories, and in the minds and the spirits of the people (Goodstriker 1996: 3). Like other Plains people, the Blackfoot have also recorded their memorized oral history visually, in pictographs, such as those which can be seen at Writing on Stone Provincial Park, and in records known as winter counts, which John Ewers has suggested may have been 'inspired by mixed-bloods who had some knowledge of the white man's concept of the calendar' (Ewers 1997: 210). The most significant event in a year involving the entire Blackfoot nation, or, in other cases, the tribe or band to which the recorder was affiliated, was represented chronologically by pictographs used as mnemonic aids. In the past these were painted onto a tanned buffalo hide, but in later days were dictated onto paper, sometimes accompanied by written explanations (Raczka 1979). Several Blackfoot winter counts continued to be recorded well into the twentieth century and some of these are now housed in archives in Alberta (David Smyth to Brown, pers. comm. 18 October 2002).

For Kainai people, conceptions of what history is and its contemporary relevance are shaped by their understanding of the concepts of authority and knowledge and their roles within Blackfoot society, both of which are grounded within a holistic and experiential view of the world (for discussion of forms of knowledge and ways of knowing from a Blackfoot perspective, see Bastien 2004). Traditionally, history and knowledge about *Niitsitapiiwa*[3] are passed down as a form of oral narrative from one generation to the next, and it is the responsibility of older people to teach the stories and cultural ways to their grandchildren, and to acknowledge their own teachers. Within Plains oral traditions generally, storytellers were narrators rather than innovators (DeMallie and Parks 2001: 1062); among Blackfoot-speaking peoples, an individual with notable skills was referred to as *aitsinniki* (storyteller), and when a listener repeated the history that had been shared, reference would be made to that person (Fox: 2001: 6). Oral narratives are considered to be the most reliable form of Blackfoot history: 'There was always great care in correcting each other when there was an error found in one of the accounts. In this way, when everybody left for home, they all left with the same story to be retold at another time. For many years I have heard these stories, and they remain unchanged. It is in this way that our history and heritage have been accurately handed down through the ages' (Goodstriker 1996: 11).

Kainai people today who lead traditional lives continue to make reference to their teachers when sharing their knowledge; however, the language barriers between old and young have led to a serious decline in traditional forms for preserving and transferring historical and other knowledge. Older people have expressed great concern about the situation, but they have also noted the importance of recording their history in a form that is understood by younger generations:

> In the past our grandfathers, our older people whom we use, and also those that are considered as our historians, have provided us with the understanding by being able to relate to each other efficiently using our language. Today it is difficult for our young people who are now responsible to carry on our ways because of the decrease in the usage of our language ... It is today very difficult just to be able to sit across from each other to talk to each other in our language about our ways, so today it is fortunate for us that we are able to write our statements [and have them] translated into English ... We have come to a situation where we have to communicate by writing and using the English language. In this way we are able to communicate with each other freely using this method. It is good and very fortunate that we are able to write our statements and I believe that is the best method to allow us to continue to exchange dialogue regardless of the age factor. (Wolf Child 4 September 2002, translated by Blackwater)

Makoiyiipoka's (Bruce Wolf Child's) statement is indicative of the commitment among Kainai people to making their history accessible to future generations in a format they will understand. His words also reflect a view shared by many of his contemporaries that though the rapid pace of change within the community has caused social stress and cultural disruption, Kainai people will continue to learn from one another and to develop ways of ensuring that their perspectives on their history are recorded.

Such perspectives take us to new ways of thinking about photographs and archival materials: reattaching indigenous narratives and meanings to photographs provides not only a counterbalance to but also a critique of anthropological theory and mainstream historical narratives. The deep knowledge in which historic anthropological images are understood within indigenous communities, the greetings of ancestors seen in such images, the memories and otherwise buried narratives triggered by them, contradict earlier claims by scholars that such photographs 'can only be properly used when they are located within their particular genre and not given any documentary status other than as physical artefacts of the photographer's culture' (Pinney 1989: 61), and that returning images to source communities is 'redundant since the mass of photographs held in archives document *us*, not other cultures, and restitution is in this context not appropriate' (Pinney 1989: 57). While anthropological photographs most definitely document non-Native academic interests, the idea that they would not be of interest to source communities and that it is not appropriate to repatriate them is simply bizarre in the face of what we know about visual repatriation projects. (It should be noted that Pinney himself has since changed his stance on the potential of photographs to source communities; see Pinney and Peterson 2003.) Furthermore, as Poignant has observed, indigenous responses to historic photographs similarly make irrelevant (within community contexts) scholarly obsessions with critiques of the dynamics of 'representation, appropriation and authenticity; issues which are seen to mediate the evidential value of photographs' (Poignant 1996: 7): here the details in the images and the deep structures of knowledge are more important than critiques of surface detail and of the dynamics of photographic composition – which are taken for granted, and set aside in community readings. This is not to deny these legitimate and indeed necessary scholarly discourses, but adds to them a parallel way of theorizing and understanding anthropological photographs.

Edwards (2001: 12) has commented on the potential of the different narratives evoked by photographs to find points of weakness and inconsistency in theory, even in the grand and certain narratives of the entanglement of anthropology and colonialism. We have found this to be true in the Kainai-Oxford Photographic Histories Project. Blackwood, for instance, worked very much within the salvage paradigm of anthropology, in which the old, the historical, the traditional lifeways of Native people were privileged and in which it was assumed that these were vanishing in the face of modernization and acculturation. Contrast this with Narcisse Blood's overview of the photographs:

> We want people to look at us more as people rather than as just another item or archival material in the museum. This is what we endured. This is what our ancestors went through. Just the fact that you're talking to a descendant of those is a testimony to the resilience, the spirit of those people and what they went through. And we still have challenges, even today, that we're facing. For us it's inspirational too, to see the kind of hardships that they went through. If they could make it, we certainly can too. So, that's my perspective. (Blood 6 December 2001)

In Blood's words, the harsh facts of colonization are accepted, but are refracted in his perception of Blackwood's photographs and become a message of resilience, determination, and strength. More broadly, in their readings of the photographs in terms of the themes of survival and transition, as well as in their readings of such lessons for the present and future, Kainai people articulated that one of the messages of Blackwood's photographs for them was that they documented Kainai 'engagement with change on their own terms, and on their own ground' (expressed in a similar but Australian context by Poignant 1996: 5), and their determination to maintain Kainai ways and identity despite such change.

Community Conclusions: Sharing Knowledge

> We have become so, I guess you could say, white-washed; our children have, and not too many of them are interested in the past at least at this point. Maybe at some time in the future ... Maybe as you get older it becomes more important that you know where you're coming from. So I think this is going to be really beneficial for our people and I'm just glad that I could be a part of it. I wish I could be there when my great-great-great grandchildren listen to this tape because I really wish I could have heard my grandmother speak instead of just looking at her picture.
>
> Georgette Fox, 27 August 2002

The dialogues that emerged in the interviews between Kainai people, Brown as interviewer, and Blackwood's photographs, as well as in the subsequent writing of this book, have underscored the complex processes through which historical voices can be brought together with contemporary perspectives to provide a deeper appreciation of the history of the Kainai community. The implications for scholars of the importance of understanding these processes are tremendous, and should foster greater cultural inclusiveness in interpreting the past as well as a more acute appreciation of the responsibilities involved in undertaking projects of this sort. At the same time, within the Kainai community, individual views on how the photographs and the discussions they have prompted can be utilized for the benefit of their own people have been clearly articulated. Some of this information can be used to create a fuller understanding of Kainai contributions to the history and culture of southern Alberta as they are more broadly understood, as well as to histories of anthropological interactions and of visual representation. However, Kainai people see roles for the images that are deeper, more personal, and ultimately more pressing. As indicated in the statement by Andy Blackwater at the beginning of this chapter and encapsulated in the title of this book, Kainai believe strongly that there are messages within photographs that can be interwoven with their efforts to pass on their cultural and historical traditions to future generations.

The notion of photographs being part of a continuum of knowledge that has the potential to link generations was articulated by some individuals from the outset of the project, and became more explicit during the second research trip in 2002, when Brown visited those people who had been interviewed the previous year to discuss their transcripts and ensure that they were satisfied with the progress that had been made. Andy Blackwater had suggested that those people who had contributed interviews should make a taped statement in which they explained why they had agreed to participate in the project and gave formal consent for the transcripts to be used as the basis of this publication, and for copies of the transcripts and tapes to be stored in an accessible location on the reserve.[4] Some of these statements were made in English; others were made in Blackfoot and have since been translated by Mr Blackwater and checked with the interviewee. Copies of these statements are now stored with each tape and transcript so that future generations of Kainai who may wish to listen to the tapes will know that they were recorded in the full knowledge that they were intended to form a resource for the community. Moreover, because many of those who recorded consent statements acknowledged their own teachers, as is appropriate in Blackfoot culture, and emphasized that their own knowledge had been passed down to them orally, this added an extra layer of authority to their statements which would be appreciated and understood by future generations of Kainai. As people recorded their statements of consent it became increasingly clear that there was a feeling within the community that the images allowed for aspects of the past to be framed in ways that made sense in Kainai cultural terms. Access to the photographs provided opportunities for community members to articulate their views on Kainai history and the ancestors who are part of that history; studying them raised the possibility of filling gaps in that history from a Kainai perspective, points observed by Rufus Goodstriker when he recorded his statement of consent for his interview transcript to be made available at Red Crow Community College and incorporated into this book:

> I am speaking to the new generation of today and to future generations. There are a lot of things that we need to make them understand about our people of the past. Those are our relatives and our forefathers (the original Blackfoot people). It is encouraging to talk to our younger generation about the ancient history and stories and legends of our people.
>
> Today I believe that now that I am older as well as those other older people we should be telling or talking to our younger people about our history so our younger people will be aware of the way of life of our ancestors. It is fortunate that a lot of our children have advanced themselves academically and now they are teaching our young ones. They need to teach our children about our way of life combined with the regular school curriculum.
>
> It is ideal today that our young people know both our ways and the white man's ways. Our way, *Niitsitapi*, is good and the white man's way is also good to learn [the white man's writing and speaking of their ways]. There are a lot of our adults that had a formal education in the past, but do not understand our ways today. A lot of our adults, too, eventually return for adult education and they are taught about the white man's ways, to try to figure out their idea of existence. It is good that these adults return for adult education today to allow them to learn more about our ways and history [in reference to incorporation of culture into education]. We need to allow the continuation of our culture and traditions, especially for the new generation of elders, so that they may transfer to their children and grandchildren our way of life. This is what I believe in. We must not be stingy with our knowledge to say that 'I will not share.' It is important that we think the other way, that we need to share. In our way that is why we have our legends, which provide us with knowledge. (R. Goodstriker 20 August 2002)

A further point that emerged in the interviews and was reinforced by the statements of consent was the importance of ensuring that the photographs and the information collated during the project are accessible to the community. Photographs of Kainai people exist in public and private collections throughout Alberta, and are already used by many community members, a number of whom enjoy very positive working relationships with museums and archives in the province. Nonetheless, there are concerns about the logistical (and sometimes cultural) barriers to visiting museums and archives, and some people spoke of their hope that a heritage facility might one day be created on the Reserve, where resources such as Blackwood's photographs could be cared for by Kainai heritage management specialists and utilized in ways which fit with Kainai traditions and expectations:

> We need these pictures in our community, wherever we can find them, and I know quite a few people have pictures. I just looked at some the other day. But many of these pictures from our community, we need to display them ... if and when, we get an archival centre ... so people in the future ... I don't think the names Shot Both Sides, Heavy Runner, Crying Head are ever going to cease to exist; they're not going to cease to exist, so those people in the future can [see these photographs]. Because, as you know, ours is all oral history. (Weasel Head 28 November 2001)

A heritage facility of this sort would provide a space for people to look at photographs and exchange stories about the subjects as well as digest the knowledge shared by interviewees. Rosie Red Crow, for example, stated that it was important not only that future generations *see* the images, but that they *listen* to the statements recorded as part of this project, since this would 'help in individual self-worth and then they shall feel more good about who they are. The important thing is for our young people to know their family history, grandparents, and so on' (Red Crow 17 August 2002). Echoing these remarks, Andy Blackwater agreed that images from the past can be used to talk about issues that are current in the community now, and that giving people the opportunity to access and use the images according to their own needs would be tremendously helpful in creating positive self-esteem:

> Look at today's problems in our community. The lack of self-worth is a real problem, and the lack of identity. Lot of our young people are going though identity crises. Lot of them don't know their history. Lot of our young people don't value our traditional cultural ways. Lot of it has to do with the lack of access to that information that will allow them to follow up, to do their own searching. And pictures like this, they can look at them. (Blackwater 26 November 2001)

Martin Heavy Head observed that 'the Bloods have always been quite interested in tracing their lineage and talking about people they are related to, and having photographs would help quite a bit [in their discussions].' Taking this one stage further, he added that photographs represent 'the community's history,' and because they 'can be reproduced quite easily now, they should be made available':

> I think that society in general is quite a bit more enlightened today. You don't just have a picture and say these are, you know, 'one person and a thousand Indians,' or whatever. You try to accurately describe who's there, because it is important for everybody involved to know who's in the picture and what their position in the community was. (Heavy Head 16 November 2001)

Interpretations and Misinterpretations

Comments concerning the importance of physical access to images were closely connected with statements many people made about the need to be able to interpret them in their own way. Shirley Bruised Head, for instance, drew parallels between this project and the *Lost Identities* photographic exhibition:

> [Photographs] provide a history and for a number of indigenous people across the world, they really don't have their history, and it's not from their point of view. It's always from somebody else's point of view. And once something like this starts, as you add information, then your history is being told from your point of view and it's all coming out from these photographs. And I think that's the major thing for communities and for groups of people to have their history told. (Bruised Head 28 November 2001)

Reading photographs through new gazes and bringing new perspectives to them is crucial to this process, as it returns elements of control to those being photographed. Though some of Blackwood's images are quite formal, and the resistance in people's eyes is noted by Kainai today, in other images she elicited easy smiles and laughter, although, as Shirley Bruised Head has noted, perhaps the laughter was at her expense:

> I like this one [plate 26]. I really like this one. Look, they look like they're all flirting with her and having a damn good time teasing her! (Bruised Head 28 November 2001)

Such perspectives not only point the way to whole new meanings of the images, but to the fact that Blackwood didn't get everything right and misunderstood a good deal. Kainai people raised serious concerns about historical inaccuracies in the statements that Blackwood recorded in her diary, and remarked upon how easily outsiders' misinterpretations of traditional cultural practices were then recorded as 'facts.' Though it is acknowledged both by community members and by historians that the relationships between anthropologists and Native peoples during this period were varied and complicated, and that there were a variety of reasons why anthropologists and others may have misinterpreted information, the fact remains that there are now statements in the written literature that are seen as damaging. Inaccuracies and misinterpretations are blamed for creating negative stereotypes that non-Native people have absorbed and perpetuated, but more importantly, reading these misinterpretations in books written by non-Natives rather than seeking advice from traditional teachers, some Native people have become confused about aspects of their culture and, at worst, have become ashamed of who they are. Kainai perspectives on the past need to be voiced, and though this process has already begun in the publication of literature and resources aimed at a variety of audiences,[5] for this project there needed to be an opportunity for Kainai people to respond to Blackwood's comments and their implications, as well as share their readings of the photographs. Frank Weasel Head's understanding of what Blackwood wrote echoes concerns expressed by several community members and demonstrates how uncomfortably written statements can fit with oral traditions:

> Frank Weasel Head: It's like, you know, Alison, it's like the other people that you have interviewed and have met with this, with some of the writings that the lady did. We said that we're not in agreement with her, because that's her point of view. Now that's believed to be the gospel truth in England at that museum. It's believed to be the gospel truth. And if we come in and we say, 'Oh no, we disagree,' it's not a matter of disrespecting Miss Blackwood or anything. They might think they're being disrespect[ful] or they're saying that she's lying or anything. But that's her belief. That's how she seen it or understood it, but it's not normally the case.
> Alison Brown: Yes, yes.
> Frank Weasel Head: It's not normally the case.
> Alison Brown: The information she got, she probably got it from the Indian Agent. I don't get any sense that she actually spoke to people here ... I should say that none of this information has been made public any-

way, you know, from her diary. There've been a few researchers who have looked at the diary but it has never been on exhibit or anything like that. If any of this information were ever to be put on display, the point would be made that this was her impression.
Frank Weasel Head: Uh-huh. See like, in talking about the posing and sadness in some of their ... in the way they dressed ... 'Went to chief's camp. He has a painted tipi. They all put on their glad *rags*.' Well yes, they were rags, the clothing, to them. But to them, that's all they had.
Alison Brown: I think that's just an expression.
Frank Weasel Head: Yes, it's an expression, but just to further illustrate with the posing, some of them, I think, that's why they have such a sad face. 'Another photographer coming out to study us, to see what we are. But I can't really say who I am because I am being told what to do, how to pose, what to wear.' That's, like I say, that's my personal [view] ... others have different [opinions]. (Weasel Head 28 November 2001)

Given that Kainai people are all too aware of how little non-Native people know about Kainai culture and history, it was thought that several additional interviews should be recorded specifically to reflect upon Blackwood's interpretation of her brief visit to the community, as recorded in her diary and fieldnotes. The main points made during these interviews are presented as appendix 2. These interviews provided an opportunity for Kainai people to situate Blackwood's statements within their own historical and cultural perspectives and provide depth and balance. It was remarked upon that these reflections on Blackwood's statements needed to be made available to non-Natives as well as Kainai people in order to provide context for her remarks, which were primarily viewed as being 'superficial' and as 'sweeping statements,' based as much on the ignorant generalizations of the Indian Agent as on her own observations (Blood 20 August 2002). Nonetheless, it was also remarked upon that while Blackwood's statements are very brief and could be misleading, they also could be of great value to researchers working on aspects of twentieth-century Kainai history by adding a further layer of documentation to the oral record. Dorothy First Rider, for example, who has undertaken considerable historical research connected with Treaty entitlement, discussed the relevance of some of Blackwood's statements, remarking that even though she 'didn't realize how important those comments may have been in the future,' her statements regarding cattle ranching on the Blood Reserve and the Indian Agent's approach to his responsibilities confirm oral testimony and are extremely interesting and valuable (First Rider 6 September 2002). Likewise, photographs themselves can be used to confirm oral histories – perspectives that may be familiar to many Kainai community members, but which have been superseded by mainstream historical analyses, or which need reinforcing within the community:

> There's a lot of oral history that remains to be verified or proven one way or another and I think that the oral history has always been, at one point or the other, [found] to be true, rather than the other way round, where it has been disproven. So, I think that's the case, that if you do find photographs of that era, then I think it would help to verify the oral history. (Heavy Head 16 November 2001)

Differing interpretations of the images are not just to be found between Kainai and non-Kainai people. As was constantly emphasized by community members, their interpretations were personal, and did not represent a collective 'Kainai approach' to reading the images. Nonetheless, while the Kainai people who interacted with Blackwood's photographs were in broad agreement about the potential of the photographs to provide connections with the past and the future, they sometimes disagreed over the names of the people in the images, and some gave very different interpretations of the information arising out of the images. This is not surprising, given the pressures to which Kainai people, and their cultural and historical knowledge and identities, have been subject over the past century; however, in listening to these versions of truth, it is clear that they are equally probable and viable. Poignant found similar dynamics while undertaking her visual repatriation project in Australia: 'Although the photographs established continuities of self and of family, and seemingly made genealogies visible, agreement about the appearance of things within the frame was not always unanimous ... even when the reasoning is culturally informed, ambiguities in appearance may give rise to different interpretations. These differences of opinion coexisted, however, without undermining the efficacy of the photographs to revitalise and sustain memories, thereby helping to ground history in memory' (Poignant 1996: 12). In the telling, in their description and in the stories they evoke, photographs serve as vital links 'between past and present, between visible and invisible' (Edwards 2001: 4), but that does not mean that the nature of these links, or of what is linked or evoked, will be at all uniform between viewers and tellers.

Much more likely, in fact, would be individual variations on common themes, which is precisely what Kainai people gave in their readings.

Photographs and Families

Many people who viewed the images anticipated their future use as educational resources and within broader historical studies; however, the photographs also acquired an active role in the present as they began to be discussed and circulated within the community. One of the most immediate uses of the images has been within informal contexts, where they have become incorporated into Kainai visible genealogies through their display in people's homes. We were delighted to have copies of any of the images made on request for those people who participated in interviews or supported the project in other ways, and it was made clear that if they wished to have a copy of a photograph of a family member, this could be provided at no charge. A running list of photograph requests was kept on all the field trips, and the photographs were printed and mailed from Oxford as soon as possible. In a number of cases, people requested these copies so that they could be shown to relatives who had not already had an opportunity to see them because they lived off the Reserve or were not available during our visits. Though sets have now been deposited in various locations on the Reserve, at this stage in the project the repository for the photographs had yet to be decided upon. In any case, these copies were to be added to personal photographic collections and we have subsequently been told of the great pleasure that many individuals have gained from having the chance to see these family photographs and share them with their relatives. Within the private space of the home, many of Blackwood's photographs now take their place within a visual family history, and accompany portraits of several generations of family members that hang on the walls or are displayed on shelves or in cabinets. In a sense, photographs *are* family. Frequently, they are talked about as though the persons they depict are with the speaker in the room and are engaging with the conversation. Their presence suggests that future generations will be aware of their roots through being surrounded by ancestral portraits. *Matsistaotoikamo'saakii* (Rita Tallman) made this point most clearly as she used the photographs that fill the walls of her front room to talk about her own family:

> Just like my mother's picture. This was taken when she was four or five years old, when they took that picture, and I really treasure it ... I've got a

> lot of old pictures like that, from my Mom and his Dad, and my kids' pictures, when they were little boys. And all these pictures you see, that's part of my family ... so these pictures, that's why I keep them ... Pictures are really precious, so when I pass away, these will all be here, and my great-grandkids will be the ones that are asking questions, and that's good. They will keep our tradition and the pictures are really important to look at. (R. Tallman 10 December 2001)

Within First Nations communities, where many traditional stories and historical and cultural information central to the identity of the community are still passed on orally, photographs have assumed a role whereby they have become part of the process of sharing knowledge and, in this way, contribute to traditional practices of teaching and learning. Indeed, the social act of looking at and 'reading' photos functions to link generations and to consolidate traditional forms of knowledge through a process described by Poignant as 'the mobilisation of memories' (Poignant 1996: 9). Photographs are used informally, for instance, when an older person explains to grandchildren or great-grandchildren about life on the Reserve in the past or about their lineage. Many of those who participated in this project remarked that it can be challenging to describe how people coped during the post-Treaty era and to explain some of the choices their ancestors made; young people's experiences are so very different that they find it difficult to appreciate that people survived with so few of the conveniences and comforts with which they are familiar:

> And those pictures, see I think they need to know what we went through, and especially those old people, what they went through, to know our past. Just like today, everything is so easy for them and they don't know what we went through. We had to live in a tent and all that, and there's no family allowance, nothing. But today, everything is so easy... But this is why I was saying that, to teach them our way. Just like the way we are, we respect. There's a lot of respect of the older people. (Prairie Chicken 27 August 2002)

Otakkoyiisaapo'p (Allan Prairie Chicken) explained that younger people's difficulties in understanding the changes the community has experienced are, in part, due to the limited opportunities on the Reserve. This has created a cycle of dependence, denying younger generations the chance to develop survival techniques appropriate to their circumstances, just as their ancestors learned the skills to survive in the pre-reservation and transitional eras. Photographs from the past can help younger generations to understand the enormity of change that took place in the years surrounding Treaty 7, and while some of the earliest photographs of Blackfoot people portray the poverty and distress that were endemic, these images can be used to gently explain the actions that Blackfoot leaders took during a time of severe stress. Shirley Bruised Head described how photographs can be used to explore perspectives that community members may otherwise not be able or ready to fully consider. In turn, engaging with what are often traumatic images can become part of a healing process, as viewers are encouraged to confront the past and come to terms with the devastation of the last quarter of the nineteenth century. The response of some visitors to Bruised Head's selection of an image of a group of destitute people beside a torn tipi for the *Lost Identities* exhibit indicates the power of photographs to generate a sense of the realities of the past:

> [They] were kind of hesitant, or ashamed, actually, to see that. They asked me, 'Why did you put it up?' That's kind of like, 'You shouldn't show that.' And I just told them, 'Well, you know, that's what happened to our people. This is why all the treaties were signed.' And then it really hit them, you know, and then they would start talking about particular stories that they'd heard about the tough times and all of that. You know, I believe it gave them a way to look at history, to look at the past, because all they've learned is from a non-Native perspective. This is what happened. So a number of young Native people, middle-aged Native people, older Native people, had been ashamed of their leaders. 'They should have fought,' that's what everybody constantly says. 'They should have fought.' But then they see that photograph and they realize why they couldn't fight. It puts it in perspective. (Bruised Head 28 November 2001)

William Farr, who has worked extensively with the Montana Blackfeet to create a photographic history, has suggested that compiling a collection of old photographs might be analogous to designing a modern-day winter count, with photographs being 'slices of time remembered' as 'mechanical picture writing' (Farr 1984: ix). Accordingly, collections of photographs such as Blackwood's can contribute to a chronological visual history of the experiences of the Kainai Nation beginning with images such as those described above, as they emphasize the speed with which the community adapted to their changed circumstances, and their recovery from the shock of the end of the bison era. Farr has suggested that photographs have the potential to visualize something of the transformations experienced by Native peoples during this era, and can supplement oral and written histories: 'Instead of filtering out the meaningful detail, as textbook generalizations so often do, these backward glances piled one upon another, composing in the process a layered reality one could almost touch ... Stripping away the heavy curtain of years, the photographs revealed the bright and surprising different world that had been lost' (Farr 1984: xi).

Reviving

It's so important that our children and grandchildren of today and tomorrow are privy to these pictures so they have an appreciation of what our grandfathers, our grandparents went through to get us to where we are today. When we try and share it in oral stories with our children and grandchildren it doesn't have the same effect. They do not get the same kind of appreciation as when they actually see it in black and white.

Dorothy First Rider, 4 December 2001

The 'meaningful detail' within photographs indicates those aspects of Kainai culture that have altered over the years, both subtly and rather more harshly, through continued processes of transcultural exchange. Blackwood's photographs engendered narratives of change and continuity, but in addition to more abstract discussions, they also prompted commentary on how photographs can contribute to the strengthening and revival of Kainai culture in more pragmatic ways. People from all generations commented on the possibilities of using photographs to teach about traditional ways of doing things, and stated that historical images will continue to be a rich source of information for future generations of Kainai. Many younger people are seeking to learn more about their cultural heritage, and pictures from the past can be used to trace ancestors' enactments of cultural rules and activities: Kainai ways of doing things. Older people support younger people's desire to learn and encourage them to take pride in their traditions, but at the same time they are concerned that sometimes things are not always done correctly, and that traditional ways are not followed as they should be. Integrating pictures into discussions describing activities or ways of behaving or dressing can help clarify cultural concepts that are difficult to express, particularly when there are linguistic barriers:

> The pictures, they really help. Just like my kids over there, my grandkids. If I just tell them the stories, like you and I without the pictures, just talk,

talk, lot of it. If you don't see it personally, then you have to ask, 'What are you saying?' 'How do you do that?' But now you go by the pictures. Okay, I'll close this book and give you an example. One of my grandkids'll come in here and I'll tell him about it. Most of it, they're gonna lack is the word. I'll give you an example of the lady, how she sits. *Awaakiyopi* is the word for how [s]he sits. *Awaakiyopi*. Well, the kids won't know, so then you *have* to show them. (Delaney 4 December 2001)

Mr Delaney shared several other examples of how photographs depicting the way things were done in the past, recorded by Blackwood's camera, can be of use to younger generations. His comments indicated the speed at which the transitions of the early twentieth century affected the ability of Kainai people to follow their cultural traditions, and he linked his remarks with the details in the foreground of the images to indicate how some Kainai traditional ways have today become 'mixed up':

Let me check this first one again. I wish that some of these pictures were taken a little to the side so you can see the braids if you check closely to each of these guys. I'm checking on this one, on their ears. It just shows here. See? ... They covered the top. You see that? ... And today, that's another way it's changing. Today, the guys, the younger generation, the ones that got braids, they put them behind their ears. They show their ears! ... They're not following, actually how ... see, that's another example for people to know. There's quite a few people, younger people now, they want to start having braids, and that's another way of helping them. Using these pictures. That's another way. (Delaney 4 December 2001)

While some comments regarding details in the photographs related to what could be thought of as general ways of doing things according to traditional Kainai culture, other remarks were more specific, and concerned the complexities of authority and ownership rights of designs. Painted designs on tipis, for example, are sacred and are handed down through transfer ceremonies. Some designs have remained in particular families, though others have moved between different families and clans (F. Taylor 1989: 171). *Naatoisipisttohkomi* (Mary Stella Bare Shin Bone), the granddaughter of *Aatso'to'aawa* (Head Chief Shot Both Sides), recalled the tipi design that is shown in plate 20 and explained that it had since been owned by her late uncle, Head Chief Jim Shot Both Sides. She also vividly recalled the tipi liners used by her second grandmother, *Misaamahkoiyinnimaakii* (Long Time Medicine Pipe Woman), seen in plate 21, and requested a copy so that she could use the same design on her own. Through translator Andy Blackwater, and using the connection she made with the tipi liners as an example, Mrs Bare Shin Bone expressed the need for those older people who have knowledge of Kainai history and practices to share their information with the community:

> So that is an example of the importance of having these photos, having them come to our awareness. We can use some of the things that are in here. Again, in her [Mrs Bare Shin Bone's] case, it is important that the ownership of the design that she is going to put on the lining is directly linked to her ancestors. So that way she is very grateful that these are here and others will be looking at them ... She is grateful, thankful, that we'll be able to use these to help the younger people, to explain to them how things were in those days, who the people were. (M. Bare Shin Bone 13 August 2002, translated by Blackwater)

Educating

To the future generations of our children, that they may take the opportunity to read those things that we today have contributed and are put into written form, especially in reference to our children that are going through the education system today, this is all I wanted to say, based on my knowledge of my experience, and living according to what I believed in, as it pertains to the way of life of the Real People, as well as in the way that our history has been and is being handed down ... It is now up to the technicians to put [it] together in a way that is going to bring out the best there is in our statements, and then make that available to our people. I do hope that it will enhance the security of our territory, these stories, to help us to retain our culture.

Charlie Crow Chief, 1 September 2002, translated by Andy Blackwater

Blackwood's photographs have already begun to participate in informal, private, learning processes; however, the notion of the photographs contributing to visible genealogies has particular relevance for more formalized teaching within the public setting of the classroom. The participants in this project – such as Charlie Crow Chief, whose statement of consent for his words to be included in this book is quoted above – have made it very clear that they would like to see community education resources as one of the primary outcomes; much of the information that was shared in interviews was given with this intention in mind and, as we explained in the Introduction to this book, from the outset we specified that the results of the research should be used to inform a community-based outcome, the form to be determined by Kainai people. Since depositing the tapes, we have received word from educators at Red Crow Community College that the tapes (especially those in Blackfoot) are rich in details which can augment existing educational resources and are already being put to good use (Duane Mistaken Chief to Brown, pers. comm. 29 June 2003), and we hope to work with the community over the next few years to develop educational materials that will fulfil the wishes of the advisors to this project.

Many teachers working within Kainai schools already organize history projects in which their students are asked to compile family trees. These projects are an opportunity for pupils to talk about their family with older relatives in order to learn about their background and from whom they are descended. Francis (Alphonse) Whiteman Left, for example, contributed to his granddaughter's school project to record her family history, and remarked on the desire for children to have access to this information:

> It is a good idea that we preserve our statements for the younger people and future generations so that they may have an opportunity to hear and understand what we have said about our ancestors. They then would learn more about their immediate family, such as their grandparents, and know how they were raised in those days that they were among us. I hear some of our young children expressing their desire to learn more about their family lineage, and believe that this is why I realize that it is important that things are documented and recorded. (Whiteman Left 9 September 2002, translated by Blackwater)

Figure 5.1 shows Mr Whiteman Left with his granddaughter's family tree, and expresses the importance historical photographs can have in community and family education. As they studied Blackwood's photographs, many people, whether professional educators or traditional teachers, commented on how useful it would be to ask schoolchildren to work on projects that incorporated historical photographs into their genealogical research, and saw great potential for intergenerational teaching using the photographs as a focus:

> It would be nice if there's an elderly person that's related to each one of them, and give certain information regarding these, these people. And

5.1 Francis (Alphonse) Whiteman Left indicating the links between Blackwood's photographs and his grandaughter's family tree, 7 December 2001. (Photograph by Alison Brown)

they'll be talking to the students, so there'll be identities made at that point to these people. These, we're all related to these ... Identification for some students, so they could say, 'Yeah, I'm related to that person.' (B. Tallman 10 December 2001)

They should get a family tree. The kids can look at those pictures and they'll say: 'This is my relative' and they'll just know. You could put it in a book and then every once in a while they'll open the book and they'll know. (C. Goodstriker 19 November 2001).

Projects elsewhere that have brought together school and college students with historical photographs have found them to be a successful means of engaging students with their past in ways that are not possible using written texts. William Farr, for example, brought photographs of the Montana Blackfeet to the Browning High School, where students were fascinated by what they saw:

> We scattered large, 16-by-20 prints on long library tables, urged young people to thumb through print files, and copied photographs from their grandmothers' albums. Students who said that they hated written history and did not want to read books would lean over to 'read' photographs. Other students asked questions or commented on a situation that they saw in an old frame. They were intrigued and excited about what they saw, and in that excitement they seemed to find themselves standing on a Blackfeet tradition that now had gained greater meaning. (Farr 1984: xiii)

Grade 12 students at the Kainai High School expressed similar interests when Brown showed them Blackwood's images in a session arranged by *Anatsoyi'kayaakii* (Alvine Mountain Horse) to discuss anthropology and to talk about how the photographs were part of their history. Partway through the class, as the slides were being shown, one student asked to look again at one of the slides, since he had recognized one of his relatives, having seen other photographs of him at home. His classmates become noticeably more interested in the photographs and began to study them and the names closely to look and see if they too could recognize a family member. Only once this family connection had been made by one of their classmates himself, as opposed to its being pointed out by one of the adults present, did the students become interested in the project, which until that point quite possibly sounded to teenage ears as a rather dull museum exercise that had little to do with them.

Using images within formalized teaching has deeper resonance within communities where shared historical experiences have so affected the ability of later generations to take pride in their identity and to see a future for themselves. Shirley Bruised Head, who worked with schoolteachers on the *Lost Identities* project, suggested that allowing children to make connections with their ancestors and better understand their past can lead to improvements in their self-worth, and in turn, their schoolwork, giving them stronger prospects:

> We [got] an English teacher and an art teacher to work with us and the stuff they produced was just unbelievable. And it got the children thinking about where their parents came from, how their lives changed and how they can make it better. So they were starting to put their past along with their future. And just by understanding it they made a great deal of progress in their schoolwork. (Bruised Head 28 November 2001)

Classroom activities such as art and drama that allow students to utilize historical images within creative settings also allow them to learn about the past and about the underlying processes of disruption that affect their community, and there are clearly possibilities for using Blackwood's images to inspire artistic work.

The photographs are also being incorporated into teaching materials developed for post-secondary education. In 2002 Red Crow Community College joined forces with the University of Lethbridge to begin teaching a two-year diploma and post-diploma program in Kainai Studies. At present, the course includes instruction in history, art, language and literature, governance systems, and justice. Narcisse Blood, Kainai Studies Coordinator, has stated that the photographs will play a central role in discussions concerning how the Kainai have responded to the impact of colonization, and that the project itself can be used to debate Kainai interrelationships with museums. With the launch in 2003 of the *Niitsitapi* Program at the Faculty of Education, University of Lethbridge and Red Crow Community College, which offers local First Nations students a teaching degree, and research undertaken by Kainai graduate students on incorporating Blackfoot perspectives within the school curriculum, there are numerous potential uses for the images and the knowledge they evoke (Tsang 2003; Mike Bruised Head to Brown, pers. comm. 2 September 2003).

New Directions

> The ways of our people today are very different from before. Today we are more white-oriented rather than being fully *Niitsitapiiwa* [Real People]. Again, it is regrettable that those people that study history of others should [not] have been around to talk to those old teachers that knew our ways better than today. Today, it is regrettable that we have lost some of these things, and they are lost forever.
>
> Bill Heavy Runner, 13 December 2001, translated by Andy Blackwater

The issues facing the Kainai Nation regarding the preservation of their cultural heritage are similar to those facing many indigenous communities throughout the world, where the effects of colonization have resulted in discontinuities in language and cultural traditions, and elders, spiritual advisors, and educators are seeking ways to protect, preserve and pass on what they have learned from their own teachers. This has led to some innovative projects that integrate new technologies with traditional teaching methods. Web-based projects are being developed which allow community members to reinterpret museum collections and archival photographs, demonstrating the potential of these resources to acquire new meanings and play an active role in the assertion of indigenous histories. One such example is the Ara Irititja Archival Project, managed by the Pitjantjatjara Council, which records historical materials about the Anangu (Pitjantjatjara/Yankunytjatjara people) of Australia. The project has created an electronic database of archival images using culturally sensitive software and the Pitantjatjara language and can be accessed and amended by Anangu community members.[6]

In North America, too, an increasing number of projects are being developed that have resulted in CD-ROMs and websites that contain images of museum objects, scans of archival documents, photographs, and associated information and are used by communities to teach traditional manufacturing techniques or are regarded as resources for self-directed education or interest (e.g., A. Smith n.d.; Oberholtzer 2001; Howard 2002). The University of Michigan's Cultural and Heritage Preservation Institute (CHPI), for instance, has worked together with schoolchildren from the Navajo Nation, the Sault Ste Marie Tribe of Chippewa Indians, and the Bay Mills Indian Community to create educational materials about Diné and Ojibwe culture using community voices. Based on these projects, the CHPI has developed a model for digital access and preservation of culture-based knowledge. Known as the Digital Collective, this system is 'a community space where non-experts and ordinary people can enter their digital objects along with their information, stories, and experiences about their own or other objects in the collective database' (K.R. Smith 2002: 7). In a similar project, archival images from the Milwaukee Public Museum have been combined with audio recordings, contemporary images, and artwork in a digital archives project: *Maawanji'iding*, the 'gathering together' of Ojibwe voices from the six Wisconsin bands of the Lake Superior Chippewa in an interactive CD-ROM. Alexandra Smith, who has been involved in developing this long-term collaborative project, has noted that Ojibwe traditions of sharing knowledge through oral histories fit very well with the development of new media:

> Traditionally, Ojibwe people have passed on knowledge, and shared common experience, through the spoken word. Long ago the people used pictographs to record and illustrate certain events; but books were never an invention of the Anishinaabe. It makes sense that this collective knowledge of a dynamic oral tradition is an invaluable part of understanding and developing innovative new media forms. We who have become dependent on the written word often have difficulty in shaking off the metaphor of the book when we sit down to dream up new media for communicating ideas and experience. The gift of a collective memory that is stored and rejuvenated in the stories that we tell each other, offers us new ways to imagine using the tools we have access to today for passing on and sharing information. (A. Smith 1998: 112)

Such developments in technology have implications for Kainai educators, who are seeking ways to bridge the gaps in cultural knowledge and its transmission between different generations. Digital formats foster rather different sets of social interactions from those experienced when looking at photographic prints, yet, as many Kainai people have specified, if they are to successfully pass on cultural and historical knowledge to future generations, considering the possibilities of new technologies for sharing cultural information may be a necessity. Rather than being a substitute for traditional teaching methods, developing projects which combine new technologies and photographic resources with culturally appropriate forms and content may provide younger generations with the opportunity to connect with their cultural heritage in ways that make sense to them on multiple levels.

Using digital technology for teaching within the Kainai and other indigenous communities is just one part of the spectrum of creative ways in which such communities seek to transmit information about heritage to the present and future generations, in order to maintain distinctive worldviews and cultural identities. The creation of Web resources does, however, raise issues of how communities such as the Kainai create relationships with institutions which hold photographs, documents, and objects relevant to their material heritage, and how such institutions can – and need to – find ways of liaising more closely with source communities. In the next chapter, we explore the implications of the Kainai-Oxford Photographic Histories Project for institutions: issues of community access to heritage materials, of ownership and stewardship, and the difficulties of establishing cross-cultural relationships between holding institutions and indigenous source communities.

CHAPTER SIX

Moving Forward: Institutional Implications

Museums can play a vital role in First Nations' cultural renewal. Many of the objects in museum collections played an important role in maintaining connections between human beings and the rest of Creation. Other objects carry with them memories of historical events and the people who experienced those times. In some cases, these were important leaders and spokesmen; in other cases they are people's grandmothers and grandfathers. Access to these objects can help rebuild relationships which have been disrupted and restore cultural memories which may be on the brink of being forgotten.

Such access can also enhance the institution. As these cultural connections are shared with museum staff, the museum may become more aware of the significance which objects have for people and of the multi-layered meaning carried by items from non-Western cultures. Communicating these meanings to wider audiences will lead to greater cultural awareness and understanding. No museum can hope to do more than this.

Conaty and Crane Bear 1998: 73

Clearly, museum and archival collections, including historic photographs, are of potentially great importance to First Nations and other indigenous communities. That Blackwood's photographs, despite their anthropometric and colonial connotations, revivified knowledge and memory and are already playing a role in transmitting knowledge from one generation to another exemplifies the positive developments which can stem from returning images to source communities or providing special access for community members to museum collections. Such processes benefit museums and archives as much as they do source communities; indeed, Wareham (2002: 205) has described the involvement of indigenous communities in heritage institutions as revitalizing for those organizations. Museums have suffered in recent decades from harsh political critiques about their elitism, the distorted nature of their representations of non-Western peoples, and their refusal to engage with living cultures in the contemporary world. They have been accused of being irrelevant, dusty relics themselves of the colonial past – hence Annie Bare Shin Bone's response that the copies of Blackwood's photographs 'should go to the schools instead of going to the museum' (A. Bare Shin Bone 27 November 2001). At the same time, museums and other institutions with historic collections, such as archives, are being urged to provide more access to broader ranges of society, and to show their usefulness in the modern world. Outreach projects working with source communities provide a way of fulfilling all of these needs and addressing these pressures. As Conaty and Crane Bear suggest, institutions – as well as the general public – might also learn something about their collections in the process.

The previous chapters have provided many strong reasons why museums and archives might engage in outreach projects involving their collections, and thus we focus in this section on what these institutions need to do in order to meet the needs of indigenous source communities. Even with the will to work together, there are enormous challenges in doing so. Probably the most important thing to bear in mind when engaging in such work is its cross-cultural nature.[1] Museums and archives emerged out of European cultural traditions and remain cultural artefacts themselves. Many of the handling, access, copyright, and other policies in force in such institutions have everything to do with ways of thinking and notions of property which derive from Western societies and do not accord with indigenous perspectives. The formal, departmentalized, hierarchical organization of the structures of museums and archives, combined with lists of rules and arcane paraphernalia, can make these spaces intimidating or off-putting for indigenous people (and, indeed, for anyone not of the middle-class or academically inclined population which normally uses these institutions). Over the course of our careers, we have found ourselves 'interpreting' museums and archives to first-time First Nations researchers in ways that the institutions themselves must do if they are serious about providing access for such audiences: explaining how to thread a reel of microfilm onto a reader, and how to focus the machine; witnessing the problems experienced when an extended-family group, including small children, came into an archives reading room to examine records pertaining to their family (the children became a distraction for the other researchers in the room); seeing the dismay on a grandmother's face when confronted with literally hundreds of binders containing indexes, and not knowing which ones to consult in order to find records on an ancestor; explaining to descendants of an individual in Blackwood's photographs why the image is copyrighted and what that means; seeing people weep or exclaim, in the middle of a crowded reading room, on finding important material, or stifle their responses because of their discomfort at the public nature of the setting; and, seeing people, after hours spent travelling to the city to search for family records, being told that the records they wanted to see were not at this institution but in another archive/department/building, and therefore not available. To someone who may have made a decision to enter an unfamiliar and alien space for the first time, all of these situations are daunting.

Traditionally, museums and archives thought of 'their' collections as belonging to them, legally and morally, and of themselves as fulfilling a primary role of preservation. These assumptions have been challenged in many ways over the past several decades, so that complex layered concepts of multiple ownership are emerging and most heritage institutions would agree that they care for 'their' collections at least in part on behalf of the groups whose material heritage such collections comprise. There is, in other words, an acknowledgment by the heritage profession that indigenous peoples have rights in their culture and its representation, and in access to their material heritage.

Access

The corollary of the concept of stewardship is the need to provide access to collections for source community members. While increasing numbers of First Nations and other indigenous researchers are going to archives and museums, there are ways in which staff can work which increase the nature and value of access. Thinking about how one's institutional procedures, terminology, indexing and descriptive language, storage and research facilities – all often developed within the classificatory thinking of the Victorian era, with its attendant language of control, and unseen by members of the communities thus described – might be perceived by members of source communities is a good way to start: 'On the part of the holding institution it requires curatorial skills to facilitate re-engagements and repatriations through appropriate procedures and tools, from open access databases and print-out catalogues in appropriately framed language. As Smallacombe has argued, however helpful and supportive individual curators might be, the welter of finding aids and indexes, too often written in an alienating or offensive style and language, merely stresses alienation and dispossession' (Edwards 2003: 93, citing Smallacombe 1999: 3–4).

While historic terminology is part of the history of museum and archival collections and should absolutely be maintained in records, it is necessary (and possible, in many ways) to separate the language associated with material at the time of collection from the language used by the institution in the present to describe and index these collections and data. How difficult does it need to be, after all, to change a computerized database keyword of 'narcotics and intoxicants' – used by at least one British museum to classify First Nations' ceremonial pipes – to a more accurate and less offensive term?[2] Museums have much to learn from indigenous cultural centres that are developing their own terminologies for collections management and from indigenous staff who can advise on such issues. However, even when museum staff try their best to utilize terminology that is less classificatory, misunderstandings will still occur, and museums and communities need to work through these problems together. Museum culture and language by their nature are exclusive and, while indigenous people often find themselves having to work very hard to translate their cultural concepts into words that museum staff will understand in order to better appreciate why they are being asked to care for certain objects in particular ways, these processes of translation are not as yet fully two-way.

Not only are institutions sometimes distressing, but the material examined may be as well, evoking tough memories as well as the emotional greeting of deceased relatives encountered in photographs and documents. Providing a more private working area, making it possible for researchers to take breaks (difficult with some security systems – we have heard some First Nations researchers comment that trying to take a break from some archives and go outside was much like entering and exiting prison because of manual searches, the need for staff accompaniment, and multiple doors needing to be unlocked), making an extra effort to explain indexing or the context in which material was acquired, and asking for advice from the researchers about cultural sensitivities and terminology are all small things which can make a big difference to the quality of a research visit. Providing information in advance of the visit where possible, on holdings as well as practicalities such as hours of operation or local accommodation, can be extraordinarily useful and welcoming. Some staff make a point of sitting down with source community researchers on their arrival and sharing a cup of tea while getting to know one another; others deem such visits also to be semi-diplomatic in nature, and are conscious that they are opportunities to forge links with communities. In all cases, making it clear that one is willing to learn and that many observations and comments can be taken on board and acted on, and showing respect for the researcher and the special nature of the relationship between source communities and their material heritage, are tremendously important.

It is not enough, however, to work with source community researchers only on the occasions when they come to the archive; it is becoming imperative to work proactively to let source communities know where pertinent collections are. This point emerged clearly in the interview with Shirley Bruised Head, one of the team members who curated the *Lost Identities* exhibition:

> Alison Brown: ... [Do] you do have any comments or advice for why it's important that museums that have these kinds of photographs make them available to communities?
> Shirley Bruised Head: I think museums have always made them available, but people were not accessing them because they didn't feel comfortable with them, or they didn't feel comfortable with the archives. I think with *Lost Identities*, people became comfortable with the idea of going to an archive and asking to see photographs on a larger scale than previously. And I think it is also important for archives to be in contact with communities, to tell communities you know, 'We have that. How would you like to work with this particular ...' whatever it is, photograph, books, objects. 'Would you like these to come back to the community so people can see them?' I think it's very important for archives to do that. (Bruised Head 28 November 2001)

Other community members commented on the problems of accessing even the most wonderful archival collections when those exist at a distance from the community itself. The Glenbow Archives, in Calgary, has an extraordinarily good collection of photographs, including many from the Blood Reserve, and the staff are exceptionally helpful in assisting the many First Nations people who come to look at the photographic and paper archives. That said, Calgary is a drive of several hours north of the Reserve and a proper search through images of Kainai people would require several days' work:

> Glenbow is not readily available to all members of the Tribe. First of all, it's two hours north of here and then, when you do go to Calgary, unless you specifically just go there to do your research, you may not just be able to go in and go through the photographs. It would have to be a conscious decision that you do, that you make, to go look at the photographs. So, if something like this were to be available on the Reserve it would certainly be so much more helpful. (First Rider 4 December 2001)

The Glenbow has attempted to increase access to its archival collections through creating an on-line database, to which it is constantly adding.[3] This resource is invaluable to the many researchers who are also precluded from visiting the archives in person, although not all community members who would like to see these images are comfortable with the technology involved. Nor does viewing images on a computer screen provide the same kind of experience as handling photographic prints. The social activity of looking at and 'reading' photographs, and telling stories evoked by them, is best facilitated by photographic prints, as Joshua Bell learned when he brought copies of archival photographs to Koriki people of the Purari Delta of Papua New Guinea. These were 'touched, with the outline of people and objects traced by fingertips and, in more private settings, held intimately while crying' (Bell 2003: 116; and see figure 6.1). Describing the physical experiences of interacting with images, Elizabeth Edwards has remarked that they are 'very different from looking at images as slides blown up in a darkened space or clustering around a computer screen to view a CD-ROM ... Different representational forms will elicit different responses and mediate the way in which photographs participate in social relations' (Edwards 2003: 91).

Prints, then – probably best mounted in a book to keep them and their documentation together – are best for interactions with older people and with family groups, and work well in tandem with traditional forms of recounting history such as the telling of stories. Computer-based forms of access work very well, however, for some members of indigenous source communities, and provide vital information and forms of access where distance from the archive is a problem; they also lend themselves to dissemination within the community, as images can be downloaded and taken to a relative's home for a chat or into a classroom for a lesson.

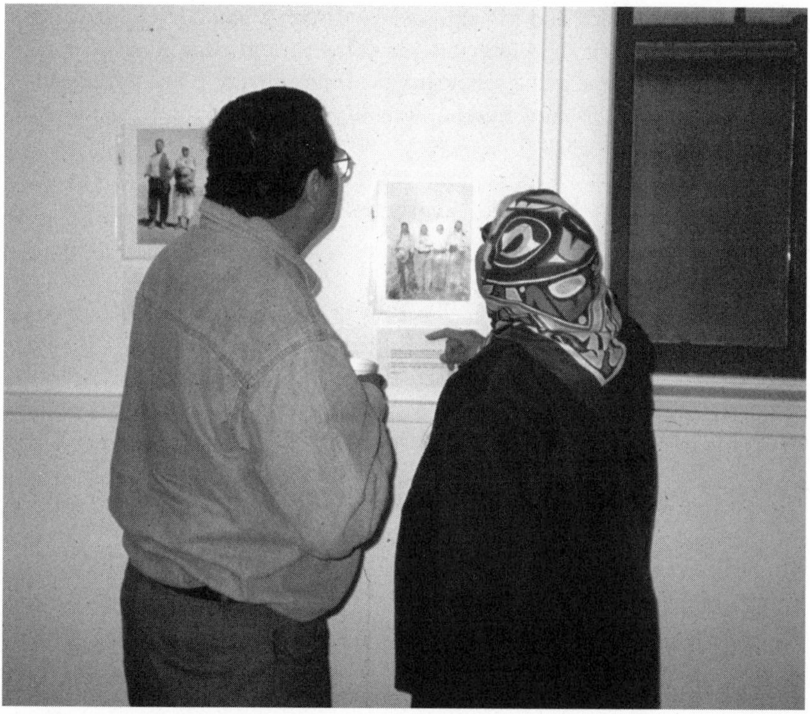

6.1 Rita Tallman and Louis Soop discussing Blackwood's photographs at Red Crow Community College, 28 May 2003. (Photograph by Alison Brown)

The importance of finding solutions to overcome physical distance has been commented on by other indigenous people. At a conference on photography in the Arctic hosted by the British Museum in 1996, George Quviq Qulaut stated:

> What I specifically have to say is the importance of the photographs and how we should be able to get them. I think one of the most important authorities, of course, our elders, are passing away very, very rapidly and every time an elder passes away part of our tradition and culture dies with us. Because of this, it is very, very important to get as many old photographs as possible. I have some friends in Rankin Inlet who actually xeroxed images and sent them through faxes to be identified. That work was very, very important because no matter how poor it was, some of these elders were able to identify some of these photographs and then we

> would relay it back and say this is the person, is so and so, thanks to modern technology. Once they are identified we can appreciate whether we should have the actual photographs, better quality photographs, for exhibiting in schools and, most importantly, in cultural centres. (quoted in King and Lidchi 1998: 240)

Likewise, Henrietta Fourmile, an Australian Aboriginal researcher, has stated with considerable feeling:

> What use is it to me to have my Yidindji and Kunggandji heritage ... invaluable cultural resources such as family histories, photographs, language tapes and mission records down south [of Australia]? I didn't even know these things ever existed until I was thirty years of age. (Fourmile 1990: 59, cited in Edwards 2003)

While distance clearly exacerbates the problem, the issues run much deeper. If you are a Kainai person, living on the Blood Reserve in southern Alberta, how would you know that photographs from your family existed at the University of Oxford in England? How many collections from indigenous source communities exist worldwide, without any knowledge of their existence in the source communities? Access begins, then, by actually telling community members that material exists, and institutions need to become far more proactive about doing so. While the creation of on-line databases is an important first step, again, unless the communities concerned are made aware of the launching of such databases, how would they know to look for them? Many indigenous communities have members who are recognized or officially appointed as the people concerned with heritage and historical research; some have cultural centres; most have official bureaucratic structures that can be worked through to find these people (some, in fact, are publicly listed, such as the NAGPRA Tribal representatives in the United States). As well, most museums and archives have professional colleagues and counterparts living nearer to the communities involved who could assist in making contact – in our case, colleagues at Glenbow were extremely generous in facilitating contacts with Kainai people in the lead-up to this project. If access is a priority in the heritage profession, then institutions cannot make the excuse that they did not know whom to contact. If museums and archives truly wish to be accessible, they will be able to find those contacts. Most of them have never tried. We argue that material such as historic photographs is so important to indigenous communities that it is time they did.

As Dorothy First Rider suggested, however, access to heritage materials needs also to happen in the community, not just in the archive. This is not simply a matter of convenience, but of indigenous intellectual and cultural access. Photographs and other 'flat' artefacts such as documents, and also artworks which can readily be reproduced or copied, are in many ways perfect vehicles for providing community access, as Martin Heavy Head suggested in his interview. It is relatively inexpensive to create a duplicate set of prints and to send them, with attendant documentation and institutional information, to a repository within a source community. Museums and archives considering sending copies of images in their collections for community use must also work with the communities concerned to identify the most suitable location for these. In our case, Red Crow Community College was identified by community members as being the most appropriate repository at this time, as the facility is readily accessible to community members, and has library staff who can care for the images. A number of other communities keep archival holdings in the Band Office, or are developing cultural centres with environmentally and physically secure areas for storing and displaying archival documents and other objects. However, the principle of access remains a priority. Phillipa Ootoowak, a participant in the British Museum's *Imaging the Arctic* conference, has observed that the steps taken by communities and museums to return copies of images (in this case to Arctic communities) are extremely encouraging, but not without difficulties:

> First, a suitably secure location is required to store these photographs (preferably humidity-controlled) and this includes responsible staffing of such a facility. Few northern communities have access to this kind of space. Second, in order to make the photographic collections accessible to the public they should be catalogued, identified, labelled and displayed in a suitable manner. This requires trained personnel, time and funding, all of which are scarce commodities in the north today. A collection of photographs stored in boxes on some shelf, however valuable, is no more accessible to the public locally than if stored in a southern institution. (Ootoowak, quoted in King and Lidchi 1998: 231)

Copies and Copyright

Inevitably, having provided copies of images, one is faced with enthusiastic responses from community members as they recognize ancestors – and immediate requests for personal copies of particular images. These are marvellous opportunities to release museum- or archive-based photographs into a wider realm in which they have deep meanings and will be treasured, and offers to institutions an especially gratifying sense of having provided real access to collections. It does, however, raise issues of budget and copyright which need to be addressed.

Different projects have handled these issues differently, and there is no single correct solution. For the *Lost Identities* exhibition, five extra prints were made of each image in the exhibition. These copies were left in the keeping of staff in attendance at each of the exhibition's venues, who were able to hand one immediately to the first people who made a request for a personal copy. As Shirley Bruised Head commented, this was part of the exhibition's success, a way of acknowledging the right of community members to have portraits of ancestors:

> ... we had them on hand. If people asked for them we were able to give it to them. And so that meant much more too, to the person. But going back to the caring and the way the exhibit was set up, we had them on hand so that people could have them and it was an immediate response to the community. (Bruised Head 28 November 2001)

In the case of the Kainai-Oxford Photographic Histories Project, significant funding from the Arts and Humanities Research Board enabled us to offer personal copies of images to family members for their own use on request (in addition to the set of prints and the CD-ROMs which were presented to the community). On one occasion, we were asked to modify image BB.A3.77 (plate 29) by isolating from the rest of the group one of the five schoolgirls portrayed for framing purposes. While altering images in this way raises legitimate issues concerning integrity and authenticity of the use of photographs among historians, it is also true that one equally legitimate value of historic photographs is as portraits of ancestors. Digital technology allows for requests for copies of images or parts of images for family use to be fulfilled without harming the integrity of the original, and, in this instance, made an elderly woman very happy: we felt that the benefits of providing this form of access outweighed the ethical arguments that heritage professionals might make about the dangers of digitally altering images. We should note that since the CD-ROM version of the photographs entered the Kainai community, community members now have the opportunity to make prints – and alter them, should they choose – for their own purposes as well.

In accordance with Pitt Rivers Museum policy, all photographs provided for research use are issued with stickers on the reverse giving accession numbers and copyright information. The latter is usually phrased in terms of ownership and reproduction rights; for example, 'Copyright Pitt Rivers Museum. Written permission to reproduce must be sought.' As we wished to make it clear to community members that they were free to use the images as they liked for their own purposes, and had anticipated that Kainai people might be critical of the Museum's policy, we discussed the matter with the Museum's Marketing Manager, Kate White, who handles copyright issues for the institution, and with Elizabeth Edwards, Curator of Manuscripts and Photographs, prior to the first field trip. They agreed that we should modify the usual wording on these statements, highlighting on the first line of the sticker that the images were provided 'for private research use of the Blood Tribe,' followed by the copyright information in smaller print. Even with these changes, Kainai people commented on the wording and its implications – that the Museum owns and controls the photographs of Kainai ancestors – in our very first meeting with the Mookaakin Foundation. In the subsequent discussions we noted that we were providing the images for community use, but that we wished the Museum to be informed if any were published. We stressed that no publication charges would be made, that the Museum simply wanted to keep track of how the images were used in formal contexts and would like a copy of any publication which included any of the images for its library. Any future plans the Tribe may develop to reproduce the images using digital formats will have to be negotiated with the Museum; however, we are confident that should such uses be suggested, we will be able to reach mutually acceptable solutions that encompass Kainai needs as well as the Museum's legal obligations under English copyright law. This pragmatic stance acknowledges that once images begin to circulate in the community it is very difficult to control use, and by letting go of control to an extent, the Museum has gained a great deal of good will – as well as achieving goals (commonly emphasized by museum funding bodies) of making part of its collections far more accessible to non-traditional museum audiences.

Policy and Praxis

Providing access for the Kainai to the Blackwood photographs in this project thus involved challenges to the Museum's policy on copyright and reproduction fees; similar projects may provide much more comprehensive challenges to procedures and policies at institutions less accustomed to working with indigenous peoples. This brings us back to the beginning of this section, in which we discussed the sometimes formidable and off-putting nature of elements of heritage institutions. What, then, are the broad curatorial and administrative processes (Edwards 2003) which can make museums and archives more open to source communities? It is, in this context, crucial to find and train staff who are interested in and willing to provide access to source communities in various ways. Institutions which are committed to creating access and working in new ways need to support their staff in doing so, by providing access to training, grants for funding travel and materials, and administrative assistance. This can be significant: the Kainai-Oxford Photographic Histories Project was funded by the Arts and Humanities Research Board for £78,000 over seventeen months. Furthermore, there are constant reminders even within institutional aspects of such projects that this is cross-cultural work: we had, for instance, large budget categories for meals and gifts to project participants, which together with payment of honoraria and travel costs are considered the culturally appropriate and respectful way to reimburse Kainai people for their significant knowledge contributions in interviews and meetings. Such costs would be open to misinterpretation by less cross-culturally aware funding bodies and administrators, but without funds for such purposes we simply could not have conducted the project.

At a broader level, institutions need to proactively develop policies which support access for source community members. Most museums have policies on collections management, access, research, and other relevant activities, and these should be reviewed specifically with an eye towards opening the institution to source community audiences. Some policies regarding access for source communities are available on-line, acting as useful models for museums wishing to develop similar documents as well as giving an overview of changing practice. These are mentioned in the text in this section, and the relevant websites are provided in table 6.1.

A number of codes of ethics for museum professionals as well as for anthropologists and social scientists now recognize the right of indigenous peoples to have access to and control over their material heritage, and the need for holding institutions to respond to source community needs for access. The UK Museums Association, for in-

Table 6.1 Ethical policies available on the internet, October 2004

Canada

Royal Ontario Museum, Toronto, Canada:
Policy on Repatriation of Canadian Aboriginal Objects http://www.rom.on.ca/about/policy/docs/caorepatriationrev.pdf

Ethical Guidelines
http://www.museums.ca/Cma1/About/CMA/ethics/introduction.htm

Royal British Columbia Museum
Aboriginal Material Operating Policy
http://www.royalbcmuseum.bc.ca/corporateservices/collectionspolicy.html

Royal Saskatchewan Museum
http://www.saskmuseums.org/about_us/first_people.php

University of British Columbia Museum of Anthropology
Management of Sensitive Materials Policy and Repatriation Guidelines:
http://www.moa.ubc.ca/collections/index.php

New Zealand

Auckland War Memorial Museum
http://www.akmuseum.org.nz/?t=288
Guiding Principles for the Trust Board's Relationship with the Taumata-a-Iwi

Australia

Museums Australia
Continuing Cultures Ongoing Responsibilities Draft Policy Statement
http://www.museumsaustralia.org.au/structure/policies/ppno/ccor.htm

United Kingdom

UK Museums Association
Ethical Guidelines
http://www.museumsassociation.org

Marischal Museum, University of Aberdeen
Collection Policy – Appendix 3: Policy toward sacred objects and human remains
Collection Policy – Appendix 4: Responding to requests for the return of items in the museum collection: a procedure
http://www.abdn.ac.uk/diss/historic/museum/information/collectingpolicy.hti

Museum Ethnographers Group
Guidance Notes on Ethical Approaches in Museum Ethnography
http://www.museumethnographersgroup.org.uk/ethglines.htm

stance, has recently written a code of ethics which states that museums will:

> Establish principles that assist people who contributed to collections to develop mutually agreed arrangements with the museum, wherever practical ... Inform originating communities of the presence of items relevant to them in the museum's collections, wherever practical ... Involve originating communities, wherever practical, in decisions about how the museum stores, researches, presents or otherwise uses collections and information about them.

Some repatriation policies also stress access. The Royal Ontario Museum's policy on the repatriation of Canadian Aboriginal artefacts states:

> The ROM recognizes the uniqueness and distinctiveness of the cultures of the aboriginal peoples of Canada, and is committed to working with them with a view to the survival of their cultures. Where objects in the possession of the ROM may assist in advancing or preserving the culture of a Canadian aboriginal people, the ROM will endeavour to provide full access to those objects to them.

National and regional museums associations have also developed policies regarding indigenous peoples. A very good one available on the Web is the Museums Australia draft document, *Continuing Cultures, Ongoing Responsibilities* (an updated response to *Previous Possessions New Obligations* [Museums Australia 1996]), Museums Australia's policy statement on Aboriginal and Torres Strait Islander collections. This includes the assertions that:

> 5. Aboriginal and Torres Strait Islander people must be given the opportunity to be involved in decisions affecting how museums store, conserve, research, display or in any other way use collections of their cultural heritage and how such collections and information are presented, whether for exhibition, publication or educational purposes.
> 6. The stories and information associated with Aboriginal and Torres Strait Islander cultural materials are of equal importance to the actual materials and must be treated with equal respect.
> 7. Aboriginal and Torres Strait Islander communities have a right to know what Australian Indigenous items are held in museum collections.

Some museums and museum associations have formed new committees to work through difficulties of access and relationships between indigenous peoples and museums, and to propose new ways of working. The Museums Association of Saskatchewan has posted information on its *First Peoples and Saskatchewan Museums Committee* on the Web, which may be useful as a model for other such working groups. A few excellent institutional policies are available on-line, such as the Royal British Columbia Museum's 'Aboriginal Material Operating Policy,' which states:

> The Museum acknowledges that all Aboriginal materials, including human remains, burial objects, ceremonial objects, communally-owned property, as well as archival records, tapes, films, photographs, and research information is part of the intellectual and cultural heritage of the respective Aboriginal peoples.

Elsewhere, particular institutional policies may not be available on the Web, but are referenced in the literature and are clearly developing across the museum profession. Stanton (2003: 139–40) has discussed how the interests of Aboriginal communities have been embedded in the policies of the Berndt Museum of the University of Western Australia. Bernstein (1992: 2) has described the strategy adopted at the Museum of New Mexico, where photographs are specifically identified in the Museum's Policy on Sensitive Cultural Materials. Museums worldwide are clearly becoming more proactive in writing policies and creating working groups to tackle the co-management of collections and to respond to issues such as repatriation. In addition, a number of indigenous organizations have been created to work within this area and, as well as providing support and training for indigenous curatorial staff, may be contacted by museums seeking guidance in matters of collections care. In North America, examples include the American Indian Museum Association (Lomawaima 1998), the Cahuilla Inter-tribal Repatriation Committee (http://www.cahuillarepatriation.org/citrc.htm), whose detailed website outlines the processes through which the CITRC works, and, of course, the Mookaakin Cultural and Heritage Foundation.

Many museums in North America and the Pacific have taken such approaches further and created boards of indigenous advisors which act as part of their governance structure, reviewing and making recommendations for policies. They also liaise with their respective communities, facilitating communication and thus access. Where the institution exists, as in the UK and Europe, at great physical distance from most indigenous communities, protocol agreements with individual communities, such as that between the Pitt Rivers Museum and the Mookaakin Foundation (see appendix 3), begin to create a climate of institutional change and responsibility to these audiences.

Such new policies are not easily implemented either in letter or in spirit, even where staff are willing. They are truly challenging to culturally based and historically entrenched ways of thinking within archives and museums, and they will continue to generate changes and challenges. Arguments are continuing in many repositories over the extent to which source communities may request that sensitive images be withheld from viewers of certain categories (non-initiated, non-Native, or women, for example, who according to cultural protocols should not view certain elements of some indigenous cultures); over demands to repatriate originals of photographs and documents, in some cases for destruction by community members; and over who should fund elements of access, the community or the institution (on these issues see Powers 1996; Kreps 2003, and specifically relating to photography, Peterson 2003, Holman 1996). Such situations challenge the very nature and being of museums and archives, as well as commonly held Western beliefs about the freedom of speech and research. In response to such protests, Edwards cites Byrne's discussion of Aboriginal and Torres Strait Islander protocols for libraries: 'Appropriate handling does not mean censorship. It means sensitivity to the contexts in which information agencies operate, the scope of their services and the nature of the communities they serve' (Edwards 2003: 95; see also Byrne 1995). Very often, sensible solutions can be worked out;[4] in any case, staff should be willing to engage in honest dialogue and to consider the cross-cultural nature of their work, and the potential benefits of different forms of access to different audiences.

Funding Bodies: Ethics and Tensions

Tensions between old and new ways of working can surface in the most elementary aspects of research projects, and some of these emerged in our relations with the funding body for our research, the Arts and Humanities Research Board (AHRB) of the United Kingdom. Like other scholarly funding agencies, the AHRB supports first-rate academic research (the definition of which is not always seen as compatible with emerging methodologies), good value of research and use of funds, and making the results of research available to other scholars. We emphasize that the AHRB was very supportive of the project, which it funded quite generously. We do not in any way wish to minimize our appreciation for their support, but seek here to describe ways in which the community-based nature of the project did not fit the perspectives and intentions of the AHRB, and the kinds of problems which might well befall other researchers taking a similar collaborative approach to research.

From the very beginning of the project, we were aware that there were ethical issues about our research that Kainai people were likely to be sensitive to, particularly issues of control over research data. In recent years many indigenous peoples have explored elements of intellectual property rights (IPR) and related trademarking and protective legislation in an attempt to prevent the exploitation of cultural knowledge for commercial gain by outsiders.[5] Other indigenous groups, including the Kainai, are increasingly seeking to restrict research concerning cultural knowledge to projects which will benefit their communities rather than just outsiders. Knowing this, we were alarmed to discover that most funding bodies in the United Kingdom expect all digital outputs from research projects they support to be made available on the World Wide Web. The AHRB grant information available to us in 2000 as we were writing the proposal states that 'it is a condition of award that significant electronic resources should be offered for deposit with the AHDS (Arts and Humanities Data Service)' (http://www.ahrb.ac.uk/research/grant/electronic.htm, accessed 13 November 2000).[6] Similarly, the UK Economic and Social Research Council 'requires all award-holders to offer for deposit copies of both machine-readable and non-machine-readable qualitative data to [a particular data archiving and dissemination organization] ... within three months of the end of the award' (http://www.esrc.ac.uk/esrccontent/researchfunding/sec17.asp). We therefore made a decision as we were writing the grant application that we simply would not – in fact, ethically could not – include any digital output to the project. Given the extent to which our relations with Kainai people have rested on our willingness to ensure that information is treated appropriately in Kainai terms (including the restriction of some interview material to its original Blackfoot so that it is available to community members only), and that Kainai themselves be involved in determining the outcome of research data, the project would simply not have proceeded if we had insisted from the beginning that we had to make all information available on the Web to meet the expectations of our funding body.

Equally difficult was the need to try and meet the expectations of our Kainai advisors, who set up the collaborative framework in which the project thrived, and those of the AHRB regarding the project schedule. This became a problem when on our planned, second visit to the Blood Reserve, we presented the draft outline for this book to members of the Mookaakin Foundation and to the Red Crow Community College Elders Advisory Committee. Both groups warmly endorsed our ideas and made useful suggestions but also made it clear that they wanted to see how those ideas developed in the manuscript. They asked us to make a third visit to go through the draft manuscript with them. We felt that, having worked in a collaborative manner to that point and painstakingly reviewed transcripts to ensure that community members had control over the data and its disposition, we could not suddenly refuse to allow community members to approve the manuscript. However, we had not anticipated this third trip, and it was not in the project outline or budget to which the AHRB had agreed; the AHRB expected the project to end by a much earlier date and all funds to be expended by that time. Since we had managed to economize enough to have a budget surplus, we reasoned that it would cost the AHRB nothing to allow us to fulfil Kainai expectations, and expected that the request would be granted readily. When we approached the AHRB and asked for an extension on the grant until we were able to take the manuscript back, and for permission to use the budget surplus for the purpose of this third trip, they were naturally concerned that we might be trying to change the nature of the project mid-stream. Their letter of response asked us to clarify how this third trip to the Reserve would enable us 'to achieve the aims and objectives outlined in your original application, and how they will be of value to the outcomes of the project' (John Edwards, Senior Awards Officer, AHRB, to Peers, pers. comm. 11 November 2002). We replied that without this trip there would not *be* a project outcome, since without community approval we would not feel able to publish. Fortunately, the AHRB approved our request, but we should note that even had they not done so, we would have found the funds to make the third visit.

We emphasize that while most research funding bodies have very similar expectations and perspectives, they may be flexible enough to accept changes to project timetables and plans as research develops. In our case we have found the AHRB staff courteous and helpful, and all of the issues discussed above were settled to our mutual satisfaction.

We recount these differences to raise broader cross-cultural issues which funding bodies and researchers need to consider: who should set research and funding agendas where indigenous source communities are concerned? How do funding bodies need to adjust to deal with the ethical and practical concerns of such communities involved in research projects? How can funding bodies, like museums and archives, work in ways which better facilitate cross-cultural communication and the kinds of reinterpretations of historic materials used in this project, which benefit both source communities and mainstream institutions? The often problematic dynamics and politics of research funding – of whose agendas and research questions are deemed better than others, of who is deemed a bona fide researcher and who isn't – were noted by Dr Betty Bastien, a Piikani scholar resident on the Blood Reserve:

> Betty Bastien: I wonder if she [Blackwood] went to Peigan.
> Alison Brown: No. She went to T'suu Tina; she was over in BC; she was in Manitoba; she was up at Norway House ...
> Betty Bastien: Do you think she got a grant?
> Alison Brown: She did, yes. She got Rockefeller funding for three years.
> Betty Bastien: I raise my eyebrows! I guess, I'll just say this – that's what happened, and continues to happen, is that foundations will fund, I guess, scientists from various disciplines to come and study ... us [and they] will give them the resources. But we can't access any of those resources to do our own research from our own worldview and in our ways of knowing.
> Alison Brown: Yes.
> Betty Bastien: And this was an expensive project. I don't know how expensive these trips were, but there must have been a lot of resources for this type of research, and for the most part, they sat in this museum for a long time. One begins to question who benefits from this type of research.
> Alison Brown: Yes. There's something wrong there, isn't there?
> (Bastien 27 November 2001)

It is important that Western institutions think about such issues, and about the implications of not dealing with them. As Banta stated in one of the first critical analyses of historic anthropological photographs: 'Armed with the camera, anthropologists can probe, scan, magnify, reduce, isolate, contrast, debase, or idealize their subjects. Through photography, they can create, disseminate, and forever seal in time their own interpretation of humankind' (Banta and Hinsley 1986: 23). Cecil King, an Odawa, objects just as forcefully from a tribal perspective to the traditional means and relations of academic research:

> We have been observed, noted, taped, and videoed. Our behaviors have been recorded in every possible way known to Western science, and I suppose we could learn to live with this if we had not become imprisoned in your words ... Our original words are obscured by the layers upon layers of others' words laid on top of them ... We want to come back to our own words, our own meanings, our own definitions of ourselves ... When will you become instrumental to our ambitions, our categories of importance? (C. King 1997: 9–10)

As this project has shown very clearly, research and research institutions can also revitalize, recover, and revivify. Policies and procedures, the daily operational processes of heritage institutions, can be barriers to indigenous source communities and their goals – or they can be bridges, helping to meet community needs. We have found in the course of this project that real determination, as well as good will, flexibility, and mutual respect, are required to understand how institutional processes and assumptions can be problematic in cross-cultural research situations, and how such problems can be overcome. This is difficult work; it goes against the grain of many institutions. It is also absolutely necessary work, both for the health of the institution and for that of source communities.

Conclusions

Now, if we can convince you that we can do a lot more to reach some better understanding than in the past, that we're not just relics, you know, for somebody else's benefit to earn a degree, or write about, or so forth.

Narcisse Blood, 6 December 2001

Even though we are scholars with prior experience of working with First Nations people, with some understanding of cultural protocol and community needs, and working from an institution which supported us in this cross-cultural work, the lessons we have learned while working with the Kainai community have been extensive and transformative. Some of our experiences have been mirrored within similar collaborative projects conducted in other parts of the world. Penny Taylor, for instance, has observed that a photographic project she was involved in concerning the contemporary lives of Aboriginal Australians during the bicentennial commemoration in 1988 was 'the product of collaboration, but also of struggle, tension, anxiety and self-doubt as the people on both sides of the camera sought to define a better way of making pictures. The aim [was] not to obscure the complexities and contradictions of that exercise, but rather to hold it up for view and examination as an essential aspect of the images themselves' (P. Taylor 1988: xvi).[1] We reflect on some of these lessons here, and hold some of the dynamics of the project up for view, in the hope that they may benefit other researchers contemplating similar work.

Narcisse Blood's comment, quoted above, was made in the context of a discussion about the collaborative nature of the Kainai-Oxford Photographic Histories Project and the effects we have all hoped this would achieve in teaching non-Native heritage professionals about the importance of working with source communities in culturally appropriate ways. It also begins to articulate the assertive mood within First Nations communities today about the forms of access they wish to have to material heritage and the control they are seeking to create over representations of their cultures and histories. In essence, many First Nations and other indigenous community members, disgusted with the distorted and partial nature of outsiders' representations of their lives and with the lack of regard for community views and needs, have begun to restrict their participation in research projects. If we wished to engage in research with Kainai people, at this historical moment, we felt that we could work no other way, and certainly some community members proved reluctant to meet with us until we signalled strongly that we were willing to work on their terms, in ways that they considered appropriate, and towards their goals. We were perfectly happy with this; it offered a way of demonstrating our respect for community members, which we wished to express. We also accept the longer-term framework of the relationships we have developed, which we very much hope and expect will last for decades to come. However, Blood's statement that 'we're not just relics, you know, for somebody else's benefit to earn a degree, or write about,' needs to be considered very carefully by potential researchers: these communities do not exist solely for the benefit of scholarly research, and projects undertaken by museums and archives with source communities need to be more than just attempts to satisfy ideas of political correctness. Research and visual repatriation need to be done in ways which satisfy community expectations and needs, and institutions need to be willing to take the larger risk, not just of making materials available for local use, but of engaging in relationships of respect and equality with these communities.

While we were strongly urged to follow a model of collaboration and co-management for this project, we emphasize that this process has never compromised our intellectual scope or freedom. We feel strongly that there is room within academia for projects such as this in which goals for both sides are negotiated and both parties collaborate and support each other, and indeed other scholars have worked in this way and continue to do so (see, for instance, Cruikshank 1998; Warry 1998; Jaarsma 2002; there are many others who could be cited). As we developed a working relationship based on trust and respect with the Mookaakin Foundation, with the Elders Advisory Committee at Red Crow Community College, and with community members more broadly, we realized that working within a collaborative framework was opening doors and ideas to us that would not otherwise have been made available: this process was stimulating, rather than hindering, our thinking. Community members made it clear that they wished us to keep our promises to send back tapes and transcripts – a very real concern voiced by Rosie Red Crow when Brown interviewed her for the first time:

> Alison Brown: That was part of our agreement, that everybody who is interviewed will have their own copy of the tape. And the pictures, if there are any of the pictures you would like a copy of ...
> Rosie Red Crow: You go right back to England? And you said you're going to have each one of those you talk to, and if you're not sending them, we don't know where to phone you or where to get you.
> Alison Brown: That's right. I promise I will send them. And Andy [Blackwater] knows how to get hold of me. He has my address. I promise I will send them.
> Rosie Red Crow: But you have to give me your address and phone.
> Alison Brown: I'll do that right now. (Red Crow 21 November 2001)

They also made it clear that we were to ask permission to quote in publications, and to give them the chance to review article texts and provide input into the manuscript for this book, and we have found that scrupulously going through this process has never led to a single request from a community member to change our thinking. It has, however, strengthened the relationship of trust between us, and at subsequent meetings and junctures people have made suggestions and corrected mistakes, and have volunteered additional stories and thoughts, but we have never felt stifled or controlled in what we thought or said. Working directly with the Kainai community has encouraged us to modify our research methodologies to fit with cultural protocols, timescales, priorities, and needs; however, we have also altered how we undertake our writing practices and interact with the academic community, to build in sufficient time in the planning of conference papers, journal articles, etc. based on this project for community advisors to read and comment on drafts. Though our working schedules have shifted somewhat to accommodate this requirement, it is a real pleasure to feel that we are working in a team, that our words will in fact be read carefully by people who are deeply interested, and that we will be offered guidance if mistakes are made.

This collaborative framework has also been built on the assumption that the relationships being forged would be long-term, would outlast the initial research project, and would encompass the Kainai Nation and the Pitt Rivers Museum broadly – not just those involved in the initial research. Working within this understanding has added a much-needed perspective on what have been intense and all too short research visits: that every part of the process contributes towards long-term relations, that we will see each other again, that there are other ways in which we can assist each other to realize goals, and that we are willing to do so. Review of the manuscript for this volume by the Mookaakin Foundation and other community members and their deep interest in the publication process have also helped to bridge stages of the project and ensure that our relationship continues. We do not know yet what form our continued involvement with the community educational phase of the project will be, but have made it clear that we hope to participate as it is deemed appropriate and that we are most willing to support community goals. In the meantime, Brown has been involved in several visits which Kainai people have made in the past two years to the United Kingdom in connection with museum business during which progress on this project was also discussed, and Peers has hosted a visit (in February 2004) by Frank Weasel Head and Andy Blackwater to Oxford so that they could see the Pitt Rivers Museum, view other collections there, and meet staff.

The most crucial element in the research process has been frequent and ongoing consultation, with the concomitant willingness to amend research goals and take guidance on board. The lesson that consultation does not form a single stage in a research project, but is a constant process which extends even after the project comes to an end, is one that has been learned in the creation of exhibitions and other museum projects involving various audiences and source communities (see essays in Peers and Brown 2003; P. Taylor 1988: xviii). There are very real challenges in maintaining mutually beneficial links after the conclusion of a project, and ensuring that communities who take ownership of museum projects do not feel sidelined at the conclusion of a specific project phase, but continue to participate in decisions affecting their material heritage. Accordingly, though individuals involved in museums and research projects frequently sustain deep friendships and partnerships with community members as projects develop, it is more difficult to ensure institutional commitment in the long term. In our case, it is intended that the agreement between the Pitt Rivers Museum and the Mookaakin Foundation will sustain a long relationship; however, the fact remains that both the community and the Museum will need to work to ensure that this does, in fact, occur.

Additionally, consultation does not provide easy answers for the difficulties posed by working with diverse and complex communities, but it does offer ways of acknowledging and dealing with such differences, and is a starting point from which to reverse the tradition of 'hit and run' research, which First Nations people have accused museums and anthropologists of practising in the past (see Lorne Carrier, quoted in Brown 2000: 210). The need to consult widely was remarked upon by *Piitaikiihtsipiimi* (Louis Soop), who was concerned that inaccurate statements are sometimes recorded by researchers who do not verify the information they receive and thereby prevent the diversities of community views from being presented, as well as perhaps recording misinformation:

> A lot of times researchers come through the reservations throughout the United States and though the reserves in Canada. They asked a limited number of people and somebody could give the wrong information, so it's not good. It is important that a number of people are consulted. (Soop 30 November 2001)

Consulting widely allows for a fuller range of community perspectives to emerge and for the complexities and diversities of viewpoints to be highlighted. Taylor's discussion of the lessons learned during the photography project she was involved with resonates with our own experiences of working with the Kainai: 'We expected to find differences of opinion, and tried to ensure that during consultation we did not omit any particular view. In this we were assisted by community members who readily acknowledged such differences as being an integral part of life and did not see it as compromising overall cohesion. We tried to ensure that the Project would benefit the communities rather than provide a vehicle for exacerbating differences that might exist' (P. Taylor 1988: xvii). As Francis (Alphonse) Whiteman Left noted in his statement of consent, 'The ancestors and those members of our clans down to our parents, there are a lot of variations among us because of the clan structure, the family structure; we kind of come from different directions' (Whiteman Left 9 September 2002, translated by Blackwater).

That we do come from such 'different directions' was often evident in the cross-cultural nature of the project itself. One set of differences and difficulties that emerged during the project, which we did not entirely anticipate, was that we constantly felt that we were translating between Kainai people, each other, our own institution, and our funding body, all of whom had different perspectives and expectations of the research project. This is, it must be said, a common problem in cross-cultural projects involving universities, museums, funding bodies, and indigenous peoples: usually each party has a very different reason and set of goals for the project. Thus, while the Kainai wished us to work towards Kainai community goals, the project was seen by Pitt Rivers Museum staff and the wider university community as fulfilling the institutional goal of increasing access to collections and working sensitively with indigenous source communities, and has often been cited as such in Museum displays, meetings with funding bodies and scholarly groups, lectures and seminars to our own and other graduate students, and publications about the Museum. To its home institution, the project is a solid example of the way in which the Pitt Rivers Museum, with its deliberately retained Victorian mode of display, is the essence of postcolonial, up-to-the-minute museum strategies.

In other ways, the project complements much existing work done by colleagues at the Pitt Rivers Museum over the past decade, in particular the approach by Elizabeth Edwards, Curator of Manuscripts and Photographs, whose work has also shown that providing access to historic resources and incorporating culturally appropriate methodology and community goals produces very positive results for museums and archives, researchers, and source communities: 'Meanings [of photographs] are made through dynamic relations between photographs and culture that do not stop at the door of the archive. To be able to argue such a position is a measure of the opening of "The Archive" itself as a cultural object, with its own social biography ... In this context, photographs are about empowerment, repossession and a different and, perhaps, contesting articulation of history' (Edwards 2001: 12).

By allowing Kainai meanings to emerge around these images, Kainai voices to speak about them, Kainai uses for them within the community, we hope we have also found a way to address those intersecting, and conflicting, pasts.

The considerable agency involved in the reinterpretation and indigenous critique of historic photographs is tremendously empowering for First Nations and other source communities. The multiple sets of meanings that photographs carry and their dual nature as visual evidence of local history and as evidence of cross-cultural interaction, encourage such shifts and redefinitions. In bringing together multiple histories – of the photographer, of anthropology, of the people photographed, of the encounter between colonizers and colonized – photographs such as Beatrice Blackwood's offer, as well, ways to begin reconciling those histories by recognizing their separate but intersecting natures and their effects on source communities in the present.

In exchange for our gifts of the images to the Kainai, we have found that they have given us these new understandings in return. In sharing knowledge, we have all benefited. We hope that this project encourages other researchers, other institutions, and other communities to embark on similar endeavours.

Statement of Consent

All Kainai people interviewed for this project have given consent for the use of their material in this book and in future educational projects developed by the Blood Tribe. We have chosen to end this book with the statement of consent provided by Mary Stella Bare Shin Bone, whose comments on the value of preserving and sharing historical knowledge have much to teach us all.

***Naatoisipisttohkomi* Mary Stella Bare Shin Bone**

Statement of Consent Following Interview, 14 August 2002
Translated by Andy Blackwater, 14 August 2002

I am going to speak in my language to whomever will have the opportunity to hear my words. The way I look at these things [the photographs], my views are limited because I did not have personal contact; I am making reference to these photographs that were brought to us. The people in the photographs that I looked at are way before my time, therefore I did not recognize many of them. But I believe it is important to look at pictures of those times as this allows us to see the way of life at that time, so that we don't lose the awareness [of our history].

The way I see things this is going to help us preserve our knowledge of our people in the past. I believe that it is extremely fortunate that they brought these photographs to us to help us recall that part of our history. In a lot of cases, what we cannot recall about us we tend to rely on the white man's version of us [written versions]. I, for myself, do not rely on or have the white man's perception. I strongly rely on our own perception in respect to our view of way of life. It is good and important that these things [the photographs] will assist us in remembering our way of life.

Because of these things that I'm referring to has encouraged me to share my knowledge of our ways so I can continue to teach the ways of our people today (and in the past), to my children and grandchildren. Also, the younger generation of Kainai, to assist them in knowing their own history. Today we have lost a great deal of our ways; it is important that this project takes place so that it may help our people, especially the young, to recall more of our history. For that reason, that I believe that this is a good thing for us, I am sharing. If I thought and believed that it is not to the benefit of our people, then I will not share my knowledge.

I am now giving permission that my statements be used in the way that has been asked of me.

Appendix One: Itinerary of Beatrice Blackwood's North American Fieldwork, 1924–7

Compiled from Blackwood Diary 1924–7

1924

September 13	Sails from Liverpool
September 24	Arrives New York
September 26	American Museum of Natural History, New York; departs for Boston p.m.
September 27	New Haven
September 30	New York
October 2	Princeton
October 3	New York
October 6	Princeton
October 11	New York
October 13	Vineland Training School (an institution for the mentally disabled)
October 15	Princeton
October 18	New York – Metropolitan Museum of Art
October 19	New York and Princeton
October 20	Philadelphia – University Museum then Vineland Training School
October 21	Vineland Training School (stays at Princeton)
October 26	Philadelphia
October 27	Vineland Training School
October 28	Princeton
November 3	Vineland Training School; spends next week between here and Princeton
November 10	Vineland Training School
November 12	Princeton
November 15	New York
November 17	Vineland Training School
November 22	Atlantic City to visit friends

November 23	Vineland Training School
November 25	Boston – Wellesley College
December 1	Princeton
December 8	Trenton – testing at State Institution for Deaf and Dumb
December 9	Vineland Training School
December 15	Philadelphia – University Museum then returns to Princeton
December 27	Washington, DC
December 29	Washington, DC – American Association for the Advancement of Science meetings

1925

January 5	Washington, DC – Smithsonian; meets Ales Hrdlicka
January 5	Baltimore – School of Hygiene and Carnegie Institute of Embryology, then Princeton
January 10	Philadelphia
January 13	American Museum of Natural History; meets with Clark Wissler. Then Princeton
January 17	Boston
January 22	Princeton
January 30	New York
January 31	Leaves New York for Nashville
February 1	Nashville – Agricultural and Industrial State Normal School for Negroes
March 7	Roger Williams University
March 14	Chattanooga
March 14	Nashville – Walden College
March 25	Middle Tennessee Normal School
April 3	Nashville
April 7	Leaves for Cleveland
April 8	Arrives Cleveland
April 13	Leaves for Nashville
April 14	Arrives Nashville
April 17	Tuskegee Institute
May 16	Calhoun – Calhoun School
May 29	Leaves for New Orleans
June 2	Bay St Louis a.m., Montgomery, Alabama p.m.
June 3	Tuskegee Institute

June 10	Atlanta – Atlanta University
June 13	Rome
June 16	Chattanooga then to Nashville
June 23	leaves for Chicago – Field Museum
June 24	Chicago – Field Museum, then leaves for Minneapolis
June 25	Leaves for Winnipeg
June 29	To Selkirk; takes boat for Lake Winnipeg
July 1	Transfer to Norway House
July 11	Oxford House
July 19	Norway House
July 24	Returns to Winnipeg
July 25	Kenora
July 27	Regina
July 29	Leaves for Calgary
July 30	Calgary
August 1	Lethbridge and Waterton Lakes
August 3	Cardston
August 5	Lethbridge, then Calgary
August 6	Banff
August 7	Lake Louise
August 8	Victoria Glacier
August 9	Field, Yoho Valley, Takkakan, and Emerald Lake
August 11	Leaves for Vancouver
August 12	Arrives Vancouver
August 14	Leaves for Victoria
August 15	Arrives Victoria
August 16	Boat to Prince Rupert
August 18	Arrives Prince Rupert, then to Hazelton
August 20	Train to Kitwanga with Harlan Smith
August 21	Kispiox; in following week, trips to Kitwanga, Kispiox Valley
September 2	Hazelton
September 4	Hagwelgate, village of Carrier Indians
September 5	Kitwanga, then Port Essington, then to Prince Rupert
September 9	Alert Bay
September 16	Victoria
September 17	Vancouver
September 21	Leaves for Seattle

September 22	Train from Seattle through Montana, North Dakota
September 24	Arrives Minneapolis
October 14	Rochester, Minnesota, then returns to Minneapolis shortly after
October 29	Duluth
October 30	Nett Lake
November 7	Red Lake
November 19	Leaves for Winnipeg
November 20	Arrives Winnipeg
November 23	Leaves Winnipeg for Minnesota again
November 24	Ogema – White Earth Reservation
November 25	Glenwood
November 26	Pipestone
December 6	Leaves for Minneapolis
December 7	Arrives Minneapolis
December 13	Leaves for Chicago
December 14	Arrives Chicago
December 17	Train for Ashland, Kentucky; then to Lackey
December 19	Arrives Hindman – measuring at school
December 30	Train for Washington
December 31	Train to Boston

1926

January 1–20	(No entries)
January 21	Leaves Wellesley for Boston
January 23	Returns to Hindman; visits different schools
March 24	Arrives Knoxville
March 31	Atlantic City (including time with friends)
April 6–13	Wellesley
April 14–May 9	Cleveland – working with Dr Wingate Todd at Western Reserve University
May 9	Leaves for Lawrence, Kansas – Haskell Institute
May 10	Arrives Lawrence, then departs for Topeka
May 11	Leaves for Santa Fe
May 12	Arrives Santa Fe
May 21	Albuquerque
June 4	Santa Fe
June 7	Albuquerque
June 12	Leaves for Phoenix

June 13	Phoenix – Indian school; administers Dodd's International Group Mental Test
June 28–July 3	Travels around reservations in area, then returns to Phoenix
July 4	Prescott
July 7	Tucson
July 11	Day trip from Tucson to Sonora, Mexico, then to Phoenix
July 13	Williams, Arizona, then to Grand Canyon, Hopi country (Supai)
July 24	Holbrook
July 26	Keams Canyon
July 29	Holbrook
July 30	Keams Canyon
August 1	Holbrook
August 3	Santa Fe; spends next few days in Southwest on archaeological tours, e.g., to Taos, Pajarito Point, Mesa Verde, Chaco Canyon
August 23	Zuni
September 1	Canyon de Chelly
September 12	Fort Defiance
September 20	Gallup
September 22	Blackrock
September 29	Phoenix
October 17	Fort Apache
October 27	Gallup via Holbrook
October 28	Acomita
October 29	Acoma
October 31	Albuquerque
November 10	Acoma then Laguna
December 5	Acoma
December 7	Santa Fe
December 19	Leaves for Chicago, then to Philadelphia

1927

January 4	New Haven. No further entries until
May 15	Leaves New Haven for Niagara Falls
May 16–23	By train to San Francisco; next two weeks at Stanford and travelling

June 13	Klamath
June 15	San Francisco
June 23	Los Angeles
June 24	San Diego
June 25	Long Beach and Hollywood
June 27	Leaves for Laguna
June 28	Acoma
July 3	Laguna
July 4	Acoma
July 6	Laguna. Spends next two months travelling throughout Southwest, measuring and looking at pictographs, etc.
September 19	Gallup, then train to Albuquerque en route to the East to return to England

Appendix Two: Beatrice Blackwood's Notations on Her Photographs with Kainai Identifications

Number	Blackwood List A	Blackwood List B	Kainai Names
BB.A3.48	Adult male, full length, full face and profile	Pete Many Fingers or Six Toed Pete. Full Blood.	*Aakaokitsii*, Pete Many Fingers
BBA3.49,50	4,5 The same man, close up, full face and profile.	4,5 Pete Many Fingers or Six Toed Pete. Full Blood.	*Aakaokitsii*, Pete Many Fingers
BBA3.20B	3 Adult male, full length, full face and profile.	5 Pete Many Fingers or Six Toed Pete. Full Blood.	*Aakaokitsii*, Pete Many Fingers
BBA3.20M	8,9 Another man, full face and profile. Close up.	8,9 Charlie Wolf Plume.	*Aiyiisoiyiisaami*, Double Train Headdress, nickname *I'kotsiisoiyik-kaawa*, Red Leggings.
BB.A3.51	Another man, full face and profile. Close up.	Shot on Both Sides. Head Chief of the Bloods. Full Blood.	*Aatso'toaawa* Head Chief Shot Both Sides.
BB.A3.52	Another man, full face and profile. Close up.	Shot on Both Sides. Head Chief of the Bloods. Full Blood.	*Aatso'toaawa* Head Chief Shot Both Sides.
BBA3.55,56	10 and 11 Young man, standing, full face and profile.	10 Sam Black Plume, Full Blood	*Pa'nii*, Sam Black Plume
BB.A3.57	12 Older man, standing by his tent. Full face only.	12 Falling over the Cutbank	*Piaana*, Falling over the Cutbank
BB.A3.58	Young couple with baby	13 Ben Strangling Wolf and wife Lucy, Full Bloods	*Aatso'to'wa* Shot at from All Sides, *Kaksi-kamo'saakii* Just Stole Woman or Day Steal Woman and their daughter Dolly.
BB.A3.59	14 The same woman and baby [This is an error, as the photo-graph numbered 13 by Blackwood is of Lucy Strangling Wolf and her family].	14 Mrs Ethel Tail Feathers. Half Breed.	*Aisstaohkomiaakii* Comes Calling Woman with Gerald Tail-feathers.

Number	Blackwood List A	Blackwood List B	Kainai Names
BB.A3.60	15 Group of women, children and dogs.	(Not listed, though the following names were typed over: Mrs Black Forehead, Mrs Weasel Moccasin, Mrs Melting Tallow. Full Bloods.)	(l–r) *Natoiyisskii* Striking Holy Face or *To'yisskii*, Plain Face Woman (Mrs Cougar/ Lynx Head) with *Siipiikamo'saakii*, Steals at Night, or Stealing at Night (Mary Eva Spotted Bull); *Pissohkomii* Calling From the Side (Mrs Jack Burning Fire) [NB also identified as *Iitohtawa* (Mrs Hungry Crow)]; and *Makaisimii* Young Drinker (Mrs Brown Chief Calf).
BB.A3.61	16 Group of women, children and dogs.	(Not listed, though the following names were typed over: Mrs Black Forehead, Mrs Weasel Moccasin, Mrs Melting Tallow. Full Bloods.)	(l–r) unidentified woman and child; *Makaisimii* Young Drinker (Mrs Brown Chief Calf); *Natoiyisskii* Striking Holy Face or *To'yisskii* Plain Face Woman (Mrs Cougar/ Lynx Head), with *Siipiikamo'saakii* Steals at Night, or Stealing at Night (Mary Eva Spotted Bull).
BB.A3.62	17 Old woman in a shawl	17 Mrs Red Leggings. Full Blood.	*Api'saakii* Coyote Woman or *Sikaipisstsaakii* Black Cloth Woman (Mrs Red Leggings)
BB.A3.63, 64	18, 19 Woman and two children (father a half-breed).	18, 19 Mrs Billy Heavy Runner and children. Full Bloods.	*Misstomohtsikitstakii* Merry Sacrifice, Good Offering or Double Offering (Mrs Billy Heavy Runner) with two of her children, possibly *Issokoiyo'maahkaawa* Heavy Runner (Bill Heavy Runner Jr.) and Lucy.

Number	Blackwood List A	Blackwood List B	Kainai Names
BB.A3.65	20 Chief's family outside his tepee.	20 Mrs Yellow Shine. Mrs Shot on Both Sides, Mrs Rough Hair and Rough Hair.	(l–r) *Mi'kaníki'soyii* Red Wing Bird Woman (Mrs Yellow Shine); Margaret Yellow Shine; unidentified girl; *Misaamahkoiyinnimaakii* Long Time Medicine Pipe Woman (Mrs Shot on Both Sides); *Naipiss-tsaakii* Cloth Woman (Mrs Rough Hair); unidentified girl; and *Istsstsiimi* Rough Hair.
BB.A3.66	21 Chief's family outside his tepee (the same taken nearer).	21 Mrs Yellow Shine. Mrs Shot on Both Sides, Mrs Rough Hair and Rough Hair.	(l–r) *Mi'kaníki'soyii* Red ing Bird Woman (Mrs Yellow Shine); Margaret Yellow Shine; *Mis-aamahkoiyinnimaakii* Long Time Medicine Pipe Woman (Mrs Shot on Both Sides); *Na'piss-tsaakii* Cloth Woman (Mrs Rough Hair) and *Istsstsiimi* Rough Hair.
BB.A3.67	22 Chief's family outside his tepee (the same taken nearer).	22 Mrs Yellow Shine. Mrs Shot on Both Sides, Mrs Rough Hair and Rough Hair.	(l–r) *Mi'kaníki'soyii* Red Wing Bird Woman Mrs Yellow Shine); *Misaamahkoiyinnimaakii* Long Time Medicine Pipe Woman (Mrs Shot on Both Sides); Margaret Yellow Shine; *Nai-isstsaakii* Cloth Woman (Mrs Rough Hair); unidentified girl; *Istsstsiimi* Rough Hair.
BB.A3.68	23 Inside the Chief's tepee.	23 Mrs Shot on Both Sides	*Misaamahkoiyinnimaakii* Long Time Medicine Pipe Woman, (Mrs Shot on Both Sides)
BB.A3.69, 70	24, 25 Couple and child, full face and profile	24, 25 Coming Singing and Wife	*Aistainsskii* Coming Singer with *Iikaiyissi'nikki* Killed Before You Did (Mrs Coming Singer).

Number	Blackwood List A	Blackwood List B	Kainai Names
BB.A3.71	26 The same woman and child	26 Coming Singing and Wife	*Iikaiyissi'nikki* Killed Before You Did (Mrs Coming Singer) with unidentified girl.
BB.A3.72, 73	27, 28 Another couple.	27, 28 Melting Tallow and wife.	Possibly Joe and Clara Heavy Head, though community members disagreed over this identification.
BB.A3.74	29 Four men.	29 The Bear, Rough Hair, Shot on Both Sides, Crying Head. Full Bloods.	(l–r) *Kiaayo* Bear, *Istsstsiimi* Rough Hair, *Aatso'toaawa* Shot on Both Sides and *Aasai-nio'tokaani* Crying Head.
BB.A3.75	30 Two boys (camera moved)	(not listed)	Two boys in the fields. They have been identified as possibly (l–r) Bernard Whiteman Left and Albert Vielle.
BB.A3.76 (x-ref. B54.20h); also BB.A3.78, same girls in same order	Blood Reserve School	(not listed)	Back row, l–r: *Kimmata'pssii* (Lily Shot Both Sides, Mrs Bare Shin Bone); *Iinakay* (Annie Good Rider, Mrs Brewer); Minnie Snake [or Bug] Eater; Rosine Two Flags; Antonia Hairy Bull; *Mini* (Minnie Sun Going up the Hill, Mrs Joe Shouting). Middle row, l–r: Annette Good Rider (Mrs Paul Russell); *Sii'pikitstakii* Making Night Offering Woman (Mary Striped Wolf, Mrs John Many Chiefs); Mary A. Skipper; *Otskapinaakii* Blue Eyed Woman (Jane Blood, Mrs Pete Bruised Head); Nancy Many Bears; Josette Melting Tallow; Susan Crazy Bull; *No'si* (Rosie

Number	Blackwood List A	Blackwood List B	Kainai Names
			Morning Owl, Mrs Dan Chief Moon); Lizzie Standing Alone; *Noyiss* (Louise Don't Tie His Shoes, Mrs Iron Shirt).
BB.A3.77	Five school girls from Blood Reserve School	(not listed)	Schoolgirls over the age of fifteen. (l–r) *Otskapinaakii* Blue Eyed Woman (Jane Blood, Mrs Pete Bruised Head); *Sii'pikitstakii* Making Night Offering Woman (Mary Striped Wolf, Mrs John Many Chiefs); Annette Good Rider (Mrs Paul Russell); *No'si* (Rosie Morning Owl, Mrs Dan Chief Moon); *Noyiss* (Louise Don't Tie His Shoes, Mrs Iron Shirt).
BB.A3.79	School girls standing up, under fifteen.	(not listed)	Back row, l–r: *Kimmata'pssii* (Lily Shot Both Sides, later Mrs Bare Shin Bone); *Iinakay* (Annie Good Rider, Mrs Brewer); Minnie Snake [or Bug] Eater; Rosine Two Flags; Antonia Hairy Bull, *Mini* (Minnie Sun Going up the Hill, Mrs Joe Shouting). Front row, l–r: *Aistaayohtowa* (Eva or Emma Mills); *Mini* (Minnie Chief Moon); Josette Melting Tallow; Mary MacDonald; Bibian Sun Dance (Mrs Mike Wolf Child); Mary A. Skipper; Nancy Many Bears; Susan Crazy Bull; Adeline Fox (Mrs Heavy Shield); Lizzie Standing Alone.

Appendix Three: Protocol Agreement

3 November 2001

PROTOCOL AGREEMENT BETWEEN
THE MOOKAAKIN CULTURAL AND HERITAGE FOUNDATION
AND
LAURA PEERS/ALISON BROWN
(ON BEHALF OF THE PITT RIVERS MUSEUM, UNIVERSITY OF OXFORD).

Introduction

This project arises from a collection of photographs taken in 1925 on the Blood Reserve by Beatrice Blackwood of the Pitt Rivers Museum. We hope that these images might be useful to the Kainai Nation in documenting Kainai history for Kainai purposes; we also hope to use them to teach museum professionals in the UK about the importance of historic photographs and artefacts to First Nations people today. The first phase of this project has been funded by the Arts and Humanities Research Board of the United Kingdom. The current grant supports travel costs for Laura Peers and Alison Brown in autumn 2001 and for a second trip to Alberta in summer 2002, as well as for honoraria to elders and other consultants, and costs associated with recording interviews or other aspects of research.

Peers and Brown are asking the assistance and participation of the Mookaakin Foundation to provide cultural guidance for this project, to help with suggesting community members to interview, and to ensure that Peers and Brown comply with the project goals and protocol as set out below.

In return, Peers and Brown agree to the terms set out below, and to assist the Mookaakin Foundation in locating grants, in locating relevant collections held overseas, and in making introductions between the Foundation and museum professionals overseas. Peers and Brown also agree to request permission from the Mookaakin Foundation, should they wish to use the Foundation's name in any future publication in addition to any which results from this project.

We realise that the project's goals will change as it becomes properly collaborative, and welcome the input of the Mookaakin Foundation members and other community members in this. Our original goals have been:

> **1. To repatriate a complete set of copies of Blackwood's photographs** and all associated documentation to the Kainai Nation, to be held in whichever repository they wish, and for any purpose that the Nation sees fit.
>
> **The negatives of the photographs are owned by the Pitt Rivers Museum, and thus are copyrighted, in accordance with English law, to the Museum. If the photographs are included in a publication, they should be credited to the Pitt Rivers Museum and the Museum should be informed. These prints are

otherwise provided without restriction for educational and research use within the community. Such further use that the community wishes to make of the photographs to be by arrangement with the Museum.

2. To interview elders and other community members to recover information about culture and history which is linked to the people shown in the photographs, to serve Kainai Nation needs.

**All records of these interviews will be subject to review by those interviewed. Copies of interview tapes will, with the permission of those interviewed, be deposited with Red Crow Community College and Glenbow Archives (subject to any restrictions that interviewees may wish to place on them). Those interviewed will also receive copies of tapes, transcripts, and other interview materials. If at any time in the future Peers and Brown or any other Pitt Rivers Museum staff member wishes to publish information collected during project interviews that has not already been published, the Mookaakin Foundation will be contacted and permission will be sought.

3. To inform museum professionals and academics in the United Kingdom: Under the terms of the project grant, Laura Peers and Alison Brown have agreed to write a short book, aimed at UK academics and museum and archival staff, on the significance of photographs in recovering historical and cultural information for First Nations communities, as well as the importance of consulting with First Nations communities on their material heritage held in overseas collections.

**We will need to quote from the interviews we do in order to write this, but will bring drafts of material prepared for publication back to all Kanai people quoted for review. We hope that an advisory/review board can be developed from Kainai community members and Pitt Rivers Museum staff in order to facilitate this process and to comment on the entire draft manuscript.

4. Community-based project using the photographs to understand and teach Kainai history. The nature of this project will be determined in conjunction with Kainai people. Laura Peers and Alison Brown will facilitate this project, including applying for necessary grant funds, and spending further time with Kainai people in the summer of 2002 and following as necessary. This project might take the form of an exhibition of the photographs, a book with the photographs and selected interview quotes, or curriculum materials for teaching about Kainai life in the 1920s.

On behalf of the Mookaakin Cultural and Heritage Foundation

Name: Narcisse Blood

Signature: Narcisse Blood

Date: Nov 3/01

Name: Pete Standing Alone

Signature: Pete Standing Alone

Date: Nov 3 01

On behalf of the Pitt Rivers Museum, University of Oxford

Name: ALISON BROWN

Signature: Alison Brown

Date: Nov 3 01

Appendix Four: Kainai Reflections on Beatrice Blackwood's Diary

In this Appendix we present Beatrice Blackwood's fieldnotes and diary entries from 1 August to 4 August 1925, when she arrived in Lethbridge and visited the Blood Reserve. Each day's entry (printed here in italics) has been interspersed with reflections on her observations made by four Kainai community members, Andy Blackwater, Narcisse Blood, Martin Heavy Head, and Dorothy First Rider, during interviews undertaken in the summer of 2002. These interviews arose following concerns that were raised during meetings with the Red Crow Elders Advisory Committee, and also in some of our initial discussions with Mookaakin Foundation members. First Nations peoples are often disturbed by what they see as mistakes concerning their cultural traditions that have become fossilized in the archival record. They argue that scholars using archival documents to write Native histories should endeavour to identify misinterpretations and present multiple perspectives of texts in their analyses in order to broaden the often monologic non-Native scholarly voice found within the textual and documentary record. The comments made by Kainai community members in response to Beatrice Blackwood's diary and fieldnotes provide a parallel narrative to these historical resources and demonstrate how Kainai readings can enrich interpretations of them some eighty years later. It is an opportunity to demonstrate the superficiality of documents created during a whistle-stop tour of the Reserve such as Blackwood (and other anthropologists) had, and a chance to provide alternative and fuller explanations for statements recorded in haste. For Kainai people today, this is their chance to reply to Blackwood's observations about their ancestors, though, as with all interviews conducted as part of this project, the perspectives shared are those of the individuals.

Blackwood Diary 1924–7 (Blackwood Papers, Box 12)

Sat August 1

8.30 train for Lethbridge. Very slow through country getting increasingly flatter, with towns plonked down with no particular reason for being where they are rather than anywhere else. Mostly wheat and oats – some pasture. A town consists of a couple of parallel streets and some cross streets, often planned but not laid – a half dozen grain elevators (store-houses). Lethbridge (1pm) rather larger. Places I never wish to see again – L – Lethbridge. Left 1.40 for Cardston – 3 elevators, a dairy an hotel and a number of houses and shacks, and a large marble edifice which is a Mormon temple. Cardston has a flourishing Mormon colony – off-shoot from Salt Lake City. The Indian Agent, Mr Faunt, has gone up to Waterton Lakes Park for the weekend, so I went up too – on a Ford truck with the man who carries the freight – 34 miles in 3 1/2 hours on mountain roads with a 3/4 [illegible] load. Grand viewing of the Rockies. Waterton Lakes Park is a continuation of the U.S. National Park called Glacier Park – the international boundary goes through Waterton lake. There is a large camping site, an hotel, a number of chalets and cottages and space for any number of tents. Found quarters in a cottage (Mrs Baker).

NARCISSE BLOOD
Well anyways, when she came and took pictures, obviously she was very bored and you had shared with me [some of her intent], but also here she talks about not wanting to be here again, places that she doesn't want to see again, it was very ... Why she was here I think we'll never know, but obviously she took these pictures and I think there wasn't too much follow up now that we can look back on it, and the only thing we can rely on is the diary that she left that she didn't want to be here.

DOROTHY FIRST RIDER
This diary will be of particular value to ... research that the Blood Tribe is currently involved in, even though I myself at this time am not involved, the interest is still there. [It] should also be of value to other researchers that are pursuing those particular interests, especially in the land claims, and some of the understandings from the Tribe that we have as to the encampment of the Mormons in the late 1800s, early 1900s, and then, presently, still residing on those sites.

The comments that she made, although they are very brief comments about the town of Cardston and what that particular town of Cardston consists of, leaves no doubt that even at the time she went through there, which was in the mid-1920s, there was not much to the town except for what she has indicated. And that's three elevators, a dairy, a hotel, and a number of houses and shacks. We are realizing that the Mormons had encroached upon our territory in the late 1800s under a supposedly ninety-nine-year lease, so for whatever reason the town was not flourishing, if her observations are correct. So I find that very interesting.

Martin Heavy Head

Well, to me it shows she's not familiar with the climate and geography. People wouldn't just plonk down a town anywhere. They'd have to have water. It's quite dry round here and water is a very important consideration.

Sun August 2

am. Went in a motor launch along Waterton Lake. A little snow in some corners of the mountains but not much. U.S. boundary marked by a narrow clearing in the trees. pm. Went up into the hills along the new Altamira Highway now under construction – it will lead into the States. About three miles of it is finished – went passed the end along a narrow trail into the mountains along the edge of a river with many falls.

Talked to the Indian Agent about the Bloods. He says that they are a high type of Indian – far superior to the Crees. You can guide them but not drive them. They get nothing from the government but the treaty money. He encourages them not to ask for things, but to be independent. They are settling and farm – and building houses as they can afford to. There are not many half-breeds. If a white man marries an Indian she remains an Indian and gets treaty but her children do not. No one not of the band may live on the Reserve so it generally happens that a woman thus married would move off it. The illegitimate child of an unmarried woman is treated as an Indian whatever the father ('I give her the benefit of the doubt,' said Mr Faunt). They still have their Sun Dance but much watered down and without the torturing. It is held in the middle of July.

Andy Blackwater

She was quite clear as to which route she took, how long it took her and what kind of vehicle – she took a Ford truck, by the way. She then made her way to the Rockies – Waterton Lakes Park – and she stated that Waterton Lakes Park is also a continuation of the National Park across on the US side, called Glacier Park. It is the international boundary that divides the two. She also was very clear as to the clearing of the bush, which divides the two countries, Canada and the US. She stated that the US boundary was marked by a narrow clearing in the trees, which today still exists as a marking of the boundary.

She then talked to the Indian Agent, Mr Faunt. He was the Indian Agent at the time in 1925. He made a very positive remark about the superiority of the Blood Tribe, Kainaiwa. I was raised with that kind of self-portrayal of our people that we are very superior, because we are very warlike, very fierce and all that. We were very independent even at that time. The statement that he made that he, the Indian Agent, encourages them, which is us, not to ask for things but to be independent. 'They are settling and farm – and building houses as they can afford to. There are not many half-breeds' because we did not allow too many outsiders to come upon our territory and at that time it would be the Reserve. Also he states that he, the Indian Agent, or anybody, can guide them, which is us, but not drive them. That is a very accurate statement, at least that the Indian Agent gave her.

Also, she made a statement that if a white man marries an Indian lady she remains an Indian and gets Treaty, but her children do not. That's not quite accurate. The Indian Act existed at the time; it became the law that we had to abide by. It states that if a white man marries an Indian lady, she loses her status, also her children lose their status. So she made this statement, which is not quite accurate. In our practice, traditional way of life, once a person or a lady marries another person from another clan, she becomes part of that household, but not necessarily the clan. She'll never lose her clanship. She is expected to be part of the camp and the lodge of her spouse's family, so she does become part of that family. Now, we can perhaps agree with an Indian woman marrying a white man, naturally we would expect her to move into that household and into that community of the white person that she marries. That we can agree to. But the things that we disagree, is that there is no law in the land that can undo her birthright as an Indian or First Nations person. So, to us it is unheard of – anybody to take away your birthright as Aboriginal or First Nation person. That we disagree with. We've always disagreed with. There has been in our case, today there is some that have married onto the Reserve, but they remain like Piikani. A Piikani man marrying a Blood woman, the Piikani may live in our community for the rest of his life, but will always be considered as a Piikani. And the other way, if one of our ladies marries to Siksika or Piikani or any place, they'll always be considered as a Blood woman, or Kainaaki. They never lose that identity. You can never take that away from a person.

She then did mention that we still have our Sun Dance, 'but much watered down and without the torturing' ... The Sun Dance is always complete ... The statement that 'without the torturing,' which is the piercing part of Sun Dance, was an additional event that takes place whenever a younger warrior makes a vow to go through a piercing. They make a vow to survive or to come back safe from a warpath, or a vision quest, or in times of danger they'll make a vow to the Creator to be allowed to survive, in turn they'll go through a piercing ceremony at the Sun Dance. Also, not every year we have a Sun Lodge. It's those times a young lady, a very innocent lady, that's pure, will make a vow to make a Sun Lodge and that's another addition to our Sun Dance. The Sun Dance is for other purposes, not just for piercing and building a Sun Lodge. So, just in addition to her statement, to help others understand that whatever is taking place at our Sun Dance has remained the same for as long as I can remember and beyond that.

Making a statement that the Sun Dance is 'much watered down' at that point in time has a lot to do with the government policy and it goes through the Indian Act ... They tried to stop the annual Sun Dance using the excuse that it took us away from our harvesting of the agricultural grain, harvesting the hay. They argued that it took us away from that kind of activity which was, in terms of time, needed to be done, apparently at the same time as the Sun Dance ... They even desecrated the Sun Lodge. But our leaders and spiritual leaders at the time took a position on that and they reminded them that when they, the white people, had their Sunday ceremonies, we never interfered with their ceremonies. As well, we didn't desecrate their churches.

Narcisse Blood

It is interesting that the comment that the Indian Agent makes here, 'They are settling and farming.' She's quoting where he makes a comment that we're not dependent and we are encouraged not to be dependent on government money and I think it is important to understand just what had happened. R.N. Wilson's paper, *Our Betrayed Wards*, really goes at length to describe what had happened and, in our earlier discussions, I had talked about the Greater Production Farms, which was an effort to help support WW1 efforts to the Allied Forces in Europe. And the Blood Tribe was one of them, a place for one of those farms. They referred to them as Greater Production Farms ... I think if you read R.N. Wilson's *Our Betrayed Wards* you really see how it is outlined – the very deliberate and systematic undermining of that very successful ranching and farming, the transition that our people had to go through. And my comment was that our people were very adaptable, because to change a way of life, of living off the buffalo for centuries and for all of a sudden to have such a drastic change in a very short period of time, we were able to become what he's referring [to] here as making our own money and so forth. And it had a lot to do with the ability to make the changes, to adapt to the changes, that were taking place, but also having a real sense of identity of a people back then. To use what was our strength, our tradition, of helping each other in farming and ranching efforts. That was very successful. And it is very important to understand that this was taking place and that's why the Indian Agent makes reference to it.

And [s]he talks about our Sun Dance, that it is very watered down, without the torturing. And if you had to just rely on what's written, it doesn't tell you very much, but typically, anthropologists and sometimes, unfortunately, the academic community will make conclusions just based on what's written ... We had some discussions about what he referred to as the torturing, which was the piercing, and it was a very personal decision of the individual that made a vow to escape maybe certain death or danger when our people used to go on war paths or coups. To get out of that they make a vow to our Creator to the sun that, 'If I get out of this situation I'll offer my body to you at this next Sun Dance at the centre lodge and go through a piercing. Help me get out of this situation.' So the negative connotations that come out of this is that it is something we did for the sake of torturing and this is a statement that was based on the ignorance of the Indian Agent.

But also, writing down what the Indian Agent talks about, how he views the Bloods, our people, back then, and making some comparisons to the Crees. I don't know if this man had any dealings with them but he makes this statement and it's written.

Dorothy First Rider

Also, another interesting comment that she has made is of course that the Bloods were very superior to the Crees! But aside of that she makes some reference to the Indian Act and to the enfranchisement Act which is very interesting ... that is that Indian women would not lose their status, I think that's what she indicated over here, but her children would not be of Treaty status. But she doesn't make any mention of if they were legally married if the Indian woman would lose their status. Of course, this is something that the Tribes and other First Nations have to deal with, especially in the early 80s. As a result the Tribe now has their own membership code and this was developed and put into place in 1985 and it was amended, I think it was in 1996, whereas no Indian woman would lose status and no non-Blood woman would gain status through marriage any more ... So although she doesn't go too much into these, the notations that she does make in some of the comments are very interesting.

Another comment that I find very interesting is where the Indian Agent makes the statement that the Blood Indians receive nothing from the Government except for the Treaty money. What I deem from this is that the Indian Agent, although he is supposed to be acting as a fiduciary, in a fiduciary capacity, does not do anything or go out of his way to encourage the Blood Tribe to go after any Treaty entitlements, and such Treaty entitlements would be the issuing of farm implements under Treaty; cattle under Treaty, which we still haven't settled with the Crown to this day in 2002; the right to housing; the right to education, etc., etc. In fact he encourages them not to ask for anything.

So that's kind of interesting for an Indian Agent to be taking that kind of a view, but I imagine that's the kind of briefing that they did receive at the time.

MARTIN HEAVY HEAD
She says she came in and spent two days in Waterton and then followed the Indian Agent out to the Reserve, 'A high type of Indian. Far superior to the Crees.' I find that a lot of people that spend time with the Bloods take on the same sort of attitude; being very anti-Cree. Anti-whatever. I don't know.

'You can guide them but not drive them.' And like I said earlier, there was that idea of naming the Indian Agent as 'Our father' *kinonna*. The Indian Agency is called *Iikaitoonio'pi* the place where our father lives, and it's sort of the idea of what the reality is, and not making any euphemistic statements about the relationships between the government and ourselves; it was a very direct kind of thing – that we were totally dependent on them. That was the idea.

This thing, 'They still have their Sun Dance, but much watered down and without the torturing.' Torturing was outlawed, but I don't know if it's that watered down. 'It is held in the middle of July' because kids were at school, so people had to wait till the kids got out of school and then they'd take them to the Sun Dance.

And of course, all of this, 'If a white man marries an Indian she remains an Indian but her children do not,' in the Indian Act she wouldn't remain an Indian and she wouldn't get her Treaty ... This statement about a Blood woman marrying a white man and leaving the Reserve and so on and so forth, that wasn't quite following the Indian Act. That was a totally different idea. It was very well spelled out that she had to leave.

Mon. August 3

Went with Mr Faunt down to Cardston and on to the Indian Reserve. Sat in his office while he dealt with the various Indians who came to see him about all sorts of things – from buying a rake to getting married. They are far more like the traditional Indian than the Crees are – tall, big-boned, large faces with very high cheekbones – and big hooked noses, the men wear their hair in two long plaits tied together in front on their chests. The women all wear shawls except some who had European dress.
pm. Drove round the Reserve – saw the hospital and the school which is under the care of the RCs. There is a good deal of t.b. but not much venereal disease. There were not many people in hospital. They go off in summer and come back with worse coughs as soon as it gets cold. They bear confinement very badly and can't be kept in bed even when they are quite bad.

Got some baby hair – asked for adult pubic hair and was told by the sister that full-blooded Indians have no body hair at all. When they see a European with axillary hair they laugh as we do at a woman with a beard. This confirms what Mrs Dent said at Norway House. Talked with the sisters at the school – some have been there 25 years without a break – it costs too much to go to Montreal where most of them belong. They said that the Indians were difficult to work with but they could see some progress.

Went to the Chief's camp. He has a painted tepee – they all put on their 'glad rags' to be photographed. Mr Faunt says they have some very fine things but don't bring them out except on special occasions – and will never sell them. He sent a lot to the Fair at Regina for exhibition. Visited a new house one of the Indians is having built, also his barn – modern in every respect. This man owns a large amount of land, 3–400 head of horses, and herd of cattle, and a six-cylinder car – with which he is at present touring in Montana. The Indians visit their kindred tribe in Montana a great deal, and Mr Faunt encourages them to get their wives from there. Two families own cars at the present time – others had them but couldn't keep them up. Many of them own large numbers of cattle and horses. The land is good and he expects a good crop this year if it doesn't get burnt up. There are about 11,000 Indians on the Reserve and their number is keeping up.

Saw a 'dead house' where they used to bury their dead – formerly also they buried in trees by the river – (the only place where there are any) wrapped in a blanket. Now they have graveyards – generally on the highest ground available.

Andy Blackwater

She came down from Cardston and onto the Indian Reserve ... I would imagine the reason why they would be discussing getting married would be to get the provisions, or the costs, associated with marrying. But the Indian Agent had no authority and never gave permission to people to get married. So, just a point of clarity right there. 'They are far more like the traditional Indian than the Cree' and then there's a description of us, and I suppose at the time, we were still kind of uniform in our appearance, because she also stated earlier that there was not much half-breeds running around. It was after we started having interracial marriages, having half-breeds and all that kind of thing started to alter our outward appearance. She states that the men had their hair in two long braids, or is it 'plaits,' tied together in front on their chest. This is inaccurate. The men always wear three braids and the ladies always wore two braids. The only time in ceremonies, like a sweat lodge or other ceremonies, the men would undo their braids and some would just let their hair loose, or hanging down, and some would tie it. That's in ceremonies, they undo the braids. And that is still practised today with the ones that still do wear braids ......

In the afternoon she states that she drove around the Reserve and saw the hospital and the school which she states is in the care of the Roman Catholics.

The school and the hospital that she's referring to in this case is in Standoff. The Roman Catholics took a contract with the government to run these schools for the government. So they were actually run by the government but managed by the Church. So they were not out here just for the goodness of their hearts. They were here because they had to fulfil the conditions of the contract. But they did good.

She states that there's a lot of TB, which is pretty much a common knowledge among us. We refer to it as *isttsíkssaisskinaan*, a phrase that is used to indicate the sound of the coughing, the different ways of coughing, and this is one of them. Hearing the way a person coughs, we know that it is TB ... 'There are not many people in the hospital and some of them come back with worse coughs as soon as it gets cold. They bear confinement very badly and can't be kept in bed even when they are quite bad.' I think as she fails to, or she was not aware, that there was much traditional practice of healing that still took place around that time. Our people always resort to the traditional medicinal type of healing, the brews and the herbs and whatever. We still use the sweat lodges for purifying as well as what we call faith healing. So maybe she wasn't given that information, that these people do seek other methods ... But it may be perceived that there was no other method and we were just being careless. Of course, it might be important to note that some of the medicine that we had developed, certain cures for some of the illnesses and diseases, we had developed certain cures for them. But these new ones, such as venereal disease and other types of disease, especially smallpox, we had not developed any traditional medicine to deal with. So therefore there might have been times when these people were affected by the European type of medicine and we had no cure at the time. So they couldn't deal with it. Especially smallpox. But I heard that smallpox, some of them did use the sweat lodges and that saved some of them.

Then she goes on to say that she wants to get a sample of hair from the different parts of the body but of course she was informed that our people were not as hairy as the rest of the people elsewhere, which is correct. She also does make mention of the sisters at the school. Apparently the sisters were quite aware of the distinction in terms of hair between other races. So the sisters did help her to make that statement, and the notion of having too much hair as compared to a lady having a beard. But again, here she does make some mention of the plight of the sisters or the nuns having to be here for twenty-five years without a break. But the church, because of the contract, were compensated properly for the work that they were doing, but she fails to mention this. That it was through a contract that the government gave the Anglican and the Catholic, the different churches, the management contracts. So it might be perceived that they were doing it from their heart, but money was a driving force.

She states that only on those special occasions that they put on their Sunday best. But here again other than that, you don't get to see those. Very seldom do they bring them out, the family treasures. I would imagine at about that time we were then being used in exhibitions and fairs. They were being used as special attractions. And today we look back and we disagree with that now, today, that we were used as items of curiosity. You know, curiosity items. Items that were conversation pieces. We disagreed with that because we did not have to try to appease people, but it was at that point that people began to change. But I guess that being proud, we like to show off, but the underlying thing is that we were being used as if we were items that came out of the museum.

She states that we had already, at that point in time, started having more modern homes, ranch type settings with barns, animals, horses. And vehicles were also coming into our community. And then she makes reference to some of us going down to the US to our brothers and sisters at the Blackfeet reservation. And also that we went there quite frequently. 'The Indians visit their kindred tribe in Montana a great deal.' Yes. We were one. But unfortunately at the time and she didn't put that in, the Indian Agent did not share the information that we were so restricted, we were so confined, on our Reserve. There were four police outposts stationed almost in each corner to keep us confined. And if we were to visit Piikani or Siksika or Amsskaapipikani, the Blackfeet, we had to get permits, to visit. It's almost like a visa today, to visit somebody. We were so restricted, so confined. Even what we produced, like horses, cattle, grain, and those were strictly controlled. Everything that we produced in terms of grain, in terms of livestock, all had to go through the Indian Agent, and they controlled it. And we had to ration our own grain. It was strictly controlled. So that is some information that maybe she should have been told. But of course, the Indian Agent wouldn't.

She also states that she saw a dead house. It was around that time, prior to that, we went through the smallpox. We went through the devastation. And that almost killed us off. At least more than half of our people died because of that. There were so many deaths at that time that they didn't have enough time or enough healthy people to bury them. So what they did, they had little houses, little shacks that already existed and they just moved them to wherever and they just stuck the people in there. And we still have some of those down at Old Agency. I don't know if you've seen them. We still have one where the dump is, up on that hill ... But like I said, at the time, because of the disease, the nature of the disease, we just started burying the people. But once some of our people got Christianized, that's when they started burying. So any graves that we might find today, if they were underground, they had a Christian burial, or they were Christianized. So if we were to remove them to another site they would get the same Christian burial because they were Christians. And that is according to their own wishes and the family's that they would bury them. They were wrapped in blankets, but after they made boxes for them. So that is, she made a fairly accurate description.

NARCISSE BLOOD

Again, the sweeping statements that were made ... but again, they also give you glimpses of ... when she just describes what's going on because it was then you started getting the residential schools. And also, the pictures depict that, where she talks about the hospital and the schools and so forth. And I think it is also significant to look at this. When our people changed their lifestyle, well, first of all, the diseases really hit us, our numbers really went down, so the 11,000 that she cites as the population of the Bloods is, I think, wrong. I think we were a lot lower than that, but I know we're much higher in terms of numbers, but you also have to keep in mind that with the changes that took place, first of all the disease had a devastating effect on our people. There were more people that died from smallpox in particular than any battles. So that did a lot to subdue our people and then bold moves like taking the children and putting them into residential schools. But you also have to keep in mind when there's a change in diet and a change in lifestyle, then there were also diseases that were still being brought in. When she talks about the coughs and the hospitals. When our people started moving into European style houses a lot of our people died from influenza and I think tuberculosis started coming in at that time too and a lot of it had to do with stale air. And when we look at it from today's perspective, housing builders are starting to say, 'We need circulation.' So if you stay in a tipi, then you always had that flow of air and I think research tells us today that it was the stale air that often causes problems with regards the colds and other infections we have. So now there's an effort to change that. But this would be a direct result of a sudden change. And I'm sure the diet had something to do with it even though we were still practising berry picking; roots were still being picked, and there was still some hunting going on. But then I think you also have to keep in mind that with the buffalo gone there were different animals that had to be hunted probably a little bit more.

The other thing I wanted to talk about was she makes a comment that, or the Indian Agent makes the comment that, we visited our relatives to the south quite a bit, as an observation. For us, the forty-ninth parallel was not very significant. Maybe to the Indian Agent it was, but to us it wasn't. Thus, the comment is that we went down to Montana. And I don't think the concept of

Montana really came in for a long time because that was our traditional territory and we are all related.

DOROTHY FIRST RIDER

There are some things in here that I'm curious as to why she would mention those, but before I get into that she also makes an interesting statement that there is a lot of tuberculosis among the community, among the members, but not much venereal disease. That's an interesting comment. I know when I was doing some research when I was in university in Regina there was unfortunately a lot of Aboriginal women that seemed to have contracted the disease because of the circumstances they were forced to go and try and engage in some sort of livelihood to be able to support their children, their families, because times were very difficult in those days. A lot of them were referred to as 'outside Fort Indians,' I think, was the term that had been used ... and they seemed to have contracted the disease. But nobody seems to delve into that kind of research. It's just something that's talked about. So she mentions it over here, so maybe it is the fact that not too many of our women engaged in those kinds of practices. I know historically a lot of the women would work for the people, the families, in Fort Macleod and in Cardston, as housekeepers, and that's how they made their subsistence. Also, since healthcare was supposed to be a Treaty right as well, according to Beatrice Blackwood, the health of the Blood Indians was not very good. They had a lot of health problems, especially with the tuberculosis. They were plagued by bad colds [and] healthcare was supposed to be a Treaty right, and it is supposed to be a Treaty right, but they were not getting the care, even then, that they should have been receiving.

The Blood people seem to have been economically stable at least in most respects at the time of her visit. She indicates that there was a man that owned a large amount of land and he had three to four hundred head of horses and a herd of cattle and that confirms the research that I was involved in a few years ago when we were launching our court case in regards to the mismanagement of our cattle, the beef cattle that we never received under Treaty. At that time a lot of the people were engaged in ranching. They were very adept at this and according to our research they did not only have range cattle but they had good quality cattle and these cattle were worth a lot of money. They proved to be very adept at ranching; they knew how to take care of them, especially their horses, as well ... And they never received cattle under Treaty, so what a lot of the Blood Indians did was that since they owned a lot of horses they would sell their horses and they would purchase cattle from the sale of those horses, and that's how our cattle industry began on the Reserve. So to this day we still haven't settled our cattle entitlement under Treaty, but that's some of the research that we managed to uncover and it goes hand in hand with some of the oral testimony that has been passed down from the elders from one generation to another. But I'm glad that it is confirmed by the comments she made, although she didn't realize how important those comments may have been in the future.

One comment here about the 11,000 Indians living on the Reserve in the early 1920s may have been an error on her part but you can ask Annabel [Crop Eared Wolf] for her documentation and find out whether there should have been 1,100 or 11,000 people.

The dead house is an interesting comment and unfortunately that house is no longer there; the structure is completely gone, but the site is still there. It should be used as a historic site. We should take an initiative from the Bloods to see that it is identified as a historic site, maybe with a plaque to indicate what this used to be and what it was used for.

Martin Heavy Head

So this whole idea of her saying 'not much venereal disease,' I wonder if it is the case about Freud being a big influence at the time ... The same with Esther Goldfrank ... But she was quite obsessed about sex and things like that. So I wonder if it was the influence of Freud, or just what it was. But I find a lot of the stuff you read in anthropology has so much to do with sex!

Are there people with braids? Is there anybody with three braids? ... There's no way to tell with this guy. Is that another braid? Don't think so. It's pretty well two braids. Well, if they're saying three braids, I don't think so. I think it was always two as far as I know. Some people tend to want to make the final statements. This is what it was, and that's the way it was. And sometimes they are wrong. So, I don't know.

People, well even today, people hate going to the hospital, and when people lived in the tipis, because of the circulation, in a lot of ways once you got used to it, it was much healthier than living in confined spaces. Especially if you had TB, you know it would just run rampant.

Tue. Aug. 4

am – wandered around the Agency – watched them corral horses and catch some for work. There are a lot of young colts but most of them are 'small stuff' and not much good.

pm – went to the school and measured 20 children who were there for the holidays. They are kept at school all the time from puberty until 18 or until they get married. Menstruation begins very early – often at 8 years old, and child-bearing will go on up to 50. It is not always easy. The children were not a very healthy bunch, several had open wounds, and others had swollen ones which they had not reported ('They don't say anything about them till they hurt.') They are treated with iodine. Some showed signs of white blood – only one had hazel eyes. Went down to Cardston (Cahoon Hotel) for early morning train.

ANDY BLACKWATER

She continues to wander around with the Agent watching the day-to-day activity in terms of dealing with the livestock. She then describes what ... we call ... cayuse ... They are smaller built horses but they are very hardy, very tough. And a lot of these saddle bronco riders, rodeo, they used to use a lot of these cayuses because they are very tough, but they are smaller ... But I don't know, like I said it has been a little over 300 years since the horses came back. We had horses way back then, but they were smaller. But the horse that came through the Spaniards, that's what they say, they brought them as far as the Nez Perce country, in Oregon, and in the horse raids that they went on for coup, if you caught some of those horses then they were introduced. But we managed to develop horseman skills in a short period of time. Of course, we moved faster and quicker and were more independent in hunting, but that helped kill off the buffalo too. With the guns. With the fur trade.

So, then she made another observation that, 'Went to the school and measured twenty children that were there for the holidays. They are kept in school all the time from puberty until 18 or until they get married.' She talks about the childbearing years ... She goes on to talk about her observation of the children that were kept in school. Some of the children that were brought into the schools remained there, some were orphaned, and because of the disease that occurred prior to that a lot of our children were without homes, and even relatives weren't able to deal with them. So, a very few of them landed up having to stay full time. Especially in those summer months when they should have been back in the community. She also, of course, here it is important to note that again there was a federal Indian policy through the Indian Act that says that a child of a certain age has to be at school, and if not there's a penalty to the point that the parents may be charged and imprisoned, because they won't send their children to school. It did occur; there was some that went to [jail]. In most cases children are brought into the schools and forced into the schools, taken away from the parents, and they had to stay till they were sixteen or eighteen. Sixteen, you can get married. If you get married at sixteen then you leave. Otherwise you might have to stay till you are eighteen. The ones that were eighteen were the ones that were brought to the Industrial school at Dunbow. And that was, of course, the result of the overall policy of the federal government, the assimilation of our people into the mainstream. And that had a very devastating result on our people today.

And the other thing that she also did make a statement, 'the children were not a very healthy bunch. Several had open wounds, and others had swollen ones which they had not reported.' She also goes on to say the type of treatment they used, the iodine. Well, naturally, iodine stings, you know? Especially when applied to an open wound. And 'some showed ... white blood – only one had hazel eyes.' I would imagine they failed to realize that we were used to another diet. Our diet was quite different. From then, they were subject to a different diet. And this new diet, even though they would give them milk, and eggs and butter and all that, our bodies were not conducive to, you know, they were not really agreeable – that kind of new diet. So in terms of benefiting from that, it was limited, because our bodies were not used to it. We're used to a different diet of meat and all that. And the meat that we are accustomed to is very lean. We weren't accustomed to animal fat, sugar, flour, bread, butter, eggs. We are not accustomed to all of that, even though all that might be deemed to be very healthy, we are not accustomed to it. We are naturally, our immune system was affected. We were so susceptible to coughs. Just an ordinary cold, it would go to extremes to some of us ... Every year you could always tell, a certain time of year. You knew you were going to develop a real bad cold. It kind of, it was almost a certain frequency.

Narcisse Blood

On Tuesday August 4th she brings up a point that 'the children are not a very healthy bunch' and I know this is one of the concerns that we had. I don't think we were very healthy at those residential schools because of the diet and being away from your parents forcibly. In our traditional ways of doctoring it's not just the ailment, but the whole person. And yes, children are going to get sick if they are lonely and if they are being told things like, 'You're not to speak your language. You'll be punished for your language.' But again, she makes an observation, and I would make the comment as an observation that you're almost blaming the victim, and that's based on ignorance again of a very superficial view and just writing what you observe without knowing the background of what's happening. And yes, our people were really unhealthy, spiritually, emotionally, and very much mentally. And you need all those faculties in place to be relatively balanced so you can battle any diseases that you are hit with.

Dorothy First Rider

She also mentions the children that were at the residential school. She measured twenty children that were there for the holidays. And those children at the time she wrote this, in 1925, did remain at the residential school, even during the holidays. She mentions the young girls' menstruation starting very early. I know later on a lot of them would not begin this process until their early teens, but now it's gone back to them beginning very early, so that's an interesting comment.

She also makes the comment that a lot of them have several open wounds and others have swollen ones which they had not reported and somebody made the comment that they don't say anything until they hurt. Indian people, the Blood Tribe, Aboriginal people, usually accept things that they have no control over, so if they had no control over their pain, they just kind of accepted their particular circumstance, be it right, or be it wrong, whether they should have received the healthcare or not, probably because the healthcare wasn't there; the medical attention wasn't given. There was not much they could do about it so they just accepted it. It would be good if somebody was to do an article on the residential school and also emphasize this.

The comment that she makes about some show signs of white blood and only one had hazel eyes ... Because of the length of time that it took for non-Native contact to have an impact or to reach the Blackfoot here in Western Canada attests to the fact that we were not impacted by non-Native society, even into the twenties there was not that much impact, and there were not that many mixed marriages, although the story is different when you get into Saskatchewan, Manitoba, Ontario, etc., where a lot of them today have lost their Aboriginal features. But that's not really prevalent here on the Blood Reserve and I think people here are very proud to say, 'I am of Aboriginal descent. I am of Blackfoot descent, or Blood descent.' Along with that we've still managed to maintain and still practise our religion, our traditional ways, maintain some of our values etc., where unfortunately in the eastern part of Canada they have totally lost their language and their original ways.

Martin Heavy Head

When they first introduced cattle farming or ranching at the turn of the century, there was no big cattle market, so people, the farmers and ranchers at that time kept cattle for no real good reason. Like, they were told by the Indian Agent to raise cattle. So they raised them and having access to free grazing they did have large herds of cattle and large herds of horses, and we actually became quite rich. But there was no place to sell the cattle. There was no cattle market for them to go and sell the cattle. The only place that would buy the cattle was the Indian Agent, to give as rations on the Reserve. So they had a slaughterhouse right on the Reserve, and I think it was around this time, or possibly before that. So people were very glad to go and sell their cattle to get rid of some of these cattle. They were taking care of them without really knowing what they were doing. But of course later on the big cattle markets developed and they could sell their [cattle]. And then, this visiting. People would go and visit all the time. Even months at a time.

'Blood Indians Notes' (Blackwood Papers, Related Documents, File A3, Fieldnotes)

[Page 1] The Bloods are a band of the Blackfoot Indians – their Reserve is in Southern Alberta just over the U.S. border – it is very large – and includes some of the best grain-growing land in Canada. They are fast becoming settled. Some of them are successful farmers and quite wealthy. They mostly live in houses in winter – which they have paid for themselves – but prefer tents in the summer. Their band now numbers 11,000 and is increasing. There is not very much white mixture. If a Blood woman marries a white man she leaves the Reserve and her children are not paid Treaty – though she herself may receive it. The illegitimate child of an Indian woman on this Reserve is counted as an Indian no matter who was the father. If a white woman marries an Indian her children count as Indians but this is very rare, and usually such a man would be educated and would not live on the Reserve in any case.

[Page 2] The adults have the appearance which is always considered typically Indian. They are very tall – many of the men over 6ft and have very large faces – narrow foreheads, very prominent cheekbones, very wide bizygomatic and very wide bigonial heavy square jaws – rather full lips and often broad noses – though the index would be low because of the very great nasal height – the noses are also very long and extremely convex in most cases. The U.F.I. and T.F.I. are very high. The men wear their hair in two plaits over their shoulders, it is often very long and thick. Some of the younger men have cut it short. The school girls all bob theirs, so I could not get any long pieces. The children often have a Mongolian fold in one or both eyes, but it seems to disappear about puberty. The adults sometimes have their eyes set somewhat obliquely and give the appearance of having a fold but it is not a true fold on examination.

Their faces are tanned – almost to copper colour in some cases, but on the unexposed parts they are light, for the girls an average would be N2R9 W5 Y4 on [page 3] the Bradley colour top. The hair is very dark brown or black – I have seen no exceptions to this in a large number. The Agent and the people at the hospital say they have never met with red hair. And the eyes dark brown unless there is white blood – which shows in the features also in all the people I have looked at.

The children have rounder faces and less pronounced features – the maxillae are not so prominent and the jaws have not the same square appearance, though the bigonial width tends to be larger than the m.f.d. in most cases.

The older people have frequently an edge to edge bite and the teeth are much worn. The younger ones have an overbite and the teeth are often irregular. The gums are not pigmented.

The girls mature very early – menstruation often begins at 8 years old – and 12 is common. They go on bearing children till 50 or over. Confinement becomes increasingly difficult as they lead a 'white man's life.' At first they would not come to the hospital but now they come freely, and infant mortality is decreasing. They marry often at 16, or earlier – and sometimes [page 4] have their first child at 14 – they are played out early in these cases. Marriage is often 'Indian fashion': by exchange of presents, and when the man gets tired of his wife he gives back the presents and goes to live with someone else. This is stopped by the Agent whenever possible but is difficult to change. They give their children away to other families quite freely. They all have Indian names. A child will not bear his father's name, but each member of a family might have a different name, e.g. 'Chief Moon,' 'Many Bears,' 'Don't Tie His Shoes' etc. This, added to the practice of adoption, makes it difficult to trace relationships and it is not improbable that there is a good deal of consanguineous marriage, though this is not allowed where it is known. The children, however, are now given an English Christian name, and their father's name, the Agent sees to this when paying Treaty, and is frequently asked [page 5] to choose the Christian name. There are R.C. and Methodist missions around but they haven't made much impression and but few of the children are baptized.

They used to bury the dead by wrapping them in a blanket and tying them up in a tree (the only trees on the Reserve are along the river) but do not any more. Now they dig a hole on top of a bit of rising ground and bury in a wooden coffin. At one time they left their dead in specially built houses – 'dead houses' this also is obsolete.

They still hold a Sun Dance in July each year, but much modified. They are not allowed to torture either men or animals. The great feature of the Sun Dance used to be the consumption of large numbers of buffalo tongues. They would slaughter beasts by the thousand, take their tongues and their hides and leave the rest. Now they have to use ox tongues of all the beef that is slaughtered for some time before saved for the occasion.

[Note on reverse of page 5] Note later. The Sun Dance and also the painted tepees are associated with an elaborate ritual which has been worked out by Dr Clark Wissler – see Anthropological Papers of the American Museum of Nat. History, Vol. VII, 1912.

[Note on reverse of page 3] The children are kept at boarding school all the time from puberty till 18 or till they get married. They were not a very healthy bunch, several had tubercular glands.

ANDY BLACKWATER

On the first page, she's quite accurate. She makes mention of the US border, the success of the farmers, becoming quite wealthy. They lived in houses in the winter, but preferred to live in tents and tipis in the summer. Talks about the population. Again makes mention that there's not much white mixture. She again makes reference to interracial marriages, what happens to the status of the Indian person, the Indian lady and the white lady, which I've already commented on. She does mention that it was very rare that an Indian man marries a white lady.

On page 2 she makes reference to the description of the Indian man – facial features. And again she makes mention of the hair, the braids. Here's where she mentions that once they go to school they cut their braids off, wear different hairstyle. She says the girls also were made to wear a different ... She does make mention of the Mongolian Fold, which perhaps needs more clarification. Then it goes on to continuation of dealing with the outward appearance. She talks about teeth. These are her observations.

Those people that she visited were the chiefs, and the houses; those are the people that today we refer to as *Issoitapiiksi*, the Riverside People. A lot of them were from the Fish Eater clan but even at that point in time the clans started to live, like a clan will disperse to other parts of the Reserve, so in these areas, like the Riverside community was made up of a certain clan but a mixture of others. So the features also, like today, you go to Glenwood, you go to Levern, and you look at the people in that immediate area, they kind of would be different. You go to another part of the Reserve, they tend to look different, feature-wise. So, maybe she needed to visit other parts, because this is a very big community, to get the full scope.

The interesting thing to note at this time was when we settled on the Reserve, the name of the clans became more regional, as opposed to the earlier names. Like *Issoitapiiksi*, Riverside People, it is almost like a clan. Then we have *Spikskoitapiiksi* – All Tall Tree People, Tall Tree People. It's an opposite of the area between Cardston and Fish Creek area where there's no trees, so that's a reverse. It's kind of humorous. Then you have the Thirty Tree People, east of Cardston. Then you have *Tatsikiitapiwa* the Standoff People now, *Tatsikiitapiwa*. Then, *Issoitapiiksi*, then *Aakaiksamaiksi*, or *Pinaapitapiiksi*, and this is one of the older clan names [and in this context means 'the people from Old Agency']. But within those you have All Short People, based on the characteristics of those, All Tall People, based on the characteristics of that clan, and then All Black Face People, *Mo'toisikskiiksi*. Then you have *Aakaipokaiksi*, Many Children clan, based on you know. So, the clans, the larger clans, still had at that time, outstanding physical characteristics. It may not have been the best thing in this case for her to have just visited Levern. The All Short People.

Here is a statement that she makes which is not accurate. 'Marriage is often Indian fashion by exchange of presents. And when a man gets tired of his wife, he gives back the presents and goes to live with someone else.' That is not an accurate statement. Marriages occur through traditional ways, based on survival. Primarily the principal in this is for survival. So naturally, if I want my daughter to be able to survive, to have her basic needs met, then naturally I would look for the best hunter, the best provider. Not necessarily the most handsome man. Even at that point in time it was still practised that your daughter would still have a good, easier [life], but you don't want to put your daughter where she would have to struggle, where she would be abused. So, a lot of arranged marriages did occur. But being that we were going through a transition, of being Christianized, these things start to change. The role of the provider was altered. So, it became sort of a thing like today, it's not necessarily based on survival any more. But of course, a young lady always tries to marry a rich [man], you know. It started to alter at that time. But you never give back the presents. In fact, if you're going to marry you give presents, you don't get presents. The girl might get presents, not necessarily presents, but your wife might be provided for in terms of those things that she needs to be a good wife. But you, you don't get, I haven't heard of returning presents. That is not an accurate statement. And of course it is very difficult to interpret, to try to understand, what does she mean by 'when a man gets tired of his wife'? I would imagine the Indian Agent was the one that told her that. So that's not accurate.

'This is stopped by the Agent whenever possible, but is difficult to change.' I would imagine this is where they tried to ... some were still in the practice of having more than one spouse, so I would imagine this is where the laws of the land state you can only have one wife at a time. So the Indian Agent is trying to implement those laws. But the interesting thing that happened prior to that and around that time is the coming of the Mormons. The Mormons, they practised that. They could have two, or as many wives as they wanted. And us, we practised the same out of necessity, not out of pleasure. So, maybe our ancestors felt that there was something in common; for the first time something was in common, so we accepted the Mormons.

Anyway, she talks about 'they give their children away to other families quite freely.' This is where traditional adoption needs to be looked at, and the principles of traditional adoption. I've already alluded to some of that. It is an honourable thing to be adopted by another set of parents, then you have another set of brothers and sisters, even grandparents. And this is all based on natural law; we don't undo what was meant to be. So that apparently which laws would she be citing, or what is, you know, it would be difficult for us to say specifically where she's coming from. It could be understood that these parents just didn't want their children; they were dumping that responsibility. But maybe it needs further elaboration.

The names I've already made some mention on that. Like we all have Indian names, and as a child you have a name that is reflective of your character or your characteristics. As you get older you earn another name. Maybe later on then you earn another name, through marriage, based on your marriage. And usually the name you have is a former clan name. So, like I had stated earlier, you have a name and they'll ask you which clan you're from, then you state your clan. So the way that family names are used, we use the clan name. Usually everybody is quite aware of a name, a certain name will belong to a clan. The nuns and the priests and the Indian agents had great difficulty in following through with names. They failed to realize there is and there was a clan system that is closely associated with names ... She does make some mention of names, first names, like Chief Moon, Many Bears, Don't Tie His Shoes. Now, Don't Tie His Shoes, I would imagine is inaccurate, because this *Kataino'siwa* is associated with a very old person who probably never wore shoes. So that is an incorrect translation. She adds that she encounters from the Indian Agent I suppose, that the Indian Agent is encountering difficulty with names for record keeping. And that is when they started giving Christian names.

The only other one that is totally incorrect, 'The great feature of the Sun Dance used to be the consumption of large numbers of buffalo tongues. They would slaughter beasts by the thousand and take their tongues and their hides and leave the rest.' They would use oxen and cattle. They only use a hundred. A hundred tongues. It corresponds to the hundred willows that are being used for the Holy Woman's *Ookan*, sweat lodge. It's a hundred. Fifty willows on one; half are coloured black and red. So they correspond. It may mislead. 'They take their tongues and their hides and leave the rest.' It was the buffalo hunters that came out and I suppose some of our people may have assisted those buffalo hunters, but they were hunting the buffalo right off the trains. They had Buffalo Bills and all of those people, and they slaughtered the buffalo by the thousands. They left the carcass; all they took was the hide, so this may also mislead, that it was us that did the slaughtering and wasting of the meat of the buffalo. We did practise conservation. We only took what we can use, and leave the rest for later. That is our principle. We do not accumulate. We might accumulate some for winter provisions, to carry us from that point in time to the next harvest time, so we might do that. But we don't have means of transporting all of these items from one camp to another, so we just cure enough or dry enough for where we are going to settle for the winter, to have enough provisions for that. And then we go out and gather whatever we need for the next winter. It's not going out to slaughter. Our people, according to our own historians, had to go right down to Yellowstone and that area when the buffalo became very scarce, and that's why Chief Red Crow was almost late for the treaties because he was down there hunting for the winter while the treaties were being arranged. He took it very lightly; it was just one of those treaties that the government or whoever is just going to break or breach. So they started going that far in different directions due to the scarcity of the buffalo.

DOROTHY FIRST RIDER

The comments that she makes on the Reserve being very big, a very large Reserve and that the Reserve in southern Alberta is just over the US border is very true and also supports the research we were doing on one of our claims, which is referred to as the Big Claim, where the Canadian government at the time took it upon themselves to move our border fourteen miles north to accommodate the US government and the forty-ninth parallel that it instituted, and the customs officers there and some of the large cattle holders and some of the large mainstream non-Native ranchers and farmers that were in that area. And that's why the border was moved and our Reserve was lessened by fourteen miles to the north. So, like I said this is an extremely valuable document and if you hadn't brought it I don't know how much longer it would have taken us to be able to uncover information of this importance.

She makes another interesting comment in terms of our physical appearance. A lot of the men are over six feet and to this day a lot of our men are still very tall. They are still over six feet tall compared to some of the other Aboriginal people, some of the other tribes, especially in northern Alberta where they tend to be very small; in BC where they are very short, very stocky, etc. I don't know what relevance it would have but yes, we are very tall. The children according to her observation have rounder faces and less pronounced faces and I don't know why the physical appearances would differ from that of their parents. There must have been an introduction of some other physical traits by another, maybe from the people that were coming in from the US. I don't know.

'Confinement becomes increasingly difficult as they lead a white man's life.' I imagine by the 1920s people were becoming a little more dependent on the type of medication that was offered, for example, she makes reference to the hospital, where they have difficulty confining people that require medication but now they come freely. I imagine that some of this can be attributed to the fact that people did not have the faith, and they also were still practising a lot of the traditional means of attending to the sick people on the Reserve, whereas now, maybe the trust was there in allowing hospitals to be able to cater for medical attention.

It was [true] at the time people did marry very young. Some of them married when they were sixteen; some of them even younger than that. It seemed to have been an accepted way of life. You got married at sixteen and you began raising your family and now, well, there are still some people who believe in marrying quite young but I think the tendency is to wait until your twenties and even thirties. There's not that much pressure any more. They really didn't have careers and they were not encouraged to pursue careers. A lot of them, like I said, were housekeepers. A lot of them worked at the hospital, and that basically was it. They were not encouraged to go into any kind of careers. I know at the time if there was the pursuit of higher education there was the danger of losing Treaty status and that was right within the Indian Act, so people did not pursue those types of professions. And that was not changed until 1953, so when she was writing this in 1925, people were still not encouraged to go into any kind of professions.

She says that marriage is still 'Indian fashion through exchange of presents.' I don't know about that. I never heard of it. 'When a man gets tired of his wife he gives back the presents and goes to live with someone else.' I'll have to ask. It's a curious statement.

'They give their children away to other families quite freely.' I imagine an outside onlooker would think that we still practise this today but actually what happened at that time was we had our own form of adoption, whereas if a parent or parents, whether it was a single parent or a family, did not have the ability to raise a child properly then they would give that responsibility to a family member that wanted to take on that responsibility. So what we have today are foster parents; we have guardians; we have people that are taking care of children that are taken away by the courts and placed, and they used to be placed with a lot of non-Native families, whereas today the courts and Children's Services are attempting to place them within their own cultural setting so we practised it at that time without it being formally referred to as a placement for children.

The notation that she makes about everybody having their own names, for example, 'Chief Moon, Many Bears, Don't Tie His Shoes, etc.' We are very proud in the Blood Tribe that we maintained our names, whereas especially in Saskatchewan, a lot of them, when the Roman Catholics were introduced into that area changed the names of those First Nations there and they all gave them French names. And that's why you have a lot of, mostly the First Nations in Saskatchewan, have French surnames, and we here on the Blood Reserve and within the Blackfoot community have our original names.

The Sun Dance, where she references the torture ceremony, I imagine for an outsider looking in, it would simply be an act of torture, without them understanding what led to that particular act of torture. It wasn't a form of torture. People would make a pledge when they required additional prayers or if they made a pledge and they stated that someone was really sick and they would do this and the child was saved, or someone was saved, so it was a form of personal sacrifice. But for the outside audience I guess it would just be a means of torture and they wouldn't understand why people were doing that. And it's still practised today.

MARTIN HEAVY HEAD

'They give their children away to other families quite freely.' Well, I think before the reservation days the children were the centre of the whole clan and they knew that their survival depended on their children, so they had to raise their children to be very generous, very kind, to be strong and to be brave. Because they would be the ones fighting for them when they were old men and women. It would be their kids that would be providing food for them and safety and shelter and so on. So they had to raise their children with those attributes in mind. But of course, when these people moved from the previous lifestyle to become settled on reserves and become dependent on the white man, that whole idea changed. They were now no longer dependent on the band system; they were dependent on a foreign government. And as I said earlier, the Bloods were very much aware of this. In fact, they called the Indian Agent their father, and where he lived was where the father lived, kind of thing. So I think there was a very real understanding of the situation they were in. But there was some carry over from the previous days, in that if you all lived in the same camp and you're all related, then it doesn't matter who raised the children. So this giving of the children 'very freely' was a very real thing and must have continued on into the reservation days because there was never any idea, in fact, if somebody else loved the children as much as you do, or more than you do, then why not? You know, why not get them to raise the child. Because they'd still be in the same camp. You'd still see them every day. So I think that was very much the idea with that.

'They all have Indian names.' It was considered at the time that getting your name was like baptism. If you were to die without a name, you would go to wherever you would go without a name. You wouldn't have an identity. You have to have a name. It's kind of like baptism. 'A child will not bear his father's name, but each member of a family might have a different name.' Again, that's kind of referring back to European customs and having a first name and a surname. But then of course, you're identified by the clan that you come from, so the clan becomes kind of the surname, which is the case anyway.

This idea of the Agent choosing the Christian name, well, among the Bloods, and the Blackfoot in general, it's quite an important deal to get a name. And one of the things that they used to talk about was when they went to school at Dunbow, they would go there and they'd just have some name. So they had to try and identify them at these residential schools, so I guess one of the things they did was they would put a bunch of names in hats, and people would come and pick out a name. And even if somebody already had a name, they'd go up and choose a new name, because it was an honour to get a new name!

'They are not allowed to torture either men or animals.' I wonder why ... she's probably thinking about ritual sacrifice of animals [like] in some other cultures. This is wrong. 'They would slaughter beasts by the thousand. Take the tongues and their hides and leave the rest.' That was as a result of dealing with the fur trade. You know, it probably did happen. Probably Blood Indians did take part in it at some time or another, but that didn't have anything to do with the Sun Dance. It was the trading of hides. My grandfather was telling me that they had those buffalo hunting rifles, very long, and they would have to collect as many hides stacked on top on each other as the same height as the rifle. That's what they would trade for a buffalo rifle.

'The great feature of the Sun Dance used to be the consumption of large numbers of buffalo tongues.' Yeah, I think they did used to use a hundred buffalo tongues, but the hundred buffalo tongues were actually cut into small pieces and dried, and then when the woman comes out she would feed everybody. It was a public thing. Everybody in the place would be fed. Now I think they only use four. So a lot of it is ... And then 'they would slaughter beasts by the thousand' again I think that was the fur trade.

Notes

Introduction

1 The Kainai (or *Akainai*) are a Blackfoot-speaking people. The Blackfoot Nations recognize three tribes among themselves: the Kainai; the Piikani (Peigan), who comprise the *Apatohsipikani* in southern Alberta and the *Amsskaapipikani* (Blackfeet), whose reservation is in Montana, and the Siksika (also known as Blackfoot or Northern Blackfoot). The name the Kainai use for themselves is often translated as Many Leaders/Chiefs, a name said to have originated when a visitor to the Tribe asked to see the leader and was approached by several men claiming this title (F. Taylor 1989: 24). Another story about the origin of the name Kainai arose when one of three brothers (*Siksikawa*, *Piikani*, and *Kainaiwa*) came back from a quest with many scalps of men (*Ninnaiks*) and was thus named '*Aakainawa*/Many men/chiefs' (Arima 1995: 1, citing Schultz and Donaldson 1930: 24–5; Duane Mistaken Chief to Brown, pers. comm. 27 April 2004). They became known as the Bloods following a translation error of the Blackfoot word for Weasel People, the name by which they were known among the Blackfoot-speaking Nations in recognition of the weasel-tail shirts they wore. The Blackfoot word for the weasel in its white (winter) phase is *aapaiai*, whereas the word for blood is *aáápan* (Crow Chief 30 November 2002; Duane Mistaken Chief to Brown, pers. comm. 27 April 2004).

2 For the purposes of this book we define the term 'source communities' as the descendants of those groups whose material heritage is now in museum collections.

3 In Canada the collective term 'First Nations' is applied to federally recognized Native communities and is generally preferred over the term 'In-

dian,' though this is still current in much Canadian legislation. Whenever possible, museums and researchers should use the specific name used by the Nations with whom they work. We use 'Kainai' to refer to people from this Nation, as that is what they call themselves in their own language, *Kainaiwa*, though they frequently use the name 'Blood' when speaking in English. At some places in this book, however, we use 'Blood' to indicate colonial perspectives (as in Blood Tribe or Blood Reserve, a name given by the federal government and still the official government designation for the Kainai reserve). In other places in the text we use the terms Aboriginal, Native, and non-Native, to imply broad First Nations perspectives that are neither tribally nor nationally specific.

1: The Photographs and Their Contexts

1 Joseph Thomas Faunt (1882–1949) was born in Haddington, Scotland and emigrated to Canada in 1903. He worked in Montreal before travelling to western Canada in 1905, eventually settling in Fort Macleod. He moved to the Blood Reserve with his wife and young family in 1921 when he was appointed Indian Agent, a post which he left in 1926. Faunt's family recall that he often spoke of his respect for Kainai people, and that the tribe honoured him for his assistance. He subsequently worked as Indian Agent on several other reserves, including Peigan (1943–4), Morley, Winterburn (1945), and Hobbema. We are most grateful to Tim Faunt, Bob Faunt, Campbell Hardie, and Kira Lyttik for generously providing us with additional information and insights into Joseph Faunt's career.

2 On Blackfoot history in general, see Lewis 1942; Ewers 1958; Raczka 1979; Hungry Wolf 1980; Dempsey 1980, 2001, 2003; Nugent 1993; Bullchild 1985; Blackfoot Gallery Committee 2001; Smyth 1976, 2001.

3 In his winter count, Percy Creighton of the Blood Tribe recorded 1878 as 'the year the buffalo went out of sight' (Goldfrank 1945: 12; see also Ewers 1958: 279).

4 Duane Mistaken Chief has noted that in the context of tradition, this term refers to the 'laying down of arms' (Duane Mistaken Chief to Brown, pers. comm. 8 September 2004).

5 Treaty 7 was signed at Blackfoot Crossing on 22 September 1877 by the Siksika, *Apatohsipikani*, Kainai, and also the Tsuu T'ina and Stoney Nations (Bearspaw, Chiniki, and Wesley/Goodstoney). In 1996, elders and scholars of the region published the results of a major research project documenting the First Nations' perspectives on the Treaty and its cultural and historical contexts (Treaty 7 Elders et al. 1996).

6 In his glossary to Bastien's *Blackfoot Ways of Knowing* (2004), Duane Mistaken Chief explains *Ihtsipaitapiiyo'pa* as 'sacred power, spirit or force that links concepts; life force; term used when addressing the sacred power and the cosmic universe; sun as manifestation of the Source of Life; great mystery; together with *Ihtsipaitapiiyo'pa* identifies the meaning and purpose of life' (Mistaken Chief in Bastien 2004: 228).

7 The 1921 Census recorded a population of 14,557 Native people residing in the province of Alberta. The national Native population was recorded as 110,596 (Dominion Bureau of Statistics 1927: 939). The 1924 Census of Indians and Eskimos in Canada calculated the population of the Blood Tribe as 1,158 individuals; 587 were males and 571 were female (Department of Indian Affairs 1924: 2), though it is worth pointing out that on two occasions in her diary and fieldnotes Blackwood erroneously recorded the Blood population as some 11,000 people.

8 Only the Siksika chose to remain in the reserve originally allocated to them.

9 For further information on the organization and history of Kainai clans see F. Taylor 1989: 312–16 and Zaharia and Fox 1995a: vi–vii.

10 During the *aako'ka'tssin* (circle camp), the ceremonial and social gathering held each summer at the sacred Belly Buttes (*Mookowansin*), the camp continues to be organized according to clan, as it has been for generations.

11 William Graham (1867–1939) was Commissioner for Indian Affairs for the Prairie Provinces from 1920 to 1932 (Graham 1991; Titley 1995).

12 For surveys of Native agricultural activity in the Prairie provinces see Carter 1990 and Buckley 1993.

13 Horses played a profoundly important social, and sometimes ceremonial, role within Kainai ways. Though some scholarly research has addressed the economic impact of the loss of livestock during this era, the death of so many horses had implications that stretched beyond economics in a period when the relationships between Kainai and horses were changing rapidly. *Nina Piiksii* (Mike Bruised Head) has noted that Kainai 'were equal with our horses before the residential school. The residential school experience taught us that horses were simply beasts of burden whose purpose was to help us break the land and pull heavy equipment. Our horses were being crossbred with foreign breeds. They were no longer our pets and our friends. They were no longer sacred' (quoted in Baillargeon and Tepper 1998: 22).

14 On the whole, the Prairie economy was fairly strong across the 1920s (see Friesen 1984: 383–4). On the development of Euro-Canadian settler society in Alberta generally from the Treaty period through the 1920s, see Friesen 1984; D.C. Jones 2002; Palmer and Palmer 1990.

15 St Paul's Anglican Mission School was established by the Rev. Samuel Trivett on an area of the Reserve called *Omahksinni* (Big Island), directly across the river from what has since become known as Old Agency.

16 Much correspondence in the DIA and Blood Indian Agency papers attests to this concern; for example, in a letter from Ottawa to the Indian agent it was noted that 'A serious objection to these dances is the attendance thereat of Whitemen from Macleod and other points. It is thought that it would be advisable if you would post up warnings that any Whitemen attending these dances on the reserve will be liable to be prosecuted' (Department of Indian Affairs, Blood Indian Agency Correspondence 1912–15, J.D. McLean to W.J. Dilworth, 23 March 1914. GAI M1788/98.

17 Linda Poolaw's essay about her father, Horace Poolaw, gives an insight into the work of one of the earliest Native photographers in North America. Poolaw worked as a photographer from 1920 to 1975 (Poolaw 1998).

18 On critical evaluations of photographs of First Nations people, see Scherer 1975; Lyman 1982; Lippard 1992; Bush and Mitchell 1994; Johnson 1998.

19 See also Edwards: 'the detail [of photographs] comes to stand for general truths which are perhaps external to the dynamics of the image itself' (Edwards 1992: 10).

20 Dawson's images are held by the Provincial Archives of Alberta and the Glenbow Archives.

21 This image can be found at the Provincial Archives of Alberta, reference number A.17475, and is reproduced in Silversides 1994: 21.

22 The Blackfeet Reservation in Montana was established for the *Amsskaapipikani* (Southern Piegan) following a series of treaties and sales in the nineteenth century, beginning with the Lame Bull Treaty of 1855.

23 See Kehoe 1995 for brief discussion of the Blackfoot peoples as subjects of study.

24 The collections of the Victoria Memorial Museum are now part of the Canadian Museum of Civilization.

25 Reiss's own work is regarded as less stereotypical than many of the representations of Native peoples produced by his contemporaries, and his portraits remain popular today (Tanner 2000).

26 Sheridan received many gifts during her time on the Blood Reserve, some of which are now in the Hastings Museum, England, along with several of the photographs which were used to illustrate *Redskin Interlude* and plaster moulds of her Kainai sculptures. See also B. Taylor 1984.

27 The resulting image captioned 'Rough-Hair arranging his war bonnet on the author's head' is illustrated in Sheridan 1938.

28 James Willard Schultz (1859–1947) worked as a fur trader on the Blackfeet

reservation during the last quarter of the nineteenth century. He was married to a Piikani woman and lived on the reservation till his wife's death in 1903. He spoke Blackfoot fluently, and wrote numerous popular books based on his experiences and the stories he heard while living with the Blackfeet people. Though Schultz is regarded as a storyteller who took liberties with factual history, he undoubtedly was far more aware of the realities of the transition that Blackfoot people were experiencing during the late nineteenth and early twentieth centuries than some of the more scholarly writers who were later to publish on Blackfoot history and culture.

29 Wilson (1863–1944) was a keen amateur ethnographer, and many of the notes he took while employed as agent at the Peigan Indian Agency (1898–1903) and subsequently for the Blood Tribe (1904–11) are available in the Glenbow Archives.

30 See, for instance, Glenbow NA-668–2.

31 These photographers include John F. Atterton, Harry Pollard, Arnold Lupson, and Tomer J. Hileman.

32 Copies of photographs created by Anderton, Atterton, Pollard, and Lupson can be found in the Glenbow Archives and the Provincial Archives of Alberta.

33 For comparative discussion of Australian Aboriginal responses to studio photography see Aird 2003.

34 Glenbow Archives NA-3910-36a, NA-3910–59 to NA-3910-61.

2: Anthropological Contexts

1 The Tuskegee Institute was founded by Booker T. Washington in 1881 as a college for African Americans in Tuskegee, Alabama. It is now an American National Historic Park site.

2 Blackwood's papers are in the Photographs and Manuscripts Department of the Pitt Rivers Museum. References to her teaching papers are from the Blackwood Papers, Boxes 13, 16, 17, 21, 22, 23.

3 Comment in a lecture script, Blackwood Papers, Lecture Notes, Box 13. 'Plains' lecture notes also marked in Blackwood's hand, 'most of this is in "Lands and Peoples" drawer,' p. 16.

4 Blackwood Papers, Lands and Peoples Lecture Series, Box 23, 'Plains Indian' lecture and slide lists. Two slide lists; first n.d. but followed by second list dated 'Michaelmas Term 1954.'

5 Blackwood Lantern Slides: drawer 'Plains Indians,' Pitt Rivers Museum Manuscripts and Photographs Department.

6 On the following page, she has inserted by hand, 'No scientific justification for generalisations on mentality' (Blackwood Papers, Lecture III, Box 21).

7 Linton was Assistant Curator of the North American Indian collections at the Field Museum, Chicago, 1922–8. In 1936 he published (together with R. Redfield and M.J. Herskovits) the 'Memorandum for the Study of Acculturation' in *American Anthropologist.*

8 This point is worth commenting on in relation to Blackwood's Kainai photographs. Headgear is essential in the summertime in Alberta, when temperatures frequently reach the mid-30s Celsius, and it is worth observing that all of the Kainai men and boys Blackwood photographed had hats. The only men wearing them, however, are the man whom Blackwood identified as Melting Tallow (figs. 24–5) and *Aistainsski* (Coming Singer) (fig. 1.2 and fig. 23); all the others were photographed with their hats held behind them, at their sides, or tucked under their arms. In the series of photos taken outside the tipi (figs. 18–20), only one (fig. 18) shows *Isstsstsiimi* (Rough Hair) with his head covered by a scarf; this he removed for the subsequent shots, suggesting that this had been at Blackwood's request.

9 Quotation from Blackwood Papers, Lecture notes and working papers, Box 16, 'Methods of Physical Anthropology' (typewritten manuscript, n.d. but contextually ca late 1940s; pp. 16–17).

10 We have added a column indicating the identifications provided by the Kainai community for the people Blackwood photographed.

11 As did her measurements of skin and eye colour in whites at the University of Minnesota and in Appalachian villages; of African Americans at the Tuskegee Institute of Alabama; and of American Indians in a number of communities (Blackwood 1930: 146, 148, 152).

12 These notes, and the children's drawings referred to, are in a manuscript box in storage at the Pitt Rivers Museum, labelled '1994.15/Drawings and hair samples collected by Miss Blackwood/NORTH AMERICA.'

13 Captions for her lantern slides are recorded on cards in a file: PRM Photographs and Manuscripts Department, catalogue cards for lantern slides, box 'North America.' This caption is for slide 28 in the Blackfoot series.

14 Rosie Red Crow identified this child as Margaret Yellow Shine. It is noticeable that Blackwood recorded only the names of the schoolgirls, and not those of the several other children that she photographed (but presumably did not measure).

15 PRM Photographs and Manuscripts Department, catalogue cards for lantern slides, box 'North America.' This caption is for slide 31 in the

Blackfoot series. Blackwood's note that elk teeth were a sign of wealth shows a superficial understanding of what they represented for Kainai people. As it took one elk to get two teeth, a dress to be ornamented with two hundred teeth, for example, would require a hunter to kill one hundred elk. This would indicate the industriousness of the hunter – a desired trait among Kainai – and his ability to provide for others, ensuring their survival (Duane Mistaken Chief to Brown, pers. comm. 8 September 2004).

16 We are indebted to Peter Geller, Lavina Clarke, Maureen Matthews, Roger Roulette, David Pentland, and Kevin Russell for information on this phrase and its use to mean 'England.'

3: Working Together

1 As well as the Glenbow Museum gallery described in this chapter, Kainai people have worked with staff from the British Museum and Royal Ontario Museum to produce a temporary exhibition, *Ákaitapiiwa/Ancestors*, which brought scattered parts of a collection made on the Blood Reserve around 1900 back to the region for a brief time (Brownstone 2002; King and Wood 2002). Three of Blackwood's photographs were used in this exhibition, and were accompanied by captions relating biographical information about the subjects.

2 A bundle was returned to the Kainai Nation from Marischal Museum, Aberdeen, Scotland, in 2003. This was the first bundle housed in a European museum to be repatriated to the Kainai.

3 Dr Gerald Conaty, Senior Ethnologist at Glenbow Museum, is also on the board. Institutions the Foundation has worked with include the National Museum of the American Indian, the Provincial Museum of Alberta, the Peabody Museum, Glenbow Museum, the Canadian Museum of Civilization, and Parks Canada (Mookaakin Cultural and Heritage Foundation n.d.).

4 The Glenbow and the Mookaakin Foundation signed a Memorandum of Understanding in 1998 in which they agreed to assist one another in furthering their goals (Mookaakin Cultural and Heritage Society and Glenbow-Alberta Institute 1998).

5 At the time of publication, this second project outcome has yet to be defined, but our Kainai advisors have stated that they would like to see educational materials produced for use within their schools. It is possible that with Kainai people we will curate an exhibition of the photographs to be shown at a central location on the Reserve and which may then travel to the Pitt Rivers Museum.

6 Comments of this sort have often been expressed during e-mail and telephone conversations with Kainai people since the project began. We have also enjoyed additional visits with friends from the community in conjunction with trips we have made to Canada and they have made to Europe, during which it has been possible to discuss the project's progress.
7 These materials were handed over to Red Crow Community College on 28 May 2003 along with educator packs for use in Kainai schools, which included CD-ROMs of the photographs, lists of names of those people in the images, copies of Blackwood's research notes, and contact details for the Pitt Rivers Museum.
8 For similar community-prompted exploration of views see Taylor's discussion of a community-based photographic project in Australia (P. Taylor 1988: xvii).
9 It should be noted that providing honoraria can raise complex issues concerning the 'value' of knowledge and the processes through which it is transmitted. Some individuals regard the assumption that honoraria will be offered by researchers, or accepted by interviewees, as a break with tradition and an unfortunate reflection of a society that has, by necessity, become money-focused. More generally, Native peoples and researchers have accepted that interviewees contribute crucial knowledge and perspectives which are equivalent to those of lawyers, professors, or other professionals who would expect financial compensation for their time and expertise.
10 We would like to thank Alvine Mountain Horse for inviting Brown to visit her grade 12 students and talk with them about the images.
11 Kainai and other Blackfoot people living on different reserves or in the cities of Lethbridge or Calgary also heard about the images through chatting with friends and relatives who had already seen them, and it was sometimes possible for Brown to meet with them – for instance, during occasional visits to Calgary.
12 Often when individuals requested copies of particular images, they stressed that they were intended as gifts for friends or relatives, who were closely related to the subject, rather than for themselves, though requests for personal copies were also frequent, and we were happy to be able to oblige.
13 Allowing people time to study the images at their own pace has been essential, as, with each viewing, more is remembered. Sometimes, at a first viewing, people would be recognized, but their names would not be recalled until later, when the viewer had time to consider the images properly without feeling pressured by the presence of a researcher.

14 P. Taylor (1988: xx) notes scepticism expressed by Aboriginal people that her research team would send photos back as promised, and indeed this seems to be a very common doubt based on hard experience.
15 It was striking that during the second research visit, from June to September 2002, the protocol agreement was rarely mentioned. We can only assume that this was because all parties were adhering to what had been agreed, giving no one cause to draw attention to it. Likewise, on subsequent visits, little reference has been made to the agreement.
16 Though a small number of interviewees responded soon after receiving their tapes and transcripts, others did not have an opportunity to go through their transcripts and preferred to wait till Brown returned before doing so. Accordingly, they were able to witness any editing of the set of tapes intended for the community that was required. Following this review procedure, revised transcripts were given to the interviewees, and when we returned to Oxford, the master copies were also edited according to interviewees' requests.
17 We would like especially to thank Georgette Fox, Alternate School Counsellor at Red Crow Community College, who did much of the organization for this event, Andy Blackwater for advising on protocol, Myrna Chief Moon and her team for cooking, and Red Crow Community College for hosting us.
18 Photographs have been widely used in European and North American mainstream society as memory aids and links to oral tradition (in part, this is the function of family photograph albums). See also Kaplan's discussion of using photographs in Benin: photos 'served as links to oral tradition and memory among informants, and they stimulated, supplemented, and supported ethnographic study' (Kaplan 1990: 338).
19 On other source community uses and reappropriations of historical images, see Pinney 1989: 57; Kaplan 1990: 322.
20 On techniques used to 'read' photographs and artefacts, see Banks 2001: 44 (discusses the widespread, cross-cultural ability to 'read' photographs); Edwards 2001: 15, citing Poole 1997 on 'visual economy' (which equates well with the layers of textual explication in close reading); and Pearce 1994 (uses a semiotic, text-based approach to decode levels of meaning in an object).

4: Reading the Photographs

1 Mike Mountain Horse (1888–1964), a Kainai who became a writer following active service in the First World War, included a short chapter on the

'Origin of Indian Names and Other Customs' in his memoir, *My People the Bloods*. In it he described three distinct types of name used by Kainai people: 'the baby pet name, the hereditary name, and the war or battle name' (Mountain Horse 1989: 89).

2 See Kingston 2003 for comparative discussion of a project linking names, people and archival film footage from the King Island Native community, Alaska.

3 During interviews, several people commented that they wished the photographs were not black and white so that they could see the colours of *Isstsstsiimi*'s blanket.

4 By this period, fake elk teeth carved from wood or bone were often used rather than genuine teeth.

5 The smiling girl in the school photographs is *Noyiss* (Louise) Don't Tie His Shoes.

6 Photographs have been used in various therapeutic applications, for instance in family therapy, mental health treatment, and work with troubled youth. The use of photographs in therapy is presented in major works by Krauss and Fryrear 1983; Berman 1993; Weiser 1988, 1999.

7 For a comparative discussion on the possibilities of bringing together Blackfoot and Euro-Canadian philosophies and practices, see Crowshoe and Manneschmidt's (2002) discussion of healthcare provision at the Piikani Nation.

5: The Past in the Present

1 See Schwarz 1997 for an exploration of the very troubling gazes of Navajo women in one group of historic photographs, and Pinney (1989: 61), whose survey of a broad range of anthropological photographs leads him to note that some subjects 'return the viewer's gaze with such an assertiveness that there is no doubt about who is the dominant partner in the transaction of looking.' There is also, of course, the gaze of revisionist scholars who see historic photographs and other products of earlier anthropology very differently from how their predecessors did.

2 For an overview of the historical traditions of Plains peoples see DeMallie and Parks 2001.

3 The Real People, a term which includes all the indigenous people of North America.

4 Mookaakin Foundation members did not make taped statements, as their consent was implied through the signing of the protocol agreement. All Foundation members who were interviewed did, of course, review their

transcripts, and in one of our group meetings in May 2003, we shared a joint discussion of what we have all learned through participating in this project.

5 See, for example Treaty 7 Elders et al. 1996; F. Taylor 1989; Blackfoot Gallery Committee 2001 as well as numerous educational resources and publications produced by the Kainai Board of Education and the Blood Tribe intended for community use, e.g., Fox 2001; Zaharia and Fox 1995a,b,c; Zaharia, Fox, and Fox 2003.

6 See www.pitcouncil.com.au/social_arairititja.html (accessed 29 October 2001).

6: Moving Forward

1 One work which attempts to address the cross-cultural nature of museum exhibition is Leo Pettipas, *'Other Peoples' Heritage': A Cross-Cultural Approach to Museum Interpretation* (1994), which specifically targets the histories and collections represented by museums in Manitoba, Canada.

2 Plains Cree people made this particular suggestion during a visual repatriation project involving images of objects in the collection of the University of Cambridge Museum of Archaeology and Anthropology (Brown 2000). The term 'narcotics and intoxicants' used by this museum and several others in the United Kingdom as an organizational keyword to describe ceremonial pipes caused much concern to viewers of the images, who stated that it was derogatory and misunderstood the meaning of the pipes within Plains Cree spiritual culture.

3 To access the Glenbow's photographic collections, visit http://www.glenbow.org/archives.htm

4 At the Pitt Rivers Museum, for instance, certain sensitive photographs are 'available for research use "at the print" only; they are not available for copying or publication' (Edwards 2003: 95).

5 There is a large literature on Intellectual Property Rights and indigenous peoples; see, for instance, Posey 1990; Ziff and Rao 1997; Hansen and VanFleet 2003; and for international Human Rights instruments addressing intellectual property see *Universal Declaration of Human Rights*, article 27 (United Nations 1948); *Draft Declaration on the Rights of Indigenous Peoples*, article 29 (United Nations 1994); *Convention on Biological Diversity*, article 8 (j) (United Nations Environment Programme 1992).

6 As of 2003, the wording is: 'Significant electronic resources or datasets created as a result of research funded by the Board, together with documentation, must be offered for deposit at the AHDS within three months

of the end of the project' (AHRB Research Grants Terms and Conditions of Award, September 2003).

Conclusions

1 1988 marked two hundred years since the arrival of the First Fleet in the land known today as Australia. During this year numerous events were held to commemorate the occasion, which brought into sharp focus the realities of the tense relationship between Aboriginal people and Torres Strait Islanders and settler communities. After two centuries of colonialism, which threatened to eradicate all traces of Aboriginal life, many Aboriginal people and Torres Strait Islanders found no reason to celebrate this event, but instead regarded the bicentennial as a symbol of their survival.

Bibliography

Aird, M. 2003. 'Growing up with Aborigines.' In C. Pinney and N. Peterson, eds., *Photography's Other Histories*. Durham: Duke University Press.

Anon. 1933. *Catalogue of Motion Picture Films*. Ottawa: National Museum of Canada, Department of Mines, F.A. Acland.

Arima, E.Y. 1995. *Blackfeet and Palefaces: The Pikani and Rocky Mountain House*. Ottawa: Golden Dog Press.

Baillargeon, M., and L. Tepper. 1998. *Legends of Our Times: Native Ranching and Rodeo Life on the Plains and Plateau*. Vancouver: UBC Press in association with University of Washington Press and Canadian Museum of Civilization.

Banks, M. 2001. *Visual Methods in Social Research*. London: Sage Publications.

Banta, M., and C.M. Hinsley. 1986. *From Site to Sight: Anthropology, Photography and the Power of Imagery*. Cambridge, MA: Peabody Museum Press in association with Harvard University Press.

Barron, F.L. 1988. 'The Indian Pass System in the Canadian West, 1882–1935.' *Prairie Forum* 13 (1): 25–42.

Bastien, B. 2004. *Blackfoot Ways of Knowing: The Worldview of the Siksikaitsitapi*. Calgary: University of Calgary Press.

Beaulieu, D.L. 1984. 'Curly Hair and Big Feet: Physical Anthropology and the Implementation of Land Allotment on the White Earth Chippewa Reservation.' *American Indian Fall Quarterly* (fall): 281–314.

Bell, J.A. 2003. 'Looking to See: Reflections on Visual Repatriation in the Purari Delta, Gulf Province, Papua New Guinea.' In L. Peers and A.K. Brown, eds., *Museums and Source Communities: A Routledge Reader*. London: Routledge.

Berman, L. 1993. *Beyond the Smile: The Therapeutic Use of the Photograph*. London: Routledge.

Berndt Museum of Anthropology. 1997. *Berndt News: Newsletter of the Berndt Museum of Anthropology*. Number 1. September.

Bernstein, B. 1992. 'Communities in Collaboration: Strategies for Cultural Negotiation.' Paper presented at the 90th Annual Meeting of the American Anthropological Association, Chicago.

Bharadia, S. 1999. 'The Return of Blackfoot Sacred Material by Museums of Southern Alberta.' Unpublished MA thesis, University of Calgary.

Binney, J., and G. Chaplin. 1991. 'Taking the Photographs Home: The Recovery of a Maori History.' *Visual Anthropology* 4: 431–42.

Blackfoot Gallery Committee. 2001. *Nitsitapiisinni: The Story of the Blackfoot People*. Toronto: Key Porter Books.

Blackwood, Beatrice. Correspondence. Pitt Rivers Museum, University of Oxford, Manuscripts and Photographs Department, Blackwood Papers, Box 27.

– Diary, 1924–7. Pitt Rivers Museum, University of Oxford, Manuscripts and Photographs Department, Blackwood Papers, Box 12.

– Drawings and Hair Samples collected by Miss Blackwood/NORTH AMERICA. Pitt Rivers Museum, University of Oxford, Manuscripts and Photographs Department, Blackwood Papers, 1994.15.

– Ethnology Lectures, North America. Pitt Rivers Museum, University of Oxford, Manuscripts and Photographs Department, Blackwood Papers, Box 16.

– Fieldnotes. Pitt Rivers Museum, University of Oxford, Manuscripts and Photographs Department, Blackwood Papers, Related Documents File A3 (Plains), BB.A3.46–75.

– Lands and Peoples Lecture Series. Pitt Rivers Museum, University of Oxford, Manuscripts and Photographs Department, Blackwood Papers, Box 23.

– Lecture III. Pitt Rivers Museum, University of Oxford, Manuscripts and Photographs Department, Blackwood Papers, Box 21.

– Lecture Notes. Pitt Rivers Museum, University of Oxford, Manuscripts and Photographs Department, Blackwood Papers, Box 13.

– 1927. 'A Study of Mental Testing in Relation to Anthropology.' *Mental Measurement Monographs*. Serial no. 4, December. Baltimore.

– 1930. 'Racial Differences in Skin-Colour as Recorded by the Colour Top.' *Journal of the Royal Anthropological Institute* 60: 137–68.

– 1935. *Both Sides of Buka Passage*. Oxford: Clarendon Press.

– 1955. 'A Study of Artificial Cranial Deformation in New Britain.' *Journal of the Royal Anthropological Institute* 85: 173–7.

– 1970. *The Classification of Artefacts in the Pitt Rivers Museum, Oxford*. Pitt

Rivers Museum Occasional Papers on Technology 11. Oxford: Pitt Rivers Museum.

Blackwood, B., L.H. Dudley Buxton, and J.C. Trevor. 1939. 'Measurements of Oxfordshire Villagers.' *Journal of the Royal Anthropological Institute* 69 (1): 1–10.

Bodenhorn, B. 2000. '"He Used to Be My Relative": Exploring the Bases of Relatedness among Iñupiat of Northern Alaska.' In J. Carston, ed., *Cultures of Relatedness: New Approaches to the Study of Kinship*. Cambridge: Cambridge University Press.

Brittain, V. 1960. *The Women at Oxford*. London: George G. Harrap and Co.

Brown, A.K. 2000. 'Object Encounters: Perspectives on Collecting Expeditions to Canada.' Unpublished D.Phil. dissertation, University of Oxford.

Brown, A.K., J. Coote, and C. Gosden. 2000. 'Tylor's Tongue: Material Culture, Evidence and Social Networks.' *JASO: Journal of the Anthropological Society of Oxford* 31 (3): 257–76.

Brown, J.S.H., and E. Vibert, eds. 2003 [1996]. *Reading beyond Words: Contexts for Native History*. Peterborough: Broadview Press.

Brownstone, A. 2002. 'Ancestors: The Deane-Freeman Collections from the Bloods.' *American Indian Art Magazine* (summer): 38–49, 73–7.

Buckley, H. 1993. *From Wooden Ploughs to Welfare: Why Indian Policy Failed in the Prairie Provinces*. Montreal and Kingston: McGill-Queen's University Press.

Bullchild, P. 1985. *The Sun Came Down. The History of the World As My Blackfeet Elders Told It*. San Francisco: Harper and Row.

Bush, A., and L. Mitchell. 1994. *The Photograph and the American Indian.* Princeton: Princeton University Press.

Byrne, A. 1995. *Responsibilities and Response: Aboriginal and Torres Strait Islander Protocols for Libraries*. Archives and Information Services. First Roundtable on Library and Archives Collections and Services of Relevance to Aboriginal and Torres Strait Islander People. Available on-line at: http://www.nla.gov.au/niac/libs/byrne.html (accessed 28 September 2004).

Canadian Museum of Civilization. 2000. 'Harlan Ingersoll Smith.' Essay accompanying on-line exhibition *Emergence from the Shadows*. Available on-line at: http://www.civilization.ca/aborig/jaillir/jaillhse.html (accessed 25 April 2003).

Carter, S. 1990. *Lost Harvests: Prairie Indian Reserve Farmers and Government Policy*. Montreal: McGill-Queen's University Press.

Chapman, W. 1985. 'Arranging Ethnology: A.H.L.F. Pitt Rivers and the Typological Tradition.' In George W. Stocking, Jr, ed., *Objects and Others: Essays on Museums and Material Culture*. History of Anthropology 3. Madison: University of Wisconsin Press.

Clifford, J. 1997. *Routes: Travel and Translation in the Late Twentieth Century*. Cambridge, MA: Harvard University Press.

– 2004. 'Looking Several Ways: Anthropology and Native Heritage in Alaska.' *Current Anthropology* 45 (1): 5–30.

Collier, J. 1967. *Visual Anthropology: Photography as a Research Method*. New York: Holt, Reinhart and Winston.

Conaty, G.T. 2003. 'Glenbow's Blackfoot Gallery: Working towards Co-existence.' In L. Peers and A.K. Brown, eds., *Museums and Source Communities: A Routledge Reader*. London: Routledge.

– 2004. 'Le Repatriement du material sacre des pieds-noirs. Deux approches (The Repatriation of Blackfoot sacred material. Two Approaches.' *Anthropologie et Sociétés* 28 (1): 63–81.

Conaty, G.T., and B. Carter. 2005. '"Our Story in Our Words": Diversity and Equality in the Glenbow Museum.' In R.R. Janes and G.T. Conaty, eds., *Looking Reality in the Eye: Museums and Their Social Responsibility*. Calgary: University of Calgary Press.

Conaty, G.T., and C. Crane Bear. 1998. 'History, Connections, and Cultural Renewal.' In S. Boehme et al., eds., *Powerful Images: Portrayals of Native America*. Museums West in association with the University of Washington Press, Seattle.

Council of Australian Museum Associations. 1993. *Previous Possessions, New Obligations: Policies for Museums in Australia and Aboriginal and Torres Strait Islander People*. Melbourne: Council of Australian Museum Associations.

Crop Eared Wolf, A. 1997. 'Protecting Religious Rights and Freedoms.' *Alberta Museums Review* 23 (3): 38–40.

Crowshoe, R. 1996. 'Synopsis of Keep Our Circle Strong: Peigan Cultural Renewal.' In *Curatorship: Indigenous Perspectives in Post-colonial Societies*. Proceedings. Mercury Series Paper 8. Canadian Museum of Civilization with the Commonwealth Association of Museums and the University of Victoria.

Crowshoe, R., and S. Manneschmidt. 2002. *Akak'stiman: A Blackfoot Framework for Decision-Making and Mediation Processes*. Calgary: University of Calgary Press.

Cruikshank, J. 1998. *The Social Life of Stories: Narrative and Knowledge in the Yukon Territory*. Lincoln: University of Nebraska Press.

Dawson, B. 2002. '"Better Than a Few Squirrels": The Greater Production Campaign on the First Nations Reserves of the Canadian Prairies.' In P. Douaud and Bruce Dawson, eds., *Plain Speaking: Essays on Aboriginal Peoples and the Prairie*. Regina: Canadian Plains Research Center.

Day Rider, R. 2001. 'Makoyoohsokoyi (The Wolf Trail – The Milky Way).' In L. Fox, *Kipaitapiiwahsinnooni: Alcohol and Drug Abuse Education Program*. Edmonton: Duval House Publishing in association with the Kainai Board of Education.

DeMallie, R.J., and D.R. Parks. 2001. 'Tribal Traditions and Records.' In R.J. DeMallie, ed., *Handbook of North American Indians. The Plains*. 13 (part 2): 1062–73. Washington, DC: Smithsonian Institution Press.

Dempsey, H.A. 1980. *Red Crow: Warrior Chief*. Saskatoon: Western Producer Prairie Books.

– 1982. *History in Their Blood: The Indian Portraits of Nicholas de Grandmaison*. Vancouver and Toronto: Douglas and McIntyre.

– 1986. *The Gentle Persuader: A Biography of James Gladstone, Indian Senator*. Saskatoon: Western Producer Prairie Books.

– 1997. *Tom Three Persons*. Saskatoon: Purich Publishing.

– 2001. 'Blackfoot.' In R.J. DeMallie, ed., *Handbook of North American Indians. The Plains*. 13 (part 1). Washington, DC: Smithsonian Institution Press.

– 2002. *Firewater: The Impact of the Whisky Trade on the Blackfoot Nation*. Calgary: Fifth House.

– 2003. *The Vengeful Wife and Other Blackfoot Stories*. Norman: University of Oklahoma Press.

Department of Indian Affairs. 1924. *Census of Indians and Eskimos in Canada*. Ottawa: F.A. Acland.

– Blood Indian Agency Correspondence 1912–15. M1788/98. Glenbow-Alberta Institute, Calgary.

– RG 10, Vol. 3826. File 60,511-4, Pt. 1. National Archives of Canada.

– RG 10, Vol. 3827. File 60,511-4B. National Archives of Canada.

– RG 10, Vol. 6816. File 486–6-1, Pt. 1. National Archives of Canada.

Department of Indian and Northern Affairs. 1981. *Indian Acts and Amendments, 1868–1950*. Ottawa: Department of Indian and Northern Affairs Canada.

Dominion Bureau of Statistics. 1927. *The Canada Year Book*. Ottawa: F.A. Acland.

Edwards, E. 1994. 'Visualizing History: Diamond Jenness's Photographs of D'Entrecasteaux Islands, Massim, 1911–1912 – a Case Study in Re-engagement.' *Canberra Anthropology* 17 (2): 1–25.

– 1998. Photography and Anthropological Intention in Nineteenth Century Britain. *Revista de dialectologia y traditiones populares*, vol. 53, no. 2.

– 2001. *Raw Histories: Photographs, Anthropology and Museums*. Oxford: Berg.

– 2003. 'Talking Visual Histories.' In L. Peers and A.K. Brown, eds., *Museums and Source Communities: A Routledge Reader*. London: Routledge.

– ed. 1992. *Anthropology and Photography, 1860–1920*. New Haven and London:

Yale University Press in association with the Royal Anthropological Institute.

Edwards, E., and J. Hart 2004. 'Mixed Box: The Cultural Biography of a Box of "Ethnographic" photographs.' In Elizabeth Edwards and Janice Hart, eds., *Photographs Objects Histories: On the Materiality of Images*. London: Routledge.

Ewers, J.C. 1958. *The Blackfeet: Raiders on the Northwestern Plains*. Norman: University of Oklahoma Press.

– 1997. *Plains Indian History and Culture: Essays on Continuity and Change*. Norman: University of Oklahoma Press.

Farr, W.E. 1984. *The Reservation Blackfeet, 1882–1945*. Seattle: University of Washington Press.

Fienup-Riordan, A. 1996a. *The Living Tradition of Yup'ik Masks: Agayuliyararput (Our Way of Making Prayer)*. Seattle: University of Washington Press.

– 1996b. *Agayuliyararput (Our Way of Making Prayer): Yu'pik Masks and the Stories They Tell*. Seattle and London: Anchorage Museum of History and Art in association with the University of Washington Press.

– 1998. 'Yup'ik Elders in Museums: Fieldwork Turned on Its Head.' *Arctic Anthropology* 35 (2): 49–58.

– 1999. 'Collaboration on Display: A Yup'ik Eskimo Exhibit at Three National Museums.' *American Anthropologist* 101 (2): 339–58.

First Charger, F. 1998. *History of Agriculture on the Blood Indian Reserve and Information about the Blood Tribe Irrigation Project*. Standoff: Blood Tribe Agricultural Project.

Fisher, A.D. 1974. 'Introducing "Our Betrayed Wards" by R.N. Wilson.' *Western Canadian Journal of Anthropology* 4 (1): 21–31.

Fleming, P.R., and J. Luskey 1991 [1986]. *The North American Indian in Early Photographs*. Oxford: Phaidon Press.

Foucault, M. 1970. *The Order of Things*. London: Tavistock.

– 1976. *The Birth of the Clinic*. London: Tavistock.

Fourmile, H. 1990. 'Possession Is Nine Tenths of the Law – and Don't Aboriginal People Know It.' *COMA* 23: 57–67.

Fox, L. 2001. *Kipaitapiiwahsinnooni: Alcohol and Drug Abuse Education Program*. Edmonton: Duval House Publishing in association with the Kainai Board of Education.

Friesen, G. 1984. *The Canadian Prairies: A History*. Toronto: University of Toronto Press.

Geffroy, Y. 1990. 'Family Photographs: A Visual Heritage.' *Visual Anthropology* 3: 367–409.

Gidley, M. 1982. 'A.C. Haddon Joins Edward S. Curtis: An English Anthro-

pologist among the Blackfeet, 1909.' *Montana, the Magazine of Western History* (autumn): 20–33.
– 1998. *Edward S. Curtis and the North American Indian, Inc.* Cambridge: Cambridge University Press.
Goldfrank, E.S. 1945. *Changing Configurations in the Social Organization of a Blackfoot Tribe during the Reserve Period (The Blood of Alberta, Canada).* Monograph 8. American Ethnological Society. Seattle: University of Washington Press.
Goodstriker, W. 1996. Introduction. In Treaty 7 Elders and Tribal Council with W. Hildebrandt, D. First Rider, and S. Carter. *The True Spirit and Original Intent of Treaty 7.* Montreal and Kingston: McGill-Queen's University Press.
Gosden, C., and C. Knowles. 2001. *Collecting Colonialism: Material Culture and Colonial Change.* Oxford: Berg.
Graham, W.M. 1991. *Treaty Days: Reflections of an Indian Commissioner.* Calgary: Glenbow Museum.
Grant, S.D. 1983. 'Indian Affairs under Duncan Campbell Scott: The Plains Cree of Saskatchewan, 1913–1931.' *Journal of Canadian Studies* 18 (3): 21–39.
Hail, B.A., and K.C. Duncan. 1989. *Out of the North: The Subarctic Collection of the Haffenreffer Museum of Anthropology.* Bristol, RI: Haffenreffer Museum of Anthropology.
Hall, B. 1979. 'Knowledge as a Commodity and Participatory Research.' *Prospects* 9 (4): 393–408.
Hansen, S.A., and J.W. VanFleet. 2003. *Traditional Knowledge and Intellectual Property: A Handbook on Issues and Options for Traditional Knowledge Holders in Protecting Their Intellectual Property and Maintaining Biological Diversity.* Washington, DC: American Association for the Advancement of Science. Available on-line at: http://shr.aaas.org/tek/handbook (accessed 7 August 2003).
Henare, A. 2005. *Museums, Anthropology and Imperial Exchange.* Cambridge: Cambridge University Press.
Herle, A., and S. Rouse. 1998. *Cambridge and the Torres Strait: Centenary Essays on the 1898 Anthropological Expedition.* Cambridge: Cambridge University Press.
Hill, R.W., Sr. 1998. 'Developed Identities: Seeing the Stereotypes and Beyond.' In T. Johnson, ed., *Spirit Capture: Photographs from the National Museum of the American Indian.* Washington, DC: Smithsonian Institution Press in association with the National Museum of the American Indian.
Historic Sites Service and Alberta Community Development. n.d.. *Lost Identities: A Journey of Rediscovery Information Kit.* Unpublished information pack available from Historic Sites Service and Alberta Community Development.

Holman, N. 1996. 'Curating and Controlling Zuni Photographic Images.' *Curator* 39(2): 108–22.

Howard, A. 2002. www.repatriating_ethnography.edu/rotuma. In S.R. Jaarsma, ed., *Handle with Care: Ownership and Control of Ethnographic Materials*. Pittsburgh: University of Pittsburgh Press.

Hungry Wolf, B. 1980. *The Ways of My Grandmothers*. New York: Quill.

Jaarsma, S.R., ed. 2002. *Handle with Care: Ownership and Control of Ethnographic Materials*. Pittsburgh: University of Pittsburgh Press.

Johnson, T., ed. 1998. *Spirit Capture: Photographs from the National Museum of the American Indian*. Washington, DC: Smithsonian Institution Press in association with the National Museum of the American Indian.

Johnston, A. 1987. 'Plants and the Blackfoot.' Occasional Paper 15. Lethbridge: Lethbridge Historical Society.

Jones, D.C. 2002. *Empire of Dust: Settling and Abandoning the Prairie Dry Belt*. 5th ed. Calgary: University of Calgary Press.

Jones, S. 1994. 'Beatrice Blackwood Remembered.' *Friends of the Pitt Rivers Museum Newsletter*. Special 10th Anniversary Issue: 4–6.

Kaplan, F.S. 1990. 'Some Uses of Photographs in Recovering Cultural History at the Royal Court of Benin, Nigeria.' *Visual Anthropology* 3: 317–41.

Katakis, M., ed. 1998. *Excavating Voices: Listening to Photographs of Native Americans*. Philadelphia: University of Pennsylvania Museum.

Kehoe, A.B. 1995. Introduction. In C. Wissler and D.C. Duvall, *Mythology of the Blackfoot Indians*. Lincoln: University of Nebraska Press. Originally published in 1908 in the Anthropological Papers series of the American Museum of Natural History, New York, vol. 2, part 1.

King, C. 1997. 'Here Come the Anthros.' In T. Biolsi and L.J. Zimmerman, eds., *Indians and Anthropologists: Vine Deloria Jr. and the Critique of Anthropology*. Tucson: University of Arizona Press.

King, J.C.H., and H. Lidchi, eds. 1998. *Imaging the Arctic*. London: British Museum Press.

King, J.C.H., and W. Wood. 2002. *Ákaitapiiwa/Ancestors*. Lethbridge: Sir Alexander Galt Museum and Archives.

Kingston, D.P. 2003. 'Remembering Our Namesakes: Audience Reactions to Archival Film of King Island, Alaska.' In L. Peers and A.K. Brown, eds., *Museums and Source Communities: A Routledge Reader*. London: Routledge.

Knowles, C. 1998. 'Beatrice Mary Blackwood (1889–1975).' In A. Petch, ed., *Collectors 2: Collecting for the Pitt Rivers Museum*. Oxford: Pitt Rivers Museum.

– 2000. 'Reverse Trajectories: Beatrice Blackwood as Collector and Anthropologist.' In M. O'Hanlon and R. Welsch, eds. *Hunting the Gatherers: Ethno-*

graphic Collectors, Agents and Agency in Melanesia, 1870s–1930s. Methodology and History in Anthropology 6. Oxford: Berghan Books
– 2004. 'Beatrice Blackwood (1889–1975).' In *New Dictionary of National Biography*. Oxford: Oxford University Press.
Krauss, D.A., and Fryrear, J.L., eds. 1983. *Photo Therapy in Mental Health*. Springfield, IL: Charles Thomas.
Kreps, C. 2003. *Liberating Culture: Cross-Cultural Perspectives on Museums, Curation and Heritage Preservation*. London: Routledge.
Krupnik, I., and D. Jolly, eds. 2002. *The Earth Is Faster Now: Indigenous Observations on Arctic Environmental Change*. Fairbanks: Arctic Research Consortium of the United States.
Lamontagne, O. 1969. 'Reminiscing with Sister Odelia.' *Kainai News* 2(5), 17 June: 9.
Legislative Assembly of Alberta. 2000. *Bill 2. First Nations Sacred Ceremonial Objects Repatriation Act*. 4th Session, 24th Legislature, 49 Elizabeth II.
Lewis, O. 1942. *The Effects of White Contact upon Blackfoot Culture, with Special Reference to the Role of the Fur Trade*. New York: J.J. Austin.
Linton, R., R. Redfield, and M.J. Herskovits. 1936. 'Memorandum for the Study of Acculturation.' *American Anthropologist* 38 (1): 149–52.
Lippard, L.R., ed. 1992. *Partial Recall: Photographs of Native North Americans*. New York: The New Press.
Lomawaima, H. 1998. 'AASLH Native American History Initiative.' *History News* 54 (3): 13–15.
Long Lance, S.C. 1921. 'Alberta's Most Progressive Indian Tribe.' *Calgary Daily Herald*, 27 August: 20–1.
Lutz, C.A., and J.L. Collins. 1993. *Reading National Geographic*. Chicago: University of Chicago Press.
Lyman, C. 1982. *The Vanishing Race and Other Illusions: Photographs of Indians by Edward S. Curtis*. New York: Pantheon Books.
McClintock, W. 1910. *The Old North Trail, or, Life, Legends and Religion of the Blackfeet Indians*. London: Macmillan.
– 1930. 'The Tragedy of the Blackfoot.' *Southwest Museum Papers* 3. Los Angeles: Southwest Museum. Reprinted 1970.
– n.d. 'Blackfoot Medicine-Pipe Ceremony.' *Southwest Museum Leaflets* 21. Los Angeles: Southwest Museum.
MacDougall, D. 1992. 'Photo Hierarchicus: Signs and Mirrors in Indian Photography.' *Visual Anthropology* 5: 103–29.
McMaster, G. 1992. 'Colonial Alchemy: Reading the Boarding School Experience.' In L.R. Lippard, ed., *Partial Recall: Photographs of Native North Americans*. New York: The New Press.

Makepeace, A. 2000. *Coming to Light: Edward S. Curtis and the North American Indians*. Anne Makepeace Productions and WNET.

Malmsheimer, L.M. 1987. 'Photographic Analysis as Ethnohistory: Interpretative Strategies.' *Visual Anthropology* 1: 21–36.

Many Fingers, W.G., and S. Venne. 1987. 'Struggle for Religious Freedom: Blood Reserve 1921–1933.' *Kainai News* 20 (17) 7 May: 6.

Marr, C.J. 1996. 'Marking Oneself: Use of Photographs by Native Americans of the Southern Northwest Coast.' *American Indian Culture and Research Journal* 20 (3): 51–64.

Meyer, M. 1994. *The White Earth Tragedy: Ethnicity and Dispossession at a Minnesota Anishinaabe Reservation, 1889–1920*. Lincoln: University of Nebraska Press.

Middleton, S. 1953. *Kainai Chieftainship*. Lethbridge: *The Lethbridge Herald*.

Miller, J.R. 2003 [1996]. 'Reading Photographs, Reading Voices: Documenting the History of Native Residential Schools.' In J.S.H. Brown and E. Vibert, eds., *Reading beyond Words: Contexts for Native History*. Peterborough: Broadview Press.

Mitchell, L. 1994. 'The Photograph and the American Indian.' In A. Bush and L. Mitchell, eds., *The Photograph and the American Indian*. Princeton: Princeton University Press.

Mookaakin Cultural and Heritage Foundation. n.d. Information leaflet. Standoff, Alberta.

Mookaakin Cultural and Heritage Society and Glenbow-Alberta Institute 1998. *Memorandum of Understanding*. 6 March 1998.

Morris, E.M. 1985. *The Diaries of Edmund Montague Morris: Western Journeys 1907–1910*. Trans. M. Fitz-Gibbon. Toronto: Royal Ontario Museum.

Mountain Horse, M. 1989. *My People the Bloods*. Calgary: Glenbow Museum and Blood Tribal Council.

National Science Foundation Office of Polar Programs Arctic Sciences Section and Barrow Arctic Science Consortium. 2004. *Draft Guidelines for Improved Cooperation between Arctic Researchers and Northern Communities*. Available on-line at: http://www.arcus.org/guidelines/ (accessed 28 September 2004).

Niessen, S.A. 1991. 'More to It Than Meets the Eye: Photo-Elicitation among the Batak of Sumatra.' *Visual Anthropology* 4: 415–30.

Nugent, D. 1993. 'Property Relations, Production Relations, and Inequality: Anthropology, Political Economy and the Blackfeet.' *American Ethnologist* 20 (2): 336–62.

Oberholtzer, C. 1996. '"This Isn't Ours": Implications of Fieldwork on Material Culture Studies.' *Journal of Museum Ethnography* 8: 59–74.

– 2001. *Our Grandmothers' Voices: East Cree Material Culture in Museums*. CD-ROM. Copyright Cree Regional Authority.

Paiz, N. 2004. 'The Value of Preserving the Past: A Personal Journey.' In S. Ogden, ed., *Caring for American Indian Objects: A Practical and Cultural Guide*. St Paul: Minnesota Historical Society Press.

Palmer, H., and T. Palmer. 1990. *Alberta: A New History*. Edmonton: Hurtig.

Passalacqua, V. 2003. 'Sovereign Landscapes: Native North American Contemporary Photography.' Unpublished D.Phil. confirmation of status paper. Institute of Social and Cultural Anthropology, University of Oxford.

Pearce, Susan. 1994. 'Objects as Meaning; Or Narrating the Past.' In S. Pearce, ed., *Interpreting Objects and Collections*. London: Routledge.

Peers, L. 2003. 'Strands Which Refuse to Be Braided: Beatrice Blackwood's Ojibwe Collection at the Pitt Rivers Museum.' *Journal of Material Culture* 8 (1): 75–96.

Peers, L., and A.K. Brown, eds. 2003. *Museums and Source Communities: A Routledge Reader*. London: Routledge.

Penniman, T.K. 1976. 'Obituary: Beatrice Mary Blackwood, 1889–1975.' *American Anthropologist* 78 (2): 321–2.

Peterson, N. 2003. 'The Changing Photographic Contract: Aborigines and Image Ethics.' In C. Pinney and N. Peterson, eds., *Photography's Other Histories*. Durham and London: Duke University Press.

Pettipas, K. 1994. *Severing the Ties That Bind: Government Repression of Indigenous Religious Ceremonies on the Prairies*. Winnipeg: University of Manitoba Press.

Pettipas, L. 1994. *'Other Peoples' Heritage': A Cross-Cultural Approach to Museum Interpretation*. Winnipeg: Association of Manitoba Museums.

Phillips, R.B. 1998. *Trading Identities: The Souvenir in Native North American Art from the Northeast, 1700–1900*. Seattle: University of Washington Press.

– 2003. 'Introduction: Community Collaboration in Exhibitions: Toward a Dialogic Paradigm.' In L. Peers and A.K. Brown, eds., *Museums and Source Communities: A Routledge Reader*. London: Routledge.

Pinney, C. 1989. 'Other People's Bodies, Lives, Histories? Ethical Issues in the Use of a Photographic Archive.' *Journal of Museum Ethnography* 1: 57–69.

– 1992. 'The Lexical Spaces of Eye-Spy.' In P.I. Crawford and D. Turton, eds., *Film as Ethnography*. Manchester: Manchester University Press.

– 2003. 'Introduction: "How the Other Half."' In C. Pinney and N. Peterson, eds., *Photography's Other Histories*. Durham: Duke University Press.

Poignant, R., with A. Poignant. 1996. *Encounter at Nagalarramba*. Canberra: National Library of Australia.

Poolaw, L. 1998. 'Observations of an Encounter.' In T. Johnson, ed., *Spirit*

Capture: Photographs from the National Museum of the American Indian. Washington, DC: Smithsonian Institution Press in association with the National Museum of the American Indian.
Poole, D. 1997. *Vision, Race, and Modernity: A Visual Economy of the Andean Image World*. Princeton: Princeton University Press.
Posey, D. 1990. 'Intellectual Property Rights and Just Compensation for Indigenous Knowledge.' *Anthropology Today* 6 (4): 13–16.
Powers, W.R. 1996. 'Images across Boundaries: History, Use, Ethics of Photographs of American Indians.' *American Indian Culture and Research Journal* 20 (3): 129–36.
Raczka, P.M. 1979. *Winter Count: A History of the Blackfoot People*. Brocket, AB: Oldman River Cultural Centre.
Regular, W.K. 1999. '"Trucking and Trading with Outsiders": Blood Indian Reserve Integration into the Southern Alberta Economic Environment, 1884–1939 : A Case of Shared Neighbourhoods.' Unpublished Ph.D. thesis. St John's: Memorial University of Newfoundland.
Report of the Deputy Superintendent General. 1925. *Annual Report of the Department of Indian Affairs for the Year Ending March 31, 1925*. Ottawa: F.A. Acland.
Robinson, M.P. 1996. 'Shampoo Archaeology: Towards a Participatory Action Research Approach in Civil Society.' *Canadian Journal of Native Studies* 16 (1): 125–38.
Ross, M., and R. Crowshoe. 1999. 'Shadows and Sacred Geography: First Nations History-Making from an Alberta Perspective.' In G. Kavanagh, ed., *Making Histories in Museums*. London: Leicester University Press.
Ryan, J., and M. Robinson. 1990. 'Implementing Participatory Action Research in the Canadian North: A Case Study of the Gwich'in Language and Culture Project.' *Culture* 10 (2): 57–71.
– 1996. 'Community Participatory Research: Two Views from Arctic Institute Practitioners.' *Practicing Anthropology* 18 (4): 7–11.
Said, E. 1978. *Orientalism*. New York: Pantheon Books.
Salkeld, S. 1999. 'Lost Identities: Blackfoot Elders Gather, Reminisce at Display of Old Photos Collection.' *Fort Macleod Gazette*, 9 June: 6–7.
Samek, H. 1987. *The Blackfoot Confederacy 1880–1920: A Comparative Study of Canadian and United States Indian Policy*. Albuquerque: University of New Mexico Press.
Scherer, J. 1975. 'Pictures as Documents: Resources for the Study of North American Ethnohistory.' *Studies in the Anthropology of Visual Communication* 2 (2): 65–6.
– 1992. 'The Photographic Document: Photographs as Primary Data in

Anthropological Enquiry.' In E. Edwards, ed., *Anthropology and Photography, 1860–1920*. New Haven and London: Yale University Press in association with The Royal Anthropological Institute.

Schmidt, P.R., and T.C. Patterson. 1995. *Making Alternative Histories: The Practice of Archaeology and History in Non-Western Settings*. Santa Fe: School of American Research Advanced Seminar Series.

Schneider, W. 2002. *So They Understand: Cultural Issues in Oral History*. Logan: Utah State University Press.

Schultz, J.W., and J.L. Donaldson. 1930. *The Sun God's Children*. Boston and New York: Houghton-Mifflin.

Schwarz, M.T. 1997. '"The Eyes of Our Ancestors Have a Message": Studio Photographs at Fort Sumner, New Mexico, 1866.' *Visual Anthropology* 10: 17–47.

Scott, D.C. 1931. *The Administration of Indian Affairs in Canada*. Ottawa: Canadian Institute of International Affairs.

Shade, C. 2002. Speech made on the occasion of the 125th anniversary of Treaty 7, 1877. Blackfoot Crossing, 22 September 2002. Available on-line at: http://www.bloodtribe.org/Community%20Info.html (accessed 7 October 2002).

Sheridan, C. 1938. *Redskin Interlude*. London: Nicholson and Watson.

Silversides, B. 1991. 'The "Face-Puller" – George Anderton: A Victorian Photographer on the Northwest Frontier.' *Beaver* 71 (5): 22–31.

– 1994. *The Face Pullers: Photographing Native Canadians, 1871–1939*. Calgary: Fifth House.

Smallacombe, S. 1999. 'Indigenous Peoples' Access Rights to Archival Records,' Australian Society of Archivists Conference. Available on-line at: http://www.archivists.org.au/events/conf99/smallacombe.html (accessed 28 September 2002).

Smith, A. n.d. *Fishing with Nets: Maori Internet Information Resources and Implications of the Internet for Indigenous Peoples*. Available on-line at: http://www.isoc.org/isoc/whatis/conferences/inet/97/proceedings/E1/E1_1.HTM (accessed 11 April 2003).

Smith, A. 1998. '*Maawanji'iding*: Gathering Together Ojibwe Histories, Lake Superior, Wisconsin. Project Notes from a CD-ROM Work in Progress.' *Journal of Museum Ethnography* 10: 111–14.

Smith, D.G. 2001. 'The "Policy of Aggressive Civilization" and Projects of Governance in Roman Catholic Industrial Schools for Native Peoples in Canada, 1870–95.' *Anthropologica* 43: 253–71.

Smith, K.R. 2002. 'From Oral Tradition to Digital Collectives: Information Access and Technology in Contemporary Native American Culture.' *RLG*

DigiNews 6 (6). Available on-line at: http://www.rlg.org/preserv/diginews/diginews6-6.html (accessed 28 September 2004).

Smith, L.T. 1999. *Decolonizing Methodologies: Research and Indigenous Peoples*. London: Zed Books.

Smyth, D. 1976. *The Fur Trade at Rocky Mountain House*. Manuscript Report Series, no. 197. Ottawa: Parks Canada.

– 2001. 'The Niitsitapi Trade: Euroamericans and the Blackfoot-Speaking Peoples to the Mid-1830s.' Unpublished Ph.D. dissertation. Ottawa: Carlton University.

Stanton, J. 2003. 'Snapshots on the Dreaming: Photographs of the Past and Present.' In L. Peers and A.K. Brown, eds., *Museums and Source Communities: A Routledge Reader*. London: Routledge.

Stoler, A.L., and K. Strassler. 2000. 'Castings for the Colonial: Memory Work in "New Order" Java.' *Comparative Studies in Society and History* 42 (1): 4–48.

Tanner, S.J. 2000. *Winold Reiss: Native American Portraits*. Seattle: Frye Art Museum.

Taylor, B. 1984. *Clare Sheridan*. Hastings: privately published.

Taylor, F. 1989. *Standing Alone: A Contemporary Blackfoot Indian*. Halfmoon Bay, BC: Arbutus Bay Publications.

Taylor, P. 1988. *After 200 Years: Photographic Essays of Aboriginal and Islander Australia Today*. Cambridge: Cambridge University Press in association with Aboriginal Studies Press.

Thomas, J. n.d. 'Luminance: Aboriginal Photographic Portraits.' Essay accompanying on-line exhibition *Pride and Dignity*, National Archives of Canada. Available on-line at: http://www.archives.ca/05/050101_e.html (accessed 21 May 2002).

Thomas, J., and A. Hudson. 2002. 'Edmund Morris: Speaking of First Nations.' In L. Jessup and S. Bagg, eds., *On Aboriginal Representation in the Gallery*. Canadian Ethnology Service Mercury Series 135, Hull, QC: Canadian Museum of Civilization.

Thomas, N. 1991. *Entangled Objects: Exchange, Material Culture and Colonialism in the Pacific*. Cambridge: Harvard University Press.

Thompson, J., J. Hall, and L. Tepper with D.K. Burnham 2001. *Fascinating Challenges: Studying Material Culture with Dorothy Burnham*. Canadian Ethnology Service, Mercury Series Paper 136. Hull, QC: Canadian Museum of Civilization.

Thornton, M.V. 2000. *Buffalo People: Portraits of a Vanishing Nation*. Surrey, BC: Hancock House.

Titley, E.B. 1995 [1986]. *A Narrow Vision: Duncan Campbell Scott and the Administration of Indian Affairs in Canada*. Vancouver: UBC Press.

Treaty 7 Elders and Tribal Council with W. Hildebrandt, D. First Rider, and S. Carter. 1996. *The True Spirit and Original Intent of Treaty 7*. Montreal and Kingston: McGill-Queen's University Press.

Tsang, P. 2003. 'Program Preserves Blackfoot Culture: Lethbridge to Train Native Teachers.' *Calgary Herald* 9 September: B3.

Tsinhnahjinnie, H. 1998. 'When Is a Photograph Worth a Thousand Words?' In J. Alison, ed., *Native Nations: Journeys in American Photography*. London: Barbican Art Gallery.

United Nations. 1948. *Universal Declaration of Human Rights*. G.A. res. 217A (III), U.N. Doc A/810 at 71.

– 1994. *Draft Declaration on the Rights of Indigenous Peoples*. UN Subcommission for the Prevention of Discrimination and Protection of Minorities, 46th session, U.N. Doc. E/CN.4.Sub.2/1994/56. 28 October 1994.

United Nations Environment Programme. 1992. *Convention on Biological Diversity*. Na.92–7807. 5 June.

Urry, J. 2002 [1990]. *The Tourist Gaze*. 2nd edition. London: Sage Publications.

VanStone, J.W. 1992. 'Material Culture of the Blackfoot (Blood) Indians of Southern Alberta.' *Fieldiana Anthropology* new series 19. Chicago: Field Museum of Natural History.

Wareham, E. 2002. 'From Explorers to Evangelists: Archivists, Record-keeping, and Remembering in the Pacific Islands.' *Archival Science* 2 (3–4): 187–207.

Warry, W. 1990. 'Doing unto Others: Applied Anthropology and Native Self-Determination.' *Culture* 10: 61–73.

– 1998. *Unfinished Dreams: Community Healing and the Reality of Aboriginal Self-Government*. Toronto: University of Toronto Press.

Weiser, J. 1988. 'Photo Therapy: Using Snapshots and Photo-Interactions in Therapy with Youth.' In C. Schaefer, ed., *Innovative Interventions in Child and Adolescent Therapy*. New York: Wiley.

– 1999. *Photo Therapy Techniques: Exploring the Secrets of Personal Snapshots and Family Albums*. 2nd edition. Vancouver: Photo Therapy Centre Press.

Werner, O. 1961. 'Ethnographic Photography.' Unpublished MA thesis, Syracuse University, Syracuse, NY.

West, R.W. 1998. Foreword. In T. Johnson, ed., *Spirit Capture: Photographs from the National Museum of the American Indian*. Washington, DC: Smithsonian Institution Press in association with the National Museum of the American Indian.

Wilson, R.N. 1910. 'The Sacrificial Rite of the Blackfoot.' *Transactions of the Royal Society of Canada*. 3rd series, 1909–10; vol. 3, section 2. Ottawa: Royal Society of Canada.

– 1921. *Our Betrayed Wards: A Story of 'Chicanery, Infidelity and the Prostitution of Trust.'* Ottawa: privately published.

Wischmann, L. 2004. *Frontier Diplomats: Alexander Culbertson and Natoyisy-Siksina' among the Blackfeet*. Norman: University of Oklahoma Press.

Wissler, C. 1910. 'Material Culture of the Blackfoot Indians.' *Anthropological Papers* 5, pt. 1. New York: American Museum of Natural History.

– 1911. 'The Social Life of the Blackfoot Indians.' *Anthropological Papers* 7, pt. 1. New York: American Museum of Natural History.

– 1912. 'Ceremonial Bundles of the Blackfoot Indians,' *Anthropological Papers* 7, Pt. 2. New York: American Museum of Natural History.

– 1913. 'Societies and Dance Associations of the Blackfoot Indians.' *Anthropological Papers* 11, pt. 4. New York: American Museum of Natural History.

– 1918. 'The Sun Dance of the Blackfoot Indians.' *Anthropological Papers* 16, pt. 3. New York: American Museum of Natural History.

Wissler, C., and D.C. Duvall. 1908. 'Mythology of the Blackfoot Indians.' *Anthropological Papers* 2, pt. 1. New York: American Museum of Natural History.

Wright, T. 1992. 'Photography: Theories of Realism and Convention.' In E. Edwards, ed., *Anthropology and Photography, 1860–1920*. New Haven and London: Yale University Press in association with the Royal Anthropological Institute.

Zaharia, F., and L. Fox. 1995a. *Kitomahkitaiiminnooniksi: Stories from Our Elders*. Vol. 1. Edmonton: Donahue House Publishing and Kainai Board of Education.

– 1995b. *Kitomahkitaiiminnooniksi: Stories from Our Elders*. Vol. 2. Edmonton: Donahue House Publishing and Kainai Board of Education.

– 1995c. *Kitomahkitaiiminnooniksi: Stories from Our Elders*. Vol. 3. Edmonton: Donahue House Publishing and Kainai Board of Education.

Zaharia, F., L. Fox, and M. Fox. 2003. *Kitomahkitaiiminnooniksi: Stories from Our Elders*. Vol. 4. Edmonton: Duval House Publishing and Kainai Board of Education.

Ziff, B., and P.V. Rao. 1997. *Borrowed Power: Essays on Cultural Appropriation*. New Brunswick, NJ: Rutgers University Press.

Zuyderhoudt, L. 2004. 'Accounts of the Past as Part of the Present: The Value of Divergent Interpretations of Blackfoot History.' In B. Saunders and L. Zuyderhoudt, eds., *The Challenges of Native American Studies: Essays in Celebration of the Twenty-Fifth American Indian Workshop*. Leuven: Leuven University Press.

Index

Page numbers in italics refer to illustrations.